W9-BRA-134

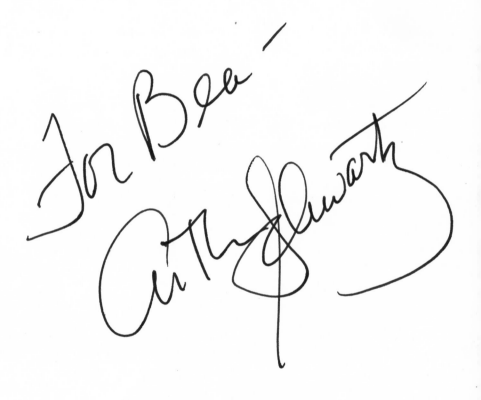

For Bea

Arthur Schwartz

Country Kitchens Remembered

Also by Marilyn Kluger
The Joy of Spinning
The Wild Flavor
Preserving Summer's Bounty

Country Kitchens Remembered

*A Memoir With
Favorite Family
Recipes*

Marilyn Kluger

Illustrated by Mary Azarian

DODD, MEAD & COMPANY
New York

Portions of this book have appeared, in slightly different
form, in *Gourmet* magazine: March and July 1971;
November 1976; May and November 1977; September
and October 1978; and September 1982. Reprinted by
permission of *Gourmet*.
"The Gift of Snow" appeared in *Good Housekeeping*,
December 1980. Excerpts taken from *Preserving Summer's
Bounty*, Copyright © 1979 by Marilyn Kluger, appear in
this book by permission of the publisher, M. Evans and
Company, Inc., New York, NY 10017.

Copyright © 1986 by Marilyn Kluger

All rights reserved

No part of this book may be reproduced in any form
without permission in writing from the publisher.

Published by Dodd, Mead & Company, Inc.
79 Madison Avenue, New York, N.Y. 10016
Distributed in Canada by
McClelland and Stewart Limited, Toronto
Manufactured in the United States of America
Designed by Claire B. Counihan
First Edition
1   2   3   4   5   6   7   8   9   10

Library of Congress Cataloging-in-Publication Data

Kluger, Marilyn.
Country kitchens remembered.

Includes index.
1. Cookery, American.   2. Country life—Indiana—
History.   3. Kitchens—Indiana—History.   I. Title.
TX715.K65   1986   641.5973   86-13418
ISBN 0-396-08760-4

For my brothers

Harold Marshall
and
James Marshall

Contents

Foreword

WHEN WRITING ABOUT my country childhood on a farm in southern Indiana and the farmhouse kitchens that were at the heart of it, the events and surroundings I describe seem to belong to a time more distant than the 1930s—even back to the turn of the century.

Certain aspects of life in our community remained as they were in an earlier time for at least a quarter of a century longer than they did in less remote areas. We were old-fashioned and behind the times in many ways simply because most of us did not have electricity, few had telephones, and many areas still had unimproved roads.

In 1935, only one family in eleven living on farms and in rural areas had electricity. By the end of World War II, rural electric lines had been strung to half the farms in Indiana, including ours, and the era I describe came to an end.

The self-sufficient family farm was not unusual in the 1930s. For families who had chosen that way of life, often following their parents' example, the thirties were not the time of scarcities and deprivation remembered by many who look back on those years.

My grandparents and parents had always led lives of independence and self-sufficiency on neighboring small farms, and the Depression did not affect our circumstances in ways my two brothers and I were especially aware of. Our lives continued as they always had, and those years are the happiest, most secure, of remembered times for all of us.

One factor adding to our security surely was that our parents combined the occupations of teaching and farming, and there was a steady, albeit reduced, income throughout the Depression. But, more importantly, both Dad and Mother knew how to live without requiring much money to provide the basic necessities of food, clothing, and shelter.

"There is no reason for folks on a farm to go hungry," my father would often say as he leaned back in his chair and surveyed a particularly bounteous meal such as Mother regularly served us on an everyday table. "Just look at this fine dinner! Laura, you have outdone yourself."

Dad took great pleasure in enumerating the foods on our table and pointing out to us the visible—and flavorful—rewards of hard work on the farm and in the orchard (his), industry in the garden (the children's), and skill in the kitchen (Mother's).

"Let's see now—there's our own milk and homemade butter, the green beans are from the garden, those are peaches from the fine orchard of old Charles E, himself—by golly! I don't believe anyone can find anything on this table that we did not raise here on our farm."

Of course, there was much more to living a good life on an eighty-acre farm during the Depression than having abundant meals on the table. But in those days, industrious people like my parents, living in the country, still had a multitude of practical skills learned from their own parents, and many of them were still necessary to daily life.

When the Marshall family came to Indiana from Kentucky in the early 1800s, Indiana had just become a state. My sturdy pioneer ancestors built a double log cabin, connected with a dog trot, on land that still belongs to our family. The Thomas Lincoln family lived only a few miles away, and my great-grandmother Marshall's father, Alexander Bolin, approached manhood with his friend, Abraham Lincoln.

There were only a few dozen families in the area at that time, and the rugged, isolated frontier life fostered self-sufficiency and hardiness. While the Indians and panthers and bears and the Lincolns had left the vicinity by the time my grandfather, James Alexander Marshall, was born in 1863, the stories of those days and the practical skills of his parents, the first generation of children born to settlers of Indiana, were passed down, parent to child. The heritage of pioneer life was still a strong influence in the boyhood home of my father, with the big old log cabin still standing on a hill nearby, and the colorful histories of Scotch-Irish and English relatives—who fought in the Revolutionary War, who migrated from Virginia, who were taken captive by Indians, who split rails alongside Abraham Lincoln, who were killed in feuds and accidents, or who survived frontier life—were recounted by grandparents whose own parents lived them. When I visited my Marshall grandparents as a child in the 1930s, the olden-days flavor of their lives was still strong, and the indomitable pioneer spirit was an ingrained family characteristic.

In the home of my maternal grandparents, Henry and Sophia (née Satkamp) Buse, the children of emigrés from Germany in the mid-1800s, the family stories were immigrant sagas rather than pioneer tales, and often they were spoken in German: There was the sad story of the little sister of my great-grandfather who died during the voyage from the homeland and was buried in cloth at sea. And there was the struggle of my great-great-grandparents to make something of their lives in America. They worked in a slaughterhouse in Cincinnati until they got enough money to buy a good farm in Seymour,

Indiana, a hundred miles westward, only to die a few years later, leaving Gerhart Buse an orphan at eleven years of age. In a less heroic migration, my great-grandfather Gerhart moved from Seymour to Stendal to avoid the Civil War. There he married Mary Rebber and reared a family. When my grandfather, Henry, grew to manhood, he went to Nebraska to homestead, but he didn't like living in a sod house, and when the flat, treeless land became so muddy that his jeans stood by themselves, he came back home to Indiana. There he bought a farm nestled equidistant between the two predominantly German communities of Stendal and Holland, and the old English-populated town of Taylorsville, later renamed Selvin, where the Marshalls had settled two generations earlier.

This is where I grew up, in an area where the colorful past retold often seemed more exciting than the 1930s days of my childhood. A sense of family and identity come naturally when one is surrounded by scores of relatives within a single community. Family history and the commonality of characteristics are there to be accepted and lived up to—or lived down. Even familial resemblences are definable. My father looked and acted "like a Marshall," and those words summed it up to anyone who knew the Marshall family, without further description.

The Marshall men were extremely strong and muscular. They were tall, large-boned, well proportioned, and athletic. They grew portly with age and good food, and they were bald by thirty. Most of them had a "Marshall head": if you sat behind a row of Marshall men at a funeral—the only time you were likely to see them in church—you couldn't tell them apart. The male Marshall head was large and round, with a bald pate ringed with dark hair. They had high, broad foreheads and wide mouths. They had beautiful Irish eyes, deep-set and blue, under bushy brows that could be serious or dancing. They smiled easily and laughed a lot. They had a lively sense of humor, superior intelligence, and the gift of gab. They were born storytellers, with a musical inclination that reflected itself in their rhythmic speech. They exuded confidence and they were not shy. They knew how to work hard and could do—and *would* do—anything they set their minds to, but they were easygoing and did not overexert themselves with physical labor. They liked to visit and loaf and talk. They had the dignity and attitude of teachers and the down-to-earth naturalness and practicality of farmers. They were as comfortable in suits and white shirts as they were in rough old work clothes. An old family chronicle states: "It would do you good to meet this fine family; sixteen children, and no black sheep to date."

Mother was just as much a Buse as Dad was a Marshall. She was taller than average, raw-boned, and lean. The Buses did not put on fat; they worked it off. Mother's capacity for hard work was as outstanding as her independence, determination, and dignity. She was every inch a lady, and she seldom lost her composure. She held her head high and her carriage was erect. She was highly ethical, idealistic, straightlaced, self-controlled, and the stereotype of a dedicated schoolteacher. She was reserved, but in command of her classroom, her home, or any situation. She could milk a cow, pitch hay, drive horses, recite Shakespeare, speak Latin, sew dresses, and wring a chicken's neck with equal aplomb— but quietly and self-effacingly. She did not depend on anyone to do anything for her, but she did *everything* for *everyone* around her. She had a tender heart and a strong will, and both were mirrored in her face. She had a nice face, with high cheekbones and a widow's peak in her fine, thick, light-brown hair. Her eyes were large and deep-set and expressive; her gaze, steady and serious. Her eyes were blue one day and green the next, depending on the color they reflected. She had an innate shyness and reticence, and she was not extravagant with her pleasant smiles. But she had a droll, dry sense of humor that she tended to reserve for her nonpublic moments—after school, after church, at home, and in retrospect. She always wore nice conservative dresses of the best quality to school, with sensible ladylike oxfords, and she was quite handsome and refined looking. But she was most pleasing to my eye when she put on her print housedresses and tied the sashes of her apron around her waist—and became the angel of our home.

I am glad I lived childhood's decade with aspects of an earlier era lending an old-fashioned flavor to that happy time. I was lucky to have a childhood with one foot in another century, as it were, lighted by kerosene lamps and warmed by kitchen ranges, when messages were delivered in person or via the dinner bell or rural mail carrier; when grandparents, aunts, uncles, and cousins lived nearby—or even next door; and we lived and were known and traveled within our own community.

Electricity was the difference between old-fashioned and modern. When President Franklin Roosevelt saw the need to "turn the lights on in the country" by establishing the Rural Electrification Administration in 1935, the soft lambent glow of kerosene lamps in country kitchens began to flicker out. When electricity surged into those kitchens I grew up in, washing clothes in washtubs and black kettles and wringer washers, ironing them with flatirons, and drying them on outdoor clotheslines became quaint chores belonging to the good old days. The icebox went to the attic ("we might need it again"), along with the coal bucket and butter churn.

When the homely, comforting, voracious, wood-and-coal-burning kitchen ranges were displaced by electric stoves, the country kitchens I remember lost their warm hearts. But not all cooks were willing to part with faithful old friends. Mother moved her kitchen range to the basement where she continued to use it regularly to bake biscuits, as only her kitchen range could bake her biscuits.

It was too good a team to break up.

Newburgh, Indiana   *Marilyn Kluger*

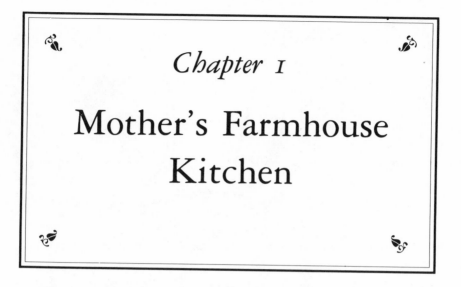

Chapter 1

Mother's Farmhouse Kitchen

THE "STARBURST SPOONER"

THE ANTIQUE PRESSED-GLASS SPOON HOLDER that I keep on a small table in my kitchen today is the same one that always stood in the middle of our kitchen table in the farmhouse in southern Indiana where I spent my childhood. I use it daily to keep extra teaspoons handy for use when needed at the table or for any purpose in the kitchen, just as my mother did a generation ago, and her mother before her. I have followed their custom because no utensil is needed more often in a kitchen, it seems, than a teaspoon. Also, the "Starburst Spooner" is a sparkling reminder of Mother's old-fashioned kitchen, with red geraniums and pink begonias blooming in its sunny windows and colorful rag rugs on the floor. I take joy in using that very spoon holder today. Protective handling of it has long been a habit, and many times I pick it up without any particular thought. But other times, unforeseen and unbidden, the old spooner becomes my crystal ball, as it were, my wellspring of memory, my Proustian madeleine. Just the familiar shape

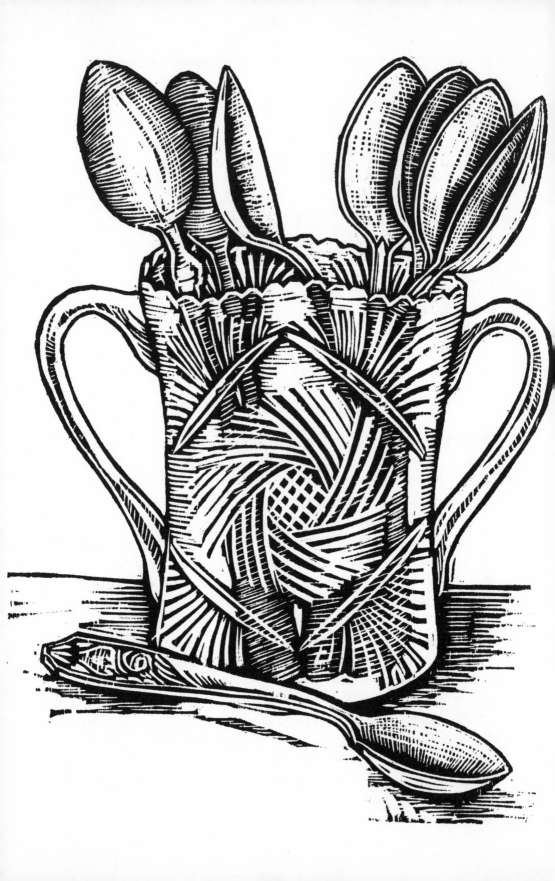

of it in my hands or the flash of sunbeams on its prismatic surface can set me dreaming of another farmhouse kitchen and my life in it.

I spent many happy hours there, especially in wintertime, keeping an eye on the fascinating round of cookery chores. From my vantage on a chair at the side of the kitchen table, I was at the same time in the middle of things and safely out from underfoot. The kitchen table was the hub of the kitchen, and the old spoon holder was always the centerpiece of the table.

FAMILY-STYLE MEALS AT THE KITCHEN TABLE

That was the table, spread with red-checked oilcloth for everyday meals and with white damask for Sunday dinner, from which was served up the best food I ever expect to eat. At every meal the pressed-glass spooner, filled with silver teaspoons standing ready for dipping spoonfuls of creamy bread pudding or hot oatmeal, was placed at the center of an arrangement of accessories necessary to the serving of our food. Around it were grouped the sugar bowl and creamer, salt and pepper cellars, butter dish, and jelly dishes. Often the collection was extended to include cruets of vinegar and hot sauce, the relish dish, and the sorghum pitcher with its hinged lid, which opened when the pitcher was tilted to allow the thick syrup to flow slowly onto a stack of steaming pancakes.

Our meals were served family-style, so around this circle of familiar table accessories were ringed bowls mounded with mashed potatoes, fresh garden vegetables, and stewed or fresh sugared fruits from the orchard. There, too, was the inevitable gravy dish, the napkin-swaddled hot breads, and, at Dad's end of the table, the ironstone platter heaped high with crusty fried chicken, or slices of smoky home-cured ham, or tender beefsteak. During hunting season, the meat on the platter might be game, perhaps quail or rabbit or squirrel.

As soon as grace was said—and sometimes before the "Amen"—my father took a serving of meat and started the platter around the table. The meat platter was passed first to my older brother, Harold, and next to my younger brother, Jimmy, who sat in the coveted seat next to Mother. There he enjoyed her extra attention and indulgences, such as having his meat and gravy-bread cut into neat, bite-sized pieces, and his biscuits split, buttered, and jellied. My place at the table was on Mother's left so that I sat between her and Dad in a refuge safe from my brothers' teasing during mealtime.

As soon as the meat platter started around, we helped ourselves to the bowls of food nearest us and passed them on to the left. There was no waiting, no formality, no cold food! The meal was on our plates within minutes after it had come from the kettles and pans on the kitchen stove. Indeed, the table was only a few feet from the sturdy black kitchen range, and it was there, within its circle of warmth, enveloped in the very aromas created by our just-cooked food, that we ate our meals. We used the dining room rarely—on Sundays when there was company, for birthday dinners, and on holidays, or when the threshing crew or corn pickers came. The kitchen table was our usual dining table.

Between meals the kitchen table served as a work table. The dishes were hardly cleared away following one meal before preparation for the next began. I was always there, whenever I was indoors, claiming a corner of the kitchen table for my crayons and paper, but keeping in touch with whatever culinary process was evolving. I waited tirelessly for my chance to pry oatmeal cookies, plump with raisins, off baking tins; to scrape sticky, sweet remnants of cake batter from mixing bowls; to roll out leftover scraps of sugar-sprinkled dough for miniature pies to bake on can lids in the hot oven alongside the apple pies Mother made.

Such were the pleasant times I remember in Mother's kitchen when I perched on a chair beside the table, elbows on the oilcloth and chin cradled in the palms of my hands, watching the kneading, slicing, rolling, peeling, dicing, mincing, cubing, grinding, stirring, whipping, beating, folding, measuring, and creaming that transformed such mundane ingredients as flour and potatoes and lard and eggs and sugar into the tasty cookies, casseroles, stews, cakes, puddings, pies, and breads that later appeared on our table. I sensed that there was something magical in cooking, and from the beginning, I wanted to be there to watch the sleight of hand that created those marvels of flavor from plain, ordinary stuff.

Though I was captivated by Mother's kitchen skills even before I went to school, my appreciation of her artistry as a cook and the scope of her efforts to provide the riches we enjoyed at her table did not come until much later, when I gained perspective and a more experienced palate.

When a family is composed of good cooks, as mine was, delicious food is taken for granted by children and adults as well. In the years of our brief lives, we children had tasted only good foods, those cooked for us by our mother, grandmothers, aunts, and hired girls who helped Mother when she was teaching school. We ate the meals they prepared for us with simple, direct appreciation, but without an inkling that our daily rustic repasts were epicurean.

All of these ladies coddled us with lovingly cooked meals. They conscientiously nourished us with vegetables, fruit, cereals, and meats, which we needed to be healthy. And they indulged us, using a modicum of restraint, with all the delights of childhood appetites.

ANGEL FOOD CAKE AND SEVEN-MINUTE FROSTING

One such delight was Mother's angel food cake, light as a cloud and standing seven inches tall, adorned by inch-high peaks of snowy Seven-Minute Frosting, which was so melt-ingly smooth that not one sugar crystal grated against the tongue. Surely angel food cake was aptly named, for it was airy and delectable and celestial enough to be eaten by cher-ubs and seraphs and angels. It seemed even more ethereal because we always had it for Sunday dinner, after church.

This was because Mother did her fancy baking on Satur-day, and it took an entire afternoon to make the heavenly creation. After the dishes were cleared off the table following the noontime meal, she brought out the large egg-white pan. It was just like the dishpan we used for washing dishes, a round, white-enameled pan with sloping sides and a red-bor-dered rim. (Actually, discarded egg-white pans served as dishpans after they became chipped.) She also gathered to-gether the tube-cake pan, the egg-white whisk, the measur-ing cup, and a large spoon. Although these were clean when taken from the cupboard, Mother placed them in the sink and scalded them with boiling water from the teakettle.

"Just a trace of grease on any of these would keep the egg whites from gaining volume," she said. "We'll just make sure they are as clean as can be."

Next, Mother gathered all the ingredients and measured them before beginning to make the cake. She was very or-ganized and exact in her preparations.

The ingredients were simple and few: thirteen egg whites, salt, cream of tartar, sugar, Swans Down cake flour, and Rawleigh's vanilla extract.

First she measured the cake flour and sifted it three times. Then she measured it carefully *after* sifting it. There would always be two tablespoons of flour or more than she had mea-sured out the first time, when she took the flour out of the box.

"See!" She scraped the surplus flour back into the carton with emphatic movements. "That's just enough extra flour to spoil my cake."

She also sifted the sugar, something she did not trouble to do when making other cakes. She wanted to be sure there were no lumps in the sugar either. She measured it out and placed it in a small bowl.

"The most important ingredient can't be measured," Mother said. "Can you guess what it is?"

The answer to Mother's riddle was *air*. But today I would say there should be a multiple answer to that question. Making a good angel cake requires skill, patience, a light hand, a strong arm, and infinite care.

When she broke the eggs and separated the whites from the yolks, she broke each one very carefully into a separate cup before placing it in the egg-white pan. The yolks of very fresh eggs break easily. If a trace of egg-yolk yellow showed in the white of an egg, Mother would put it aside.

"Just a speck of egg yolk will keep the whites from beating up light and fluffy," she explained.

The role of the eggs in the delicate creation of the angel food cake was definitely crucial. The best cakes are made with eggs that are literally fresh from the nest. It was my chore to go to the henhouse to get them, and I chose the largest brown-shelled eggs from the basket for Mother's angel cake. It was even to our advantage that the eggs were nest-warm, not cooled, as the superior egg-white foam is beaten when the egg whites are at room temperature, or about 70°F.

But Mother's angel cake was not mixed or baked according to thermometers or scientific facts. She simply had a tried-and-true recipe and a method that was failproof when she followed it faithfully in every detail.

Finally, all was in readiness, and Mother began the important business of whipping the egg whites. It was a task for which she sat on a straight-backed kitchen chair, the large egg-white pan on her knees. She beat the egg whites with a flat, fine-wire whisk, at first using small, circular, energetic motions that kept the beater under the foaming egg whites.

She added the salt and continued beating, increasing the size of the circle she circumscribed with the whisk as the egg whites became more voluminous with air. She added the cream of tartar, and continued whipping the egg whites until they formed soft peaks. Then she would stop beating every so often and, at her direction, I would sprinkle the sugar, one heaping tablespoonful at a time, over the swelling mound of egg whites. She would continue to beat until the sugar had all disappeared into the egg whites.

There was a distinctive rhythm and sound accompanying the hand-beating of egg whites with a whisk that I could recognize even without seeing what was happening. After the sugar had been whipped into the egg whites, the flour was added in a different manner. It was sifted from the flour sifter, a small portion at a time, onto the top of the airy mound. Still using the flat whisk, Mother cut down through the egg whites in a circular motion and carried the mixture from the bottom of the pan up over the flour sifted on the top, covering it with a blanket of egg whites. She turned the pan a quarter of a turn at a time and continued folding egg whites over the flour until the flour had all disappeared. Then I sifted another portion over the egg whites, and she again folded it in lightly and carefully, so as not to deflate the beaten-in air.

Finally the angel cake batter was all but finished. At last Mother took a teaspoon from the spoon holder on the kitchen table and uncapped the glorious essence of the Rawleigh's vanilla extract bottle. A teaspoonful of the flavoring was measured out and sprinkled over the top of the ambrosial mound of angel's food, and the last few folding motions lovingly tucked it in.

Quickly the angel cake mixture was spooned into the tube pan, and a knife drawn through the batter to prevent it from having air bubbles that could make tunnels in its interior during baking.

"All finished!" Mother breathed a happy sigh. "*Except* baking." She slid the cake pan into the center of the oven and closed the door. Then she lifted the cast-iron lid on top of the stove and began tending the fire.

While great care was required in mixing the angel cake, perhaps even greater care was required in baking it. Having the oven at the right temperature and keeping the heat constant was a critical factor. Too hot an oven could result in a tall cake with a dark brown cracked top, while too slow an oven could require longer baking time and result in a dry cake. The perfect angel food cake would be baked at a temperature somewhere in between, at a point Mother deemed "just right."

Maintaining the proper temperature in an oven of a wood-and-coal-burning range without a thermometer required skill beyond my comprehension. It involved a sixth sense by which Mother knew, without thermometers, gauges, or dials, when to add more wood, when to adjust the damper, and even when the cake had baked long enough. She was so familiar with the polished old stove and its idiosyncracies that she could tell when the fire was right simply by the singing of the teakettle sitting on the second cover and the feel of the heat when she held her hand momentarily in the space of the oven.

After about an hour, during which we children could not run, jump, or slam the kitchen door lest the cake should fall, Mother would open the oven door carefully, reach in, and gently pull the cake pan toward the front of the oven.

"It's done," she would announce, touching the cake with her forefinger. Mother took the cake out of the oven, and there it was, baked to perfection!

A chorus of "ohs" and "ahs" sounded in the kitchen as everyone in the house or within smelling distance of the kitchen windows congregated around the kitchen table to see the cake just out of the oven.

It rose fully an inch above the rim of the tube pan. A delicately browned crust capped the top; it was crazed with a pattern of fine cracks, revealing a glimmer of its moist white interior.

On the wave of heat escaping from the opened oven door rode zephyrs of delicate vanilla fragrance. These ephemeral fumes could be inhaled deeply and savored for only a few minutes if one lingered in the vicinity of the oven. Then they floated ceilingward, closer to the realm of angels. Oh, heavenly ambience! Mother's kitchen was an earthly paradise for one small mortal when an angel cake had just baked in the oven of the kitchen range.

When the sounds of admiration subsided, the cake pan was inverted and the angel cake was left to cool thoroughly.

"Well." Mother breathed another of her happy sighs. "It turned out very nicely." And then she began all over again. There was still the frosting for the cake to be made.

So she washed the dishes, gathered together another set of ingredients, and began cooking again. This time it would be Seven-Minute Frosting, so named because it took seven minutes to whip the sugar syrup and egg whites into a fluffy cloud of sweet confection to pile on the top and sides of the cooled angel cake.

CHURCH AND CHICKEN EVERY SUNDAY

When the cake was at last displayed on Mother's tall glass cake stand, a vision to behold and a torment to the taste buds of all who saw it under its cloche of glass, Sunday dinner seemed eons away.

And eons it was. The preacher's sermons on Sunday mornings droned on eternally for children who had to stay for church services with their parents after Sunday School. Town kids raced home at half-past ten, free as birds for the rest of the day, but we who lived five miles out in the country learned to sit still, keep quiet, and endure boredom without showing it.

But we didn't have to pay attention, unless we wanted to. Children were exempt from church until the age of confirmation. So sitting in church with the adults on Sunday mornings became a time to while away with daydreaming and introspection of a special nature, and I remember those hours as pleasant interludes rather than as captivity.

The opening hymn engaged my attention fully. It began with an awesome phrase of powerful words—"Holy, Holy, Holy, Lord God Almighty!"—sung heartily, with marked emphasis providing exactly the right timing for the choir to walk in step to as they went down the aisle toward the choir stall. The liturgy was interesting, too, as one had to be ready to stand up and sit down in all the proper places. But soon afterward, during the epistle, or lesson, or prayers, and certainly long before the minister mounted the pulpit for the tiresome sermon, my fidgeting mind had flown to the realm of its own imagination.

There, vivid images flowered spontaneously from fragments of Bible stories barely heard through a muddle of sleepiness. Random thoughts filtered through ennui, riding on waves of rich language and melodic phrasing from the King James Version. Out of the very surroundings, upon which I concentrated mightily every Sunday for years, a thousand everlasting impressions formed in my consciousness. I memorized the stained glass windows, the stenciled borders painted on the walls, and the carvings on the pews. I scrutinized the ears, necks, clothing, and hair of those who sat around me. I concentrated on the pictures on the cardboard fans placed in the racks along with the songbooks and Bibles, courtesy of Nass Funeral Home. I read the Sunday School paper and examined the contents of Mother's pocketbook. I waited for the slightest breeze from the opened transom of the window next to my seat, and suffered thirst, heat, and hunger pangs with stoicism. And I studied the painted ceiling of the dome above the altar. It was of cherubim poised in midair below a mass of puffy white clouds suspended in the bluest sky imaginable. White doves, wings outspread, hovered in the company of the angels, and light beamed out from behind the clouds, brighter than sunlight itself. When I stared at the depiction, trying earnestly to glimpse heaven just beyond the clouds, the light beams gradually brightened, before my very eyes, in the painted sky. It was an awesome hallucination and I cradled it secretly in my thoughts each Sunday when I discreetly turned my eyes heavenward to behold my private miracle.

But as soon as the word "Amen!" rang out of the pulpit, my astigmatic illusion vanished. My thoughts returned to reality. It was almost dinnertime, and Sunday dinner was the best meal of the week.

Like many other farm families in our area in the thirties, we really did have chicken every Sunday. In the summer it was always fried chicken, because that was the season when the chicks hatched in the spring had grown to size for pan frying. The young cockerels had to be eaten or sold because only a few roosters were needed for the large flock of laying hens that Mother kept for egg production. The first of the cockerels could be eaten when they were ten or twelve weeks old, when they weighed two and a half to three pounds.

Mother always bought straight-run chicks from the hatchery in the early spring, and she could never tell how many were cockerels until she counted them several weeks later when their combs began to grow. There were usually more cockerels than pullets. Out of the two hundred chicks of the springtime brood, there were more than enough cockerels to keep our family supplied with fried chicken every Sunday of the summer, as well as seventy-five or so energetic new pullets to replace fat old hens who were past their prime for laying eggs.

When egg production waned, Mother went to her recipe drawer and hunted up the recipes for one-egg cakes—or *no-egg* cakes.

"The chickens are on strike," she said.

For a time, the delectable angel food and sponge cakes disappeared from the Sunday dinner table. Instead of platters of scrambled eggs and salmon for supper, Mother made "egg-a-roosel," which my frugal Aunt Emma always used in her city kitchen to stretch her supply of country eggs brought back from visits at our house. And instead of two fried eggs for breakfast, Mother made miraculous one-egg omelets, each of which alone filled an entire plate.

Mother could stretch an egg from hither to yonder, but when her laying hens forsook their duty, Mother made the pronouncement: "Time to get rid of the boarders!" She would descend upon the hennery, examine her layers, and put colorful rings on the legs of the lazy ladies who were not doing their part. These fat hens were either destined for dinner or were sold to the peddler when the cockerels were large enough for "fryers."

There were several ways a fat hen might end up on the table—baked, stewed, or in a pot pie, chicken soup, chicken salad, chicken croquettes, or creamed in gravy with peas and pimentos. But the most likely conclusion was chicken and dumplings.

Dumplings were as important in the country kitchens in our community as biscuits and milk gravy, beans and corn bread, or potatoes and bread. Dumplings were made with stewed meats and chicken, in soups, with a pot of greens, and even in stewed fruits. They could be dropped and "light," or rolled and "slick." They could be as large as biscuits or as small as birds' eggs.

Mother most often made fluffy, raised dumplings, which she cooked in boiling chicken broth under a tight lid during the last few minutes' cooking time. Dropped dumplings took less time to mix and made less mess than rolled dumplings. Besides, Dad did not like "slick" dumplings and we knew what he would say when Mother made them.

"I ate enough of those damned 'slick' dumplings to last me a lifetime when I was a boy," he would grumble, passing the bowl on around the table. "I don't want any more of them. The rest of you folks can have my share."

Dumplings would "stick to your ribs," and they were a wintertime dish in Mother's kitchen, plentiful when she was clearing the henhouse of backsliders to make room for the coming summer's flock of new chickens.

We got our baby chicks from a hatchery in Huntingburg and transported them home in large square cardboard boxes with inner compartments and air-holes punched in the sides and tops. At first, we picked up the fluffy yellow chicks at night and returned them to the boxes to keep them warm and safe from rats. If April was cold, we sometimes brought them into the kitchen and placed the boxes near the kitchen range at night. But baby chickens are only cute for a few days, like baby pigs, and we were glad when the heat from the brooder stove was adequate to warm the brooder house and the kitchen was returned to normal use.

"April chicks—September eggs" was the calendar rule. By September, the cockerels also reached maturity, and that was the limit to how long a surplus of young roosters could co-exist in the chicken yard. At five or six months of age, the boisterous young roosters fight and crow constantly, vying for superiority, and the chicken yard is in a hubbub. So, from June to September, Mother thinned out the population of young roosters at the rate of several a week by way of the frying pan. The rest were sold, two to four a week, to the peddler from the general store in Zoar, Indiana.

PEDDLER'S WAGON ON MONDAY MORNING

The Monday morning transactions with the peddler wagon were special events in a week-to-week routine that did not include many unusual visitors. The peddler began making his rounds in the spring after the weather was settled and the narrow dirt road between our house and Zoar had been graded and dragged smooth of the deep ruts and mud holes left from winter travel. The roads needed to be fairly smooth for the peddler wagon, because it was actually a miniature general store on wheels. The peddler carried canned goods and grocery items inside compartments of the wagon body that might roll around and become dented or broken if the roads were too rough.

In spite of smoothed roads, the peddler's merchandise rattled and clanged as he drove down the road, and if anyone was outdoors and listening for it, the peddler wagon could be heard approaching before it reached the crossroads, a quarter of a mile away from our house.

In the first place, the truck's motor was loud, and the metal items, such as galvanized buckets, tied loosely to the metal-topped roof of the wagon, rang out like cymbals when the truck hit a bump in the road. Hysterical chickens, caged between the body of the peddler wagon and the truck bed, squawked in alarm. The peddler always sounded the truck's horn when he reached the crossroads, just in case we had not heard the pandemonium of his approach. He wanted the farm wives to be out by the road, ready to trade, when he arrived. Otherwise he could not keep to his schedule, and it would take all day covering his route.

When it neared ten o'clock on Monday morning, Mother was always in a rush to get ready for the peddler. It was washday, too, and the washing was well underway by that time of morning. Before the peddler came, the eggs had to be counted and in the bucket, ready to sell, the grocery list

made, and the fryers to be sold had to be caught, their legs
bound together and tied with strips of cloth.

"Bring up the rest of the eggs while I count these," Mother
would say as she brought up the first pan, mounded with
eggs, from the cool cellar and placed it on the back porch
table. Quickly and carefully, she counted the eggs by the
dozen and placed them into a white enamelware bucket,
holding three together in each hand at a time.

"Three, six, nine, twelve. Three, six, nine, twelve. Three,
six, nine, twelve." Learning to count in multiples was as
simple as counting eggs when you were a school-age child
living on a farm.

Then I was stationed on the front porch to listen for the
sound of the peddler's truck coming down the road, and Mother
went on, catching the young roosters that had been put in a
coop the night before, rinsing a load of clothes from the wringer
washer, making out the grocery list, hanging sheets on the
line.

"Call me when you hear him coming." She disappeared
behind the house, carrying the empty clothes basket, with
not a minute to waste if the wash was to be finished and the
noon meal ready at twelve o'clock, sharp.

The rhythm of my life was more leisurely. I had only to
sit in the gently swaying swing on the vine-covered porch
and listen for the peddler wagon while I guarded the egg
bucket. Our English setter, Queen, had the bad habit of
"sucking eggs," and she would steal and eat any eggs she
might find in a nest hidden in the barn or in a clump of
bushes where a hen had secreted her clutch. Dad had once
tried to break her of this habit by putting pepper in eggs
that he left in an isolated nest. But Queen was too smart to
fall for Dad's trick. She ate only the good eggs out of the
maverick nest and left the peppered eggs behind.

After that, Queen's vice became a virtue and the subject of
one of Dad's favorite anecdotes.

"That's a very intelligent dog," he would begin. "She can outsmart me. One time I thought I would break her of the habit of stealing eggs . . ."

From then on, Queen seemed to have earned the right to forage for eggs in hidden nests, if she could get them before we did. But the chicken house and buckets filled with eggs were another matter. Both were off limits.

So, on Monday mornings, I and Queen, my faithful dog, were at a like task, both of us keeping an eye on the egg bucket and an ear tuned for the clanging approach of the peddler's wagon. We sat on the vine-covered front porch, and I stroked her luxuriant coat and long silky ears while we waited for the sound of the truck. All at once, she would become alert, body tensed, ears cocked, and I would hear the truck a few seconds later.

The peddler wagon consisted of a multicompartmented wooden body, painted green, mounted on the bed of a Model T truck. It was as long as the truck bed would allow, about nine feet, and a bit taller than the cab of the truck, or almost four feet high. It was about five feet wide. Along each side of the peddler wagon body were doors that opened, like kitchen cupboard doors, to reveal cans, boxes, and sacks of grocery goods. In the two cupboards on one side of the wagon were kept the kitchen staples: oatmeal, rice, dried beans, white and yellow cornmeal, flour, baking powder, baking soda, yeast, cocoa, macaroni, salt, tapioca, pepper, coffee, raisins, marshmallows, vanilla extract, and so on. In one of the side cupboards, the peddler stored the scales with which he weighed the young roosters Mother wanted to sell along with the eggs.

She held them, two in each hand together, by their bound legs, while the peddler hung the shiny brass spring-balanced scale on a swinging bracket. He then took the fryers from Mother, one at a time, and hung them by the binding around their legs on the hook at the bottom of the scale. For a few noisy moments, the frightened rooster squawked and cackled and flapped his wings, and finally hung helpless and still, upside down. Then the peddler read the weight on the scale, untied the legs of the hapless cock-a-doodle-doo, and put him inside the chicken coop under the body of the peddler wagon.

In the same compartment where the scale and hanging bracket were kept, the peddler also kept a stalk of bananas. We had an abundance of orchard fruits and berries on the farm, so bananas, oranges, and dried raisins were practically the only fruits we ever bought. If Mother bought a bunch of bananas, it meant we were soon to be treated to banana cake, banana pudding, banana pie, or fruit salad. And there would be bananas to eat for snacks.

The two cupboards on the opposite side of the wagon held items that were less exciting to me. There was an assortment of canned fruits and vegetables, which we never needed, because our cellar shelves were better stocked with our home-canned supply than the shelves of a general store itself. Once in a while Mother bought a can of pineapple, which, like bananas, was a farm child's idea of an exotic fruit. Canned pineapple meant congealed Sunshine Salad with shredded carrots, pineapple, and lemon gelatin, or a cake turned upside down when it came out of the pan to reveal pineapple rings in a candied brown sugar syrup.

In the other compartment, on the uninteresting side of the peddler wagon, there were such necessities as kitchen matches, fly-catching ribbons, laundry starch, laundry soap, hand soap, washday bluing, coarse salt for making ice cream and pickles, paraffin, can lids and jar rings, fly spray, vinegar, lamp wicks, and garden seeds.

On top of the wagon, lashed to the iron railing, were sacks of oyster shells and laying mash for chickens, brooms, mops, galvanized buckets, a washtub, and whatever special items the peddler might be delivering to his customers.

On the front seat of the truck cab, on the passenger's side, the peddler kept egg cases for the eggs we had counted out into our bucket for trading for our groceries. The peddler counted them out again, as Mother had, placing each egg in its own cardboard compartment, layer upon layer separated by corrugated paper and wooden frames to keep the eggs from breaking in transit.

At the back of the peddler wagon a wide door opened downward, forming a shelf upon which the items we selected were gathered together, and a surface for the peddler to write on when he made out our ticket in his account book.

Shelves in the rear compartment, which was about five feet wide and two and a half feet deep, held dry goods and sundries. Straight pins, oilcloth, fly swatters, suspenders, buttons, cigars, chewing gum, ribbon, yard goods in bolts such as muslin, chambray, damask, toweling, and calico or print dress materials, red and blue paisley-patterned work handkerchiefs, bias tape, rickrack, snaps, needles, work socks, and more. On the top shelf were summer straw hats, which all of us, except Mother (who always wore a sunbonnet), wore when we worked out in the sun.

Almost everything we needed for the kitchen that we did not produce ourselves could be found on the peddler wagon. If the peddler did not have a particular item, he would bring it along the next Monday.

The peddler kept an account book with the name *Marshall* written on it. He recorded the value of the number of eggs in the bucket to our credit at the top of the page after carefully inserting a piece of carbon paper between the yellow copy and the white original. He also entered the amount credited to us for the young roosters. After Mother had called for all of the kitchen supplies she needed, and the peddler brought them to the hanging counter on the back of the peddler wagon, one by one, he listed them in the book with their prices alongside in spaces ruled off in the right-hand margin. Mother's objective was to buy a total amount of groceries costing less than the amount of money due her in trade for the eggs and roosters.

There was always a quiet, suspenseful few minutes after the peddler asked, "Will that be all, then?" while he totted up the figures. Only when he finished, did I know if the outcome was plus or minus. Mother, I am sure, had it all in her head before the addition and subtraction.

Once in a while Mother had to pay a small amount to the peddler out of her pocketbook, but more often the peddler owed Mother. This cash from the peddler made up that important household fund called "the egg money."

The egg money was used to finance small special projects in our home, to buy little luxuries from time to time. Before Mother put the egg money in her apron pocket, she gave me a few pennies. Country children who managed to be around when the peddler wagon came expected to make the last transaction of the day—for a ball of bubblegum, a stick of penny candy, an all-day sucker, a jawbreaker, a candy bar. The peddler carried a box of assorted candies, a sampling from the large glass showcase in the store at Zoar. It was a choice that had to be made quickly once the box was opened because the peddler had to be on his way. One could not stand and deliberate, pennies in hand; it was an exercise in decisivenesss.

"A bag of cinnamon red hots!" The decision always seemed forced and hurried, no matter how much thought I had given it before the open box was presented, even if I had made up my mind ahead of time. All afternoon I questioned my choice, even as I let the red hots melt slowly and spicily on my tongue.

"I wish I had bought lemon drops."

"Uuummm huummm." Mother had a way of responding when she was concentrating on what she was doing at the stove. It was reassuring and encouraging, yet somehow noncommittal.

"Zanzibars are better."

"Uummm huummm, maybe." Mother hummed.

Dad was more of a tease. "Why don't you give those red hots to your mother, since you don't like them, and let her color the applesauce pink?"

Mother made lots of fresh applesauce for the table, and for canning as well, as soon as the "Early June Transparent" apples ripened, which was somehow never in early June, but in early July. But from then on into late autumn, apples were one of the staple foods we had in abundant supply, equalled only by peaches from Dad's orchard.

DAD'S ORCHARD

When Dad built our house in the early 1930s, he planted a large orchard of apple and peach trees around it. The trees grew alongside the house on two sides, shading it. The small trees grew to maturity during the first decade of my life. Time seemed to move swiftly forward as they rushed toward fruitfulness, in direct contrast to the endlessness with which my own days seemed to progress.

One day at breakfast Dad would remark, "The apple trees are leafing out," and we would look out the window at the orchard and see the bare branches barely greening with tender leaflets.

A few days later, he would announce, "The apple trees are in full bud," and we would pull down a branch and see the tips of white on the fat green buds.

Then suddenly, overnight, the orchard would burst into glorious bloom, filling the air with a sweet, tart, innocent fragrance that intoxicated the sensibilities. I could step off the back porch and wander through an enchanted place for as long as the sensuous beauty lasted.

To walk up and down the avenues of blossoming apple

trees in April, under the canopies of flower-bedecked boughs, to the music of droning bees drawing nectar and songbirds nesting overhead, with the breeze tossing pink-tinged white petals like an unseen flower girl, was to be a player in nature's fantasia.

The orchard always held enchantment for me, although it was never quite so charming as during apple blossom time. After the petals had scattered to the winds, tiny apples appeared, and we kept close watch as they swelled to large, grass-green globes. In the meantime, Dad was preoccupied with spraying, or thinning apples where there were too many, or propping limbs bent low with too heavy a load of fruit, or mowing under the trees. There was always lots of activity in the orchard. Without the diligent toil of the orchardist, there would not have been such a pleasant place to captivate his daughter's imagination.

And, true to apple symbolism, temptation was also there. By July, we children were covertly testing the apples with the pressure of a thumb. Long before the first ones ripened— the "Early June Transparent" variety—I had daringly sampled many a green apple despite warnings of dreadful consequences. But somehow I always escaped the green apple bellyache.

"Child, you must have a cast-iron stomach," Mother would say when she learned of my escapades.

While there is no taste so unforgettable and nostalgic as that of jaw-clenchingly tart green apples, the flavors of Mother's ripe apple specialties were somewhat more felicitous to the appetite. She was endlessly clever when it came to turning out a continual flow of pies, puddings, dumplings, cobblers, sauces, and various dishes made with apples. She had a dozen or more "old faithful" recipes that all the family favored, and almost as many varieties of apples to make them with.

McIntosh were destined for cinnamony applesauce and raisin-studded applesauce cake. Crisp Rome Beauties were stuffed with pecans and brown sugar, then baked. Grimes Golden and Yellow Delicious were sliced into pies, covered with two crusts, or left open-faced for a sour cream apple tart. The spritely Winesaps were swaddled in biscuit dough or pastry and baked into apple dumplings and cobblers. Juicy Yorks topped the apple kuchen, and Aunt Blanche's apple crisp and spicy apple muffins called for sweet and tart Jonathans.

We had a luxury of apples on our table and in our cellar. In addition there were the Northern Spy, Wealthy, Baldwin, Banana, Red Delicious, and Queen. These went into our dinner buckets, which we carried to school, and comforted us on wintry Sunday afternoons when we made fudge and popped corn.

Dad grew a patch of popcorn every year. If there is such a distinction as "popcorn connoisseur," Dad was one. As he saw it, the only way to be certain of having a supply of the best popcorn was to grow it himself. He grew several varieties of popcorn over the years, including black and white kernel varieties and strawberry popcorn, but none could please him as much as the yellow-kernel variety called Brazilian Dynamite.

Half of the name, Brazilian Dynamite, was mystifying to me, but the other half was certainly appropriate. When the tiny yellow kernels popped inside the popcorn popper, noisily hitting the sides and top of the pan in hundreds of miniature explosions, each kernel truly had a speck of dynamite force inside it. After the tat-tat-tat of the staccato explosions ceased, the lid of the popper was removed, and miraculously, the one-half cupful of hard yellow grains had burst into a panful of large white blossoms of popped corn.

Mother, an English teacher with a quotation to fit many an occasion, would quote Henry David Thoreau: "Popped corn is a perfect winter flower."

How I loved those innocent Thoreauvian feasts around the

kitchen table, those bowls mounded with "cerealian blossoms." The blue pottery crock filled with popped corn temporarily replaced the "Starburst Spooner" as the centerpiece on the kitchen table on Sunday afternoons and winter evenings. Mother sat on one side and graded school papers; Harold, my older brother, sat opposite her and worked arithmetic problems; and I, with Crayolas and paper, completed the semicircle around the popcorn bowl on the kitchen table. My younger brother, Jimmy, rode his stick horse around and around the table. Dad sat nearby in his rocking chair by the stove, playing his harmonica softly (sweet strains of "Flow Gently Sweet Afton" and "Danny Boy"), or entertaining Jimmy from time to time with his repertoire of bear stories. During the school year, Jewel, the hired girl, was also there, and she was always mending or picking out nutmeats of cracked black walnuts or hickory nuts.

JEWEL, THE HIRED GIRL

Jewel used lots of black walnuts and hickory nuts in her cooking. When she was lodging with our family, we could expect the blue crock often to be mounded with sweet, chewy popcorn balls the size of handballs. These were stuck together with a syrup made of sorghum molasses, and they had nutmeats in them.

We gathered black walnuts and hickory nuts every autumn in our woods. Sometimes we also had pecans from Grandma Marshall. We hulled them outdoors before the weather turned cold, and stored them in bushel baskets in the attic. Whenever popcorn balls, or cakes and cookies, or fudge called for nutmeats, a panful of nuts was brought down from upstairs. We cracked the nuts on bricks laid on the floor behind the stove. Then we sat for an interminable time around the kitchen table, with the pan of cracked nuts in the center, laboriously digging out nut kernels, using long nails for picks. It was a tedious task, one that soon lost its charm for us children and one that Mother was too busy to fool with; so Jewel occupied her evenings by filling jars with nutmeats to use later.

Jewel indulged me more than all the other hired girls who helped Mother over the years. She was a shirttail relation, married to Dad's cousin. Her home was nearby, but not near enough for her to return home every night after supper. So she came to our house on Monday mornings after we had gone to school, and left on Fridays after supper.

Jewel cooked good meals for us, and supper was almost ready when we came home from school in the afternoon. Those welcoming aromas of supper cooking greeted our cold noses the instant we hurled ourselves through the doorway, flinging book bags and coats thither and yon, and they drew us toward the kitchen with joy.

"No snacking!" Jewel was firm.

But there was no need to raid the cupboard to find a tasty bite to hold after-school hungers at bay when Jewel did our cooking. We ate supper at four o'clock in the afternoon, before we did our chores. Jewel insisted on having early supper. She wanted to get the supper over with, the dishes washed, and the kitchen cleaned up by the time everyone came in from the barn after the evening milking and feeding the animals.

"I don't intend to be in the kitchen until midnight," she declared.

How full of ease and plenty our lives seemed when we came home to Jewel in the warm, fragrant kitchen, where the table was set, ready for supper, with six white, gold-banded plates, and the pots and pans on the stove steamed and crackled with promise. Jewel's providence in the kitchen always kept our expectations and appetites at their greatest pitch.

We converged in the kitchen, anticipating the joyful reunion around the supper table, the comfort of appeased hunger, the celebration of our evening meal.

But first, we had to pay homage to the benevolent despot of our kitchen.

"Harold, bring up the chairs."

"Jimmy, brush the mud off your shoes."

"Marilyn, put on the knives and forks."

"Someone, get Queen out from under the stove and put her *outside."*

"Hurry, now! Wash your hands and get up to the table."

"One of you call your Dad—supper's ready."

We hurried and scurried, models of obedience and helpfulness. We volunteered to help. We did not squabble. We catered to Jewel. And it came back to us, a hundredfold. Jewel expressed her affection for us and rewarded our cooperation by preparing foods to suit our individual preferences. She made cream puffs, jelly rolls, oatmeal cookies, and fudge and popcorn balls, as treats to please us children.

CHOCOLATE PIE—HEART'S DESIRE

I felt favored when Jewel made chocolate cream pie and chocolate puddings especially for me, or when she placed a cup of hot cocoa beside my plate at breakfast on cold mornings.

". . . to keep you from freezing up on your way to school," she would say.

No one else in the family was fond of chocolate, and Mother and the other hired girls made a practice of cooking to please my father or the majority's preference.

But during that particular winter, when Jewel reigned in our kitchen, I was beneficiary of her largess of chocolate desserts.

These confections were actually made with Hershey's Cocoa, not chocolate. I cannot remember our ever having the more expensive solid baking chocolate in the house. Allen's General Store in town probably did not stock it. To cooks in our locality, cocoa was the same as chocolate, and it served the same purpose. If Jewel wanted to make something chocolatey, she used cocoa.

Women of that day were not intimidated or limited by recipes. They simply made changes in them by using common sense and the ingredients they had available. They did not think of being creative or original. They were just "making do" with what they had.

When Jewel made cream pies, which she often did because we had an abundance of eggs and milk, she doubled the recipe. One pie filling was made in the regular way, but to the second batch she added cocoa. The chocolate portion was for my personal pie. It was topped with a tender, lightly browned egg-white meringue. I could eat it all by myself, if I wanted to.

Although I do not remember ever gorging myself on an entire chocolate pie, I still remember how my feelings glowed whenever Jewel made chocolate pie *just for me.* I learned the pleasure of having my heart's desire, the comfort of a satiated appetite, the joy of being coddled. Every child should know such bliss.

To this day, I find chocolate flavor endowed with a precious essence, like Proust's crumb of tea-soaked madeleine, which bears the hidden joyful past within it.

At times, in moments of epiphany, that joyful past springs to life. It may be recalled by the flavor of chocolate, angel food cake, green apples, or a mere wisp of vanilla fragrance. Sometimes it is reawakened by the imagery of baskets brimming with brown-shelled eggs, pink begonias blooming on windowsills, or puffy white clouds reminding me of Seven-Minute Frosting. Or perhaps the teakettle begins to steam and sizzle on the stove while we are eating an early supper in the kitchen at twilight. But most often it is Mother's "Star-burst Spooner" on my kitchen table that calls me back to the farmhouse kitchen of my memory.

Mother's Angel Food Cake

$1\frac{1}{4}$ cups sifted cake flour
$\frac{1}{2}$ cup sugar
$1\frac{1}{2}$ cups egg white (at room temperature, approx. 13)
$\frac{1}{4}$ teaspoon salt

$1\frac{1}{4}$ teaspoons cream of tartar
$1\frac{1}{3}$ cups sugar
1   teaspoon vanilla extract

Sift the cake flour before measuring, then sift it together three times with the $\frac{1}{2}$ cup sugar.

To the egg whites, add the salt and cream of tartar. Beat (in a copper bowl if possible) with a wire whisk until the whites begin to hold their shape. Add 1 tablespoon of the $1\frac{1}{3}$ cups sugar at a time, beating well after each addition, until all the sugar is added. Fold in the flour-sugar mixture, adding one quarter of the mixture at a time.

As you add the flour mixture, rotate the bowl a quarter turn with each folding motion and be sure the mixture is blended well after each addition. Sprinkle the vanilla extract over the batter, and fold in.

Turn cake batter into an ungreased 10″ angel food cake pan. Bake at 375°F for 35 to 40 minutes. Cool cake upside down in pan, or place tube over a sturdy bottle. When cool, loosen cake from sides and remove from pan. Ice with Seven-Minute Frosting.

Seven-Minute Frosting

2 egg whites	$\frac{1}{3}$ cup cold water
$1\frac{1}{2}$ cups sugar	Dash salt
$\frac{1}{4}$ teaspoon cream of tartar	1 teaspoon vanilla extract

Place all ingredients except vanilla in top of a double boiler. Beat 1 minute with a rotary beater or an electric mixer. Place over simmering water, and beat constantly until mixture forms peaks, about 7 minutes. Remove from heat and add vanilla. Beat until of spreading consistency.

This makes enough frosting to ice one angel food cake or one two-layer cake.

To tint, add a few drops of food coloring along with the vanilla.

One-Egg Omelet

Separate 1 large egg (at room temperature). Place the white on a sturdy dinner plate and the yolk in a small bowl. Beat the egg white with a pinch of salt on the plate, using a flat wire whisk, until soft peaks form. Add 2 teaspoons cold water to the egg yolk in the bowl and beat it vigorously with a fork. Pour the beaten egg yolk over the beaten egg white on the plate and fold the two together, using the whisk. Pour the egg mixture into a heated skillet containing a small amount of sizzling fat (1 teaspoon of bacon grease or butter), and fry the egg in one piece over medium heat, tilting the pan or lifting the edges of the egg to allow the uncooked egg to spread over the pan. Do not overcook, and turn the heat down if the skillet is holding too much heat. Turn the egg once with a spatula. Season with salt and pepper. The omelet cooks very quickly, in only a minute or so.

For a sandwich, place the egg between two slices of homemade bread, with or without butter. A leaf of lettuce may be placed in the sandwich, along with a bit of chopped green onion.

For a 1980's touch, you can also add a few chopped raw or lightly sautéed mushrooms, a sprinkling of lemon pepper, and some alfalfa sprouts. And lightly toast the bread. This makes a perfect meatless sandwich. Mother and Aunt Emma would approve—although they might draw the line at alfalfa sprouts.

Salmon Scramble

1 8-ounce can (1 cup) pink salmon	1 tablespoon butter
$\frac{1}{2}$ teaspoon salt	3 tablespoons chopped green onion
$\frac{1}{8}$ teaspoon pepper	1 tablespoon chopped green pepper (optional)
6 eggs, lightly beaten	Paprika

Drain salmon, remove skin and bones, and break into chunks. Season with salt and pepper and add to eggs.

In a skillet, melt the butter. Add the onions and green pepper and cook slowly until soft, but not brown. Add the salmon and egg mixture and cook over moderate heat, stirring constantly, until the eggs are scrambled. Sprinkle with paprika. Serve with toast and a salad.　　　SERVES 3.

Aunt Emma's Scrambled Eggs ("Egg-a-roo-sel")

Beat 3 large eggs (or 4 smaller ones) with $\frac{2}{3}$ cup milk, 1 rounded tablespoon flour, and salt to taste. Pour into a heated skillet containing a small amount of fat. Cook slowly without stirring too vigorously, pushing the cooked eggs toward the center of the pan, allowing the uncooked portion to run onto the hot pan. Let the second portion cook, and repeat, until all the egg mixture is cooked.

Sunshine Salad

1 3-ounce package lemon-
   flavored gelatin
1 cup boiling water
$\frac{1}{2}$ cup cold water

1 $8\frac{1}{4}$-ounce can crushed
   pineapple in syrup
$\frac{1}{2}$ cup finely grated raw
   carrots

Combine gelatin and boiling water, and stir until dissolved. Add cold water and stir. Let stand at room temperature until cool, about 5 minutes. Add carrots and the crushed pineapple with its syrup. Chill until set.   SERVES 6 TO 8.

Chicken Pot Pie

1 double recipe for biscuit
   dough (see p. 109)
1 cooked chicken, boned
   and skinned
6 small raw potatoes, peeled
   and sliced to $\frac{1}{8}''$
   thickness
2 cups raw shelled peas
4 carrots, sliced in rounds
1 small onion, sliced

$\frac{1}{2}$ cup diced celery
4 sprigs fresh marjoram,
   minced, or 1
   tablespoon
4 sprigs fresh parsley,
   minced, or 3
   tablespoons
3 cups light cream
2 eggs, beaten
Salt and pepper

Line the sides but not the bottom of a 3-quart baking dish with about half of the biscuit dough. In the bottom of the dish, place a layer of cooked chicken. Cover with a layer of potatoes, peas, carrots, and a portion of onion, celery, herbs, and salt and pepper to taste. Cover the vegetables with a few very thin strips of biscuit dough. Repeat layers until baking dish is three-fourths filled. Combine the cream and eggs, season with salt and pepper, and pour over the layered chicken and vegetables. Cover with a thick top crust and cut a slit in the top to vent the steam. Bake at 350°F for 45 minutes to 1 hour.   SERVES 6.

Chicken and Dumplings

5 to 6 pound stewing chicken, cut up, or 2 broiler-fryers, cut up	2 teaspoons salt
	$\frac{1}{4}$ teaspoon pepper
	1 bay leaf
3 sprigs parsley	1 recipe Fluffy Dumplings
3 celery ribs with leaves	or "Slick" Dumplings
2 carrots, pared and sliced	
1 small onion, cut up	

In a large kettle, add enough water to cover the chicken pieces. Add vegetables and seasonings. Cover and bring to a boil. Simmer for $2\frac{1}{2}$ hours or until meat is tender.

Prepare Fluffy Dumplings or "Slick" Dumplings, and cook with the stewed chicken as directed.

Remove dumplings and chicken to a platter and keep warm. Strain the broth in which the chicken and dumplings were cooked. Prepare gravy, using the following recipe.

SERVES 6 TO 8.

Chicken Gravy for Dumplings

Heat 1 quart strained chicken broth in a saucepan. Combine $\frac{1}{4}$ cup flour and 1 cup cold water; gradually add to the broth, mixing well. Cook, stirring constantly, until the mixture thickens. Add 1 teaspoon salt and $\frac{1}{4}$ teaspoon pepper. Pour over chicken and dumplings.

Fluffy Dumplings

1 cup flour	$\frac{1}{2}$ cup milk
$\frac{1}{2}$ teaspoon salt	2 tablespoons melted shortening
$1\frac{1}{2}$ teaspoons baking powder	

Sift together flour, salt, and baking powder. Stir in milk and melted shortening to make a soft dough. Drop dumplings by spoonfuls into gently boiling broth. Cover tightly and steam, without lifting cover, for 12 to 15 minutes.

"Slick" Dumplings

3 cups flour   2 cups boiling broth
1 teaspoon salt

Sift together the flour and salt. Pour the boiling broth into the flour and stir until well blended. Place dough on floured board and roll out to about $\frac{1}{8}''$ thickness. Cut into 1" squares, and drop into boiling chicken or meat broth. Cook until tender, about 15 minutes.

Chocolate Blanc Mange

6 tablespoons cocoa $\frac{1}{2}$ teaspoon salt
$\frac{3}{4}$ cup sugar   1 quart milk
6 tablespoons cornstarch   1 teaspoon vanilla

Mix together all the dry ingredients in a saucepan, making sure there are no lumps of cocoa. Stir in a small amount of the milk to blend, then add the rest of the milk, stirring constantly. Cook and stir over medium heat until the mixture thickens and comes to a boil. Remove from heat, cool slightly, and stir in the vanilla. Pour into dessert dishes while warm. Cover with waxed paper until time to serve, to prevent a thick skin from forming on top of the pudding. Serve with whipped cream or a small amount of light cream to pour over the pudding.   SERVES 6.

Jewel's Cream Pie

$\frac{1}{3}$ cup sifted enriched flour
  or 4 tablespoons
  cornstarch
$\frac{2}{3}$ cup sugar
$\frac{1}{4}$ teaspoon salt
2 cups milk, scalded
3 egg yolks, lightly beaten

2 tablespoons butter
1 teaspoon vanilla
1 9" pie shell, baked
3 egg whites, beaten until
  stiff
6 tablespoons sugar

Mix flour, $\frac{2}{3}$ cup sugar, and salt. Gradually add the milk, stirring well. Cook over moderate heat, stirring constantly, until mixture thickens and boils. Cook 2 minutes longer. Remove from heat.

Add a small amount of boiling mixture very gradually to the egg yolks; then stir the egg yolk mixture into the hot custard. Cook 1 minute, stirring constantly. Add butter and vanilla. Cool slightly. Pour into baked pie shell and let cool.

Cover with a meringue made of egg whites beaten with 6 tablespoons sugar. Bake at 350°F for 12 to 15 minutes.

VARIATIONS

Banana Slice 2 bananas into the bottom of pie shell. Add filling and meringue.

Chocolate Increase sugar to 1 cup. Melt two 1-ounce squares of unsweetened chocolate in the scalded milk, or stir 6 tablespoons cocoa into the sugar before combining it with the other ingredients.

Fresh Coconut Grate the meat of one coconut. Add 1 cup fresh coconut meat to the cooked cream pie filling. Sprinkle $\frac{1}{2}$ cup fresh coconut over the meringue before browning.

Bread Pudding

2 eggs, beaten
3 cups milk
$\frac{2}{3}$ cups sugar
$\frac{1}{8}$ teaspoon freshly grated
  nutmeg
$\frac{1}{4}$ teaspoon cinnamon

4 cups stale homemade
  bread, torn into pieces,
  not cubes
$\frac{1}{2}$ cup raisins
1 tablespoon butter

Beat together the eggs and milk with a whisk or rotary beater. Add sugar and spices. Add bread and raisins to the milk mixture. Pour into an 8" x 12" x 2" baking dish, dot with butter, and bake at 375°F for 1 hour. Serve warm with cream.   SERVES 6.

Golden Delicious Apple Pie

5 cups peeled, and sliced
  Golden Delicious
  apples
$\frac{2}{3}$ cup sugar
$\frac{1}{4}$ cup brown sugar, firmly
  packed
2 tablespoons flour
1 teaspoon cinnamon

$\frac{1}{2}$ teaspoon mace
2 tablespoons flour
  Juice and grated rind of 1
  lemon
2 9" pie shells
2 tablespoons butter

In a large bowl, combine the first 8 ingredients. Line a pie tin with pastry, add the apple mixture, and dot with butter. Cover the pie with the top round of pastry. Seal and crimp the edges. Cut a vent to let the steam escape. Brush top of pastry with a small amount of milk, then sprinkle with a little sugar to make the crust brown nicely. Bake at 400°F for 10 minutes, then reduce the heat to 375°F and bake for about 50 minutes longer, or until the apples are tender and the crust is browned.   SERVES 6 TO 8.

Jewel's Popovers

2 eggs
1 cup milk
1 cup sifted flour

$\frac{1}{2}$ teaspoon salt
1 tablespoon melted
    shortening or salad oil

Preheat oven to 425°F. Preheat popover pan while mixing batter, grease cups just before filling, and return pan to the oven so that they are sizzling hot when filled.

With a rotary beater or electric mixer beat the eggs thoroughly ($\frac{1}{2}$ minute on high speed in mixer). Add the milk, flour, salt, and melted shortening and beat until the batter is very smooth (1 minute at low speed in mixer). Fill the hot greased cups* a little less than half full. Bake at 425°F for 15 minutes, then reduce heat to 375°F and bake for 20 to 25 minutes longer. *Do not open* the oven during the first 30 minutes baking or the popovers will collapse. The sides of the popovers are rigid to the touch when they are finished. If a dry interior is desired, pierce each popover with a knife, and bake 5 minutes longer. Serve at once.

MAKES 6 POPOVERS.

Jewel's Jelly Roll

4 eggs, separated
$\frac{1}{4}$ cup sugar
$\frac{1}{2}$ teaspoon vanilla extract
$\frac{1}{2}$ cup sugar

$\frac{3}{4}$ cup sifted cake flour
1 teaspoon baking powder
$\frac{1}{4}$ teaspoon salt
Confectioners' sugar

Beat egg yolks until thick and lemon colored. Gradually beat in the $\frac{1}{4}$ cup sugar and vanilla.

---

* Popover cups may be cast iron, heavy aluminum, oven glass, or earthenware, but they must be deeper than than they are wide. The batter is thin, about the consistency of heavy cream.

Beat egg whites until almost stiff. Add remaining $\frac{1}{2}$ cup sugar, 2 tablespoons at a time, and continue beating after each addition until egg whites are very stiff. Fold egg yolk mixture into egg white mixture.

Sift together flour, baking powder, and salt three times. Add to egg mixture in thirds, folding until blended after each addition.

Line a $15\frac{1}{2}''$ x $10\frac{1}{2}''$ x $1''$ baking sheet with waxed paper. Spread the batter in the paper-lined pan and bake at 375°F for about 12 minutes.

Loosen cake carefully from the sides of the pan. Sprinkle top of cake with approximately 2 tablespoons confectioners' sugar. Cover with a clean towel, then turn the towel-covered pan upside down, turning the cake out on the towel. Remove waxed paper. Quickly trim the crisp edges of the cake with a sharp knife. Roll up the cake and the towel, starting at the narrow end. Add more sugar to the towel to make rolling easier, if needed.

Let the rolled cake cool in the towel, then unwrap. Spread with jelly, lemon filling, or thick cream-pie filling. Reroll.

Jewel sometimes used plain granulated sugar to sprinkle the jelly roll because confectioners' sugar was something of a luxury during the Depression, and we did not always have it. Sometimes sweetened fresh berries folded into whipped cream were spread inside the jelly roll cake instead of jelly.

Spicy Apple Muffins

2 cups sifted flour	$\frac{1}{2}$ cup sugar
4 teaspoons baking powder	1 egg, beaten
$\frac{3}{4}$ teaspoon salt	1 cup milk
$\frac{3}{4}$ teaspoon cinnamon	$\frac{1}{3}$ cup melted shortening
$\frac{1}{4}$ teaspoon mace or nutmeg	1 cup peeled chopped apples

Topping:

⅓ cup brown sugar, firmly   ½ teaspoon cinnamon
     packed
⅓ cup pecans, hickory nuts,
     or black walnuts

To prepare batter: Sift together the first six ingredients. Combine egg, milk, and melted shortening. Make a well in the dry ingredients and add liquid all at once. Stir until blended. Do not overmix. Add the chopped apples and pour into greased muffin wells. Fill two-thirds full. Combine topping ingredients and sprinkle over batter in muffin tin. Bake at 400°F for 25 minutes.   MAKES 12 LARGE MUFFINS.

Mother's Blackberry-Red Plum Jelly

Extract the juice from blackberries and red plums separately.

In a preserving kettle, combine equal amounts of blackberry juice and tart red plum juice, using no more than 3 or 4 cups of juice at a time. Combine the blended fruit juices with sugar, using 1 cup of sugar to each 1 cup of fruit juice. Bring to a boil over high heat and boil rapidly until mixture gels. Pour the boiling jelly into hot sterilized jelly glasses and seal with paraffin or self-sealing lids.

Aunt Blanche's Apple Crisp

4 to 6 apples, peeled,   1 cup flour, sifted
     cored, and sliced, to fill   1 teaspoon baking powder
     a deep-dish pie plate   ½ teaspoon salt
2 eggs   1 teaspoon vanilla
1 cup sugar
2 tablespoons melted butter

Arrange the prepared apples in a deep-dish pie plate.

Beat together the eggs, sugar, and melted butter.

Sift together the flour, baking powder, and salt. Add to the egg mixture and fold in until well blended. Add vanilla. Pour the mixture over the apples. Bake at 350°F for approximately 40 minutes, or until the top is lightly browned and the apples are tender.

Chicken-Fried Beefsteak and Milk Gravy

There is no set recipe for these two stand-bys in the country kitchens I remember, but there were methods that I can describe.

Chicken-Fried Beefsteak Beefsteaks were cut thin, less than $\frac{1}{2}''$ thick, and pounded to break down the connective tissue and tenderize them. Even choice cuts were treated this way. A wooden mallet with "teeth" carved in it, a wooden potato masher, or the side of a heavy plate could be used to pound the meat. Mother used the handle of our trusty "butcher knife." The steak was then coated in flour, fried like chicken in lard, and seasoned with salt and pepper.

Sometimes the steaks were breaded. A few soda crackers were crushed, an egg beaten with 2 to 4 tablespoons of milk. The pounded steak was dipped in the egg-milk mixture, then into the cracker crumbs to coat both sides. They were then fried to a tender, lightly browned crispness.

Milk Gravy Milk gravy was to us what boiled beans were to Grandma Marshall's family. And chicken-fried steak or fried chicken were not truly farm-style without milk gravy made with the pan drippings. Remove the meat from the pan. Sift flour into the sizzling-hot fat, while stirring constantly. Stir and cook the flour over medium-high heat for a minute or two, but only long enough to very slightly "tan" the flour mixture. If it is browned too much, the gravy will be dark and taste scorched. While stirring the flour-fat mixture vigorously, pour the milk in quickly in a large stream. Turn the heat down and continue stirring while the mixture thickens. Season to taste with salt and pepper.

Gravy was not something for which a country cook had measurements. Gravy-making was learned by experience, and a different sized pan or type of heat could result in a dish of gravy not quite up to standard. A well-seasoned iron skillet was the usual cooking utensil, and a tablespoon the stirring utensil. Gravy cooked in a saucepan with butter or solid white shortening is not country milk gravy; it is white sauce.

Milk gravy is made with bacon drippings, or with the fat and crusty bits left in a skillet after frying pork chops, steak, chicken, liver, rabbit, quail, squirrel, sausage, pork, or venison.

Milk gravy was spooned over mashed potatoes, over meat, over fried green tomatoes, biscuits, or plain bread. There were times when supper was simply milk gravy and biscuits.

Most farm families depended on milk gravy to round out one or more meals, often breakfast, each day, especially during winter.

As a rule, approximately equal amounts of flour and pan drippings are needed. One-fourth cup drippings and one-fourth cup flour to three or four cups of milk makes enough gravy for moderate servings for a family of four.

Milk gravy was to the farmhouse kitchens I remember what "sauce" was to less provincial cooks. It was countrified but delicious, and absolutely essential when three abundant daily meals were a necessity.

Sorghum Popcorn Balls

7 cups popped corn	1 cup sugar
1 cup black walnuts	$\frac{1}{3}$ cup water
1 cup minus 2 tablespoons sorghum syrup	1 teaspoon vinegar
	$\frac{1}{4}$ teaspoon baking soda

Mix together popped corn and nuts and place in a warm oven, 150°F, to keep hot.

Combine sorghum, sugar, water, and vinegar. Cook to the hard-ball stage, 250°F on a candy thermometer. Remove from heat and wipe crystals from the edge of the pan with a damp cloth wrapped around the tines of a fork.

Add baking soda to the hot mixture by sifting it through a sieve. Stir just enough to mix well. Pour hot syrup over popcorn and nuts, mixing well. Grease hands with butter, and taking care not to handle while syrup is hot enough to burn the hands, form the popcorn into balls.

MAKES 6 LARGE BALLS.

Cocoa Fudge

2 cups sugar	$\frac{2}{3}$ cup milk
$\frac{1}{8}$ teaspoon salt	2 tablespoons butter
6 tablespoons cocoa	1 teaspoon vanilla

In a heavy saucepan, mix sugar, salt, and cocoa. Stir in milk. Bring to a boil and cook to the soft-ball stage, 234°F to 238°F on a candy thermometer, stirring occasionally. Remove from heat and add butter. Cool slightly, add vanilla, and beat until the mixture is creamy and thick. When it has lost its glossy appearance and holds its shape, pour onto a greased platter. When solid, cut in 1" squares.

MAKES ABOUT 24 SQUARES.

Fudge With Nuts Add $\frac{1}{2}$ cup black walnuts, hickory nuts, pecans, or English walnuts to the fudge just before it thickens enough to pour out onto the platter.

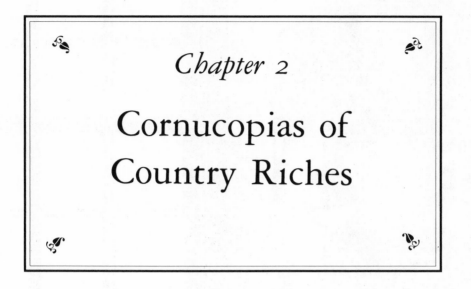

Chapter 2

Cornucopias of
Country Riches

THE PANTRY

THE PANTRY NEXT TO our kitchen in the farmhouse had a look of delicious plenty. Its pine-sheathed walls were lined with sturdy shelves that sagged gently under the weight of sparkling jars of garden vegetables, fruits, and jellies, the overflow from the cellar. Deep covered bins for pastry flour, bread flour, sugar, and cornmeal stood along one wall. On the table under the window were flat pans filled with fresh tomatoes from the garden or potatoes from the cellar, baskets of brown-shelled eggs, shiny tin pails of leaf lard, and earthenware crocks brimming with cream-topped milk. On the windowsill bloomed rose geraniums with their scented leaves, and blue-flowered chives. Even the ceiling was hung with edibles: there were always clusters of yellow onions, strings of glossy red hot peppers, and the dried beans we called "leather britches," fragrant bunches of dried, silvery green sage and pungent dillweed, and a hickory-smoked ham encased in a muslin sack. Here, too, were kept the breadboard, rolling pin, kraut cutter, nutmeg grater, turkey

45

platter, coffee grinder, cherry pitter, flour sifter, and all the other fascinating paraphernalia of cookery.

This small room with its spicy aromas, full cookie jars, and clutter of kitchen utensils was a veritable storehouse of flavorful bounties. It was my childhood land of Cockaigne where I loved to dawdle before supper, innocently nibbling a brown sugar lump while dipping a stealthy finger into the cake frosting or surreptitiously pocketing a cupcake.

But from time to time the cornucopia of riches of our country pantry diminished. Perhaps warm weather held off butchering, or the garden had not yet begun to produce, or summer's fruits were scarce, or a trip to the general store was long overdue. At such times Mother took inventory in the pantry, lifting a lid here and there, peering into flour and sugar bins, shaking oatmeal and tapioca boxes and rattling their meager contents. She wrote down a list of items and stuck the paper on a nail on the doorframe.

"We'll go to the store on Saturday," she would announce. "We are out of everything." Mother tied on her apron and put on her determined look. "We'll just make do until then."

That phrase never failed to dampen my spirits. When Mother declared that there was "nothing to do with" and spoke of "making do," it meant that the lavish hand of the kitchen was stayed, at least temporarily, and our table would be spread with "old standbys" until the stores were replenished. There was nothing to do but wait and see how bare the cupboard actually was.

Mother's standbys were those dishes she relied on when there was a dearth in the pantry. They were made of the plentiful foods of the farm—eggs, milk, cream, butter—and the pantry staples that we kept on hand in large supply, such as flour, sugar, dried beans, cereals, and home-rendered lard. A few of these standbys were totally unappealing to me as a child, but some of them were memorable dishes of delicious plainness in which I have always delighted.

CHESS PIE

My favorite among the standbys was chess pie, a treat that requires only the simplest, most inexhaustible ingredients—those we always had in abundance on the farm. Mother's chess pie was made of a delectable blend of butter, sugar, and eggs, and was baked in a deep flaky pastry shell. It also required a sprinkling of cornmeal—so little that it might even be brushed up from the bottom of an empty bin—and a squeeze of lemon juice. If there was no lemon, vinegar was used instead, with no one the wiser. Sometimes a splash of cream was added. Mother could concoct a chess pie from the last remaining staples of her barest cupboard.

Whenever Mother began to stir up a chess pie, I took my usual place on the chair beside the kitchen table where she worked. Once she had her hands in the flour, she liked to have me nearby, to scurry after something or other that she had neglected to lay out before starting to sift and mix.

"Run, now, and get some fresh eggs," she would say as she began to work the flour and lard together for the pie crust, moving her fingers deftly in those quick, peculiar motions needed to break the firm lumps of creamy shortening into small particles and to blend them with the flour.

I would dash out to the henhouse, less than a hundred feet beyond our backyard, rout the fat Rhode Island Red hens out of their straw-filled nests, and return with two large brown eggs cradled in each hand. They were still warm to the touch when I laid them on the table on which Mother was, by this time, gently pressing the dough into a flat round in the center of a floured circle on her breadboard.

"Better draw up the butter, too," she would say before I could climb back on the chair to watch her roll out the dough.

So I would scamper down the back steps again and out to the well to draw up the bucket in which the butter was kept cool and fresh, suspended just above the water at the end of a rope, from one churning day until the next. I was adept at drawing buckets from the well, this being one of my daily chores, so I would soon be back in the kitchen with the cool, moist crock of yellow butter in hand—still in time to see the dough flatten and expand under the rhythmic pressures of Mother's rolling pin.

When the round of dough was somewhat larger than the brown pottery pie plate that Mother used especially for chess pies, she would coil it around her rolling pin and adroitly unroll it over the plate so that it came out just right, with a little flap of dough hanging over the edge. This flap she cut off while holding the pie plate aloft on the palm of one hand, letting the scraps fall onto the breadboard. Next she crimped the rim all around the plate, carefully pressing the cut edge between thumb and forefinger to make a ruffled collar around the shell.

Then Mother set aside the unbaked pie shell and relinquished the rolling pin, breadboard, and pastry trimmings to me; and while I attempted to emulate her light, springy motions with the rolling pin, she quickly mixed the filling.

First she cut off a side of the large butter ball I had brought from the well. Then she dropped the yellow lump into a deep spongeware bowl and rubbed it against the sides with the back of a long-handled wooden spoon. When the butter had softened she added small measures of sugar from the crackled china cup that we always kept in the sugar bin, and after each addition she stirred the mixture vigorously until it was fluffy and creamy. Next she beat in the eggs, sprinkled the mixture with a bit of cornmeal, and added lemon juice and vanilla flavoring. The whole process hardly gave me time to finish my own small pie, using the scraps of dough, which, when sprinkled with sugar and baked, always tasted delicious in spite of my kneading and pummeling.

When Mother's filling had been poured into the waiting shell, the bowl—rimmed with sweet, sticky remnants to be scraped up with a teaspoon—was mine. Scraping bowls was one of the joys of staying close to the kitchen, the reward for running errands. A tantalizing taste of pie filling, a crumbly round of sugary crust hot from the oven—these were treats to content a small girl until suppertime.

For me, a chess pie was the redemption of a meal consisting largely of standbys. I could stoically devour even sauerkraut and sausages or boiled beans and potatoes if there was a chess pie cooling on the window ledge in the pantry.

WASHDAY FOOD

Boiled beans and potatoes appeared on our table not only when the cupboard was bare, but often on washday, which was Monday.

Food on washday always seemed, somehow, more strengthening and restorative than food on other days. Bean soup with slivers of bacon or ham, chunky potatoes, and bits of sliced onion, pickled peaches, corn bread, chess pie—it was food that stuck to your ribs and revived depleted energy and muscles made tired by hauling water and lugging newspaper-lined wooden peach baskets (which served also as clothes baskets).

Usually I tolerated washday "bean soup" without a word, picking the potatoes out of the broth and leaving most of the beans. Since I knew Mother only cooked beans when she was too busy to cook anything that needed close watching or when there was simply nothing else to cook, complaints would have been unwise. Better to stomach a few bites of beans willingly than to be told to "straighten up" and eat every last bean on my plate.

Besides, one of my father's favorite dishes was boiled dried beans. He had learned to like beans when he was growing up as one of sixteen children.

"Like them or not, we had to eat beans. Mom and Dad would have had a hard time feeding all of us without dried beans. I'll tell you, we ate a lot of beans in those days. Most folks did. And your grandmother could cook a pot of beans that made the finest eating in the world. She would soak those dried beans in water overnight and then the next morning she would put them on the stove in a big black iron kettle with a piece of salt pork in with them, and they would cook along *very slowly* until they were tender, but not mushy. Sometimes she would add a few cut-up Irish potatoes toward the last half hour when the beans were almost done. Along about noontime, she would mix up a pan of cornbread. Now that was a pan that measured two feet long and a foot and a half wide, and it took up one entire rack of the oven. And, by gollies, when dinner was over, there wasn't enough left over to feed the old dog, Strongheart. Those beans and corn bread made a meal as nourishing as a meal of meat."

Many of the stories Dad told us about his family had to do with the family's effort to achieve a good life. All the children had to work, even the little ones. And every day was washday.

"We always had clean clothes," Dad said. "Your grandmother was too busy cooking for us to do the washing, so different ones had that job. One summer when I was twelve or fourteen, I wanted to be a prizefighter and I was interested in muscle building. It was my brother Ed's job to wash the clothes. He didn't like washing much, so he said to my Dad, 'Why don't you put El on that washing machine since he wants to build muscles?' So Dad put me on that old push-and-pull washer all summer long. I washed diapers all day, every day. That was a big family; there were babies on every bed. Grace and Lois, Walter and Norman; all of them were younger than I was."

WASHDAY

Our family still had an old push-and-pull washer stored in the granary. "Better keep it; we might need it," Mother said.

She had gained the luxury of a new Maytag washer with a gasoline motor, but it still had to prove itself to her.

The gasoline motor of the Maytag made a raucous noise on Monday mornings, but it reduced the need for muscle power to wash the clothes—when it was working.

Nevertheless, washday meant at least a half day of hard work, which began with drawing up buckets of water from the front well or pumping the wheezing hand pump over the cistern near the back door. The well was fed by underground water and we caught the run-off water from the roof when it rained for the cistern. When the cistern was running dry, there was always water in the front well. When the front well was low, there was still water in one of two wells located away from the house, down by the creek. During one summer, when there was a severe drought (which caused the Dust Bowl in the southwest), we hauled the clothes down to the well by the creek with my brother Harold's wagon, and washed them there. The well was on the "old homeplace" where Grandma and Grandpa had first lived, the house where my mother was born. Washday had the air of an outing that summer. Dad put up a clothesline next to a cornfield and set up the old black kettle for heating water over an open fire. The washtubs were there on benches, and the old push-and-pull washer was hauled down with the horse and wagon, and put back into use.

We were all glad to get back to the relative luxury of washday with the Maytag when the drought was broken.

When I was old enough to master the technique of flipping the bucket at the end of the rope after it was let down into a well so that it would fill with water, and strong enough to draw it up to the top of the well and haul it over the side, drawing water was sometimes my job.

Flipping the bucket was quite a trick. The water pail had to be lowered to exactly the right distance above the surface of the water, when an expertly maneuvered snap of the wrist would turn the pail over so that it would begin to fill with water and sink while filling. It looked much easier to do than it was, and it was one of those techniques a country child was proud to master, even though it meant helping with washday chores.

Everyone around helped on washday—Dad, my older brother, the hired girl—Mother enlisted anyone she could find. Without running water and electricity, washing clothes was "heavy work." It was not beneath the dignity of the menfolk to help set up the washer and tubs, build a fire outside under the boiling kettle, or lift the washtubs to the benches next to the washing machine.

Two tubs were half filled with cold water for rinsing clothes. A third tub was filled halfway and hauled up onto the stove to provide hot water.

The big iron kettle was set up outdoors in warm weather and a fire was built under it. (Sometimes, sweet potatoes were buried in the hot ashes under the kettle to bake for washday dinner.) When the water boiled, a cake of lye soap was shaved into slivers and added to it. Periodically, the sheets and dingy dish towels were boiled in lye water—separately, of course—to whiten them. Even the rags, or work clothes that were especially dirty, were boiled in lye water before being washed, too, but colored clothes as a rule were not boiled in lye water because they would be bleached and faded looking afterward.

While Mother had moved toward modernity by acquiring a Maytag, she clung to her old ways of getting clothes clean and white.

"Getting the wash clean and the dirt out is one thing," she said. "Getting it *white* is another!"

The lye soap made cotton sheets and muslin flour-sack dish towels perceptibly whiter from the very moment they were gingerly lifted from the roiling, acrid water in the steaming kettle with the clothes stick—an old broom handle with its end porous and bleached from numerous dippings.

The boiled sheets and towels made up the "second load" of washing, following the white shirts Dad wore with his suits when he was teaching school. In the winter he needed a clean one for each day of school. In the summertime, sheets and pillowcases comprised the first load: good "colored clothes," the second; dish towels, the third load; work clothes and other colored wash, the fourth; overalls, the fifth; and rags and rugs, the sixth. The wash had been carefully sorted into piles on the floor before we began.

As each load of clothes was washed, it was put through the washing machine wringers into the first rinse water and given a good rinsing. This was accomplished by punching the tubful of clean clothing or sheets with the clothes stick or by hand. Then the wringer was swung around to a place just over the second tub, and the rinsed items were passed through it into the second rinse, which was colored blue with bluing. The bluing miraculously brightened the "whites" even more.

But the zeal for a sparkling white wash did not end with bluing in the final rinse. White sheets flapping on the front lines were banners revealing the industry and devotion of the woman of the house. Even hanging the clothes on the lines was a housewifely art. To have the wash on the line early in the morning on a beautiful day was a triumph in itself. Then there was a pattern for hanging the clothes. Mother hung the sheets evenly and precisely over the front line facing the sun, which made a crease from the line run down the middle of each sheet. Next the shirts, hung by their tails and all together; then the men's undershirts, hung by their straps. Colored clothes hung in the shade, lest the sun fade their bright colors. Socks were pinned neatly in pairs by their toes. Underwear was discreetly hung out of view from the road, hidden on the inner lines so even the hired hands passing through the yard wouldn't catch sight of Dad's "drawers" or Mother's underclothing. Rags were spread out on the grass to bleach, and if line space was short when we had a big wash, dish towels were spread out over bushes in the back yard.

Dingy grayish rags spread out on the grass benefited from a mysterious combination of grass and sunshine and became white again. It took a lot of sunning and a good breeze to get the odor of lye soap out of clothes that had been boiled. How clean the clothing smelled when we took it from the lines on a good drying day and folded it!

It was pleasant to help take the dry wash down. The arm-loads of bright dresses and spotless dish towels hugged to your body released such sweetness that the impulse to inhale deeply of their freshness and cleanness, to bury your face in the collapsing billows of pristine sheets as they were taken from the line, was irrestistible.

Folding sheets was something like a dance when two people folded them together—each grasping a corner and bringing the corners together, stepping back, then stepping forward to meet one another to join the corners together; then one partner releasing her corners and picking up the new loose edges, then stepping back, then forward, and so on until the clean fresh sheets were folded into a smooth rectangle.

After folding, the clean sheets were taken directly into the house and put back on the beds. The clean, fresh smell—concocted somehow of sunshine and breeze, clean water and lye soap—can only be achieved when the wash is dried outside on the clothesline on a sparkling day with a breeze that catches the sheets like sails in the wind and sets rows of shirts and dresses dancing like puppets on strings.

Although there are pleasant things to remember about it, washday was a hard day's work for Mother, and I was glad everyday was not washday for us, as it was for Dad when he was a boy.

THE BLESSING OF PLENTY

My father was reared in a family with sixteen children. When Dad told us how much food had to be provided to feed the multitude of brothers and sisters who sat on long benches at both sides of Grandma Marshall's kitchen table at mealtime, I understood the meaning of *plenty*.

Canned blackberries by the gallon, sour milk biscuits by the dozens, smoked bacon by the slab, fruit pies by the half dozen, yeast bread loaves by the oven load, jellies by the quart, fried green tomatoes by the crockful, and butter by the pound—the arithmetic alone boggled my mind.

"We had plenty of good food to eat, there's no question about it." Dad always stressed that point. "We had *plenty of good food* to eat. Mom and Dad spent all their time seeing to it that we would have enough."

I always loved to listen to the stories Dad told about his boyhood in that remote time, in that unique family whose high-spirited children, in spite of their number, were always well clothed, well housed, well educated, and well fed.

"We didn't have the money to go and buy—so we raised it. Dad would start out by planting an acre of potatoes. Then, after he had cut the rye, he'd plant an acre or two of beans. And we'd pick about one hundred and forty-five gallons of blackberries—now that's a fact—one hundred and forty-five gallons of blackberries! Then we would have all kinds of fruits—peaches and apples and everything canned up, and we had plenty to eat," Dad said.

When Dad told tales about his boyhood days, I understood his lifelong tendency of doing things on a large and generous scale. From childhood on, he was accustomed to thinking in acres, not feet, or planning by bushels, not gallons. He never really learned to scale down his ideas to fit his own small family of three children. Sometimes he seemed to be still thinking in terms of providing enough for a family of eighteen.

"I carried the idea of having a good garden over from your grandparents—and when Laura and I married, she was the same way," Dad told me.

When he planted an orchard, even if originally intended for family use, it ended up a grove of two hundred trees. When he "made garden," the vegetable crop would feed our family, and several others as well. When he planted a strawberry patch, he put out an acre of vigorous, prolific plants, not just one paltry row down the edge of the garden. Dad always thought in terms of having *plenty*, as he understood the meaning of plenty.

THE REWARDS OF STRAWBERRY PICKING

While I am grateful that we were never in need, having plenty, as defined by my father, in the realm of garden and orchard, was sometimes a two-sided blessing. When I recall the constant procession of luscious strawberry desserts and jams that Mother prepared for our table, I also remember the hours spent kneeling on the straw mulch between the rows when we picked box after box of the scarlet berries. After methodically picking up one row and down another row of a one-acre strawberry patch, morning after hot summer morning, with the sun burning on my back and shoulders and the less sociable of insects hovering about the brim of my straw hat, I could precisely define an acre, as well as my father's concept of plenty.

But my diligent hours among the ground-hugging strawberry vines were amply rewarded at dinnertime. Mother made immense strawberry pies filled with choice berries folded into drifts of whipped cream and cool gelatin, and strawberry shortcakes of tender, flaky, still-warm biscuits, split and buttered generously, with a layer of sweet juicy crimson berries reposing in their middles and crowning their sugary, crusty tops.

And every now and then, after the supper dishes were all cleared away and the afterglow of sunset streaked the evening sky with color as crimson as the strawberries themselves, my indefatigable mother got out her large egg-white pan and began making our most beloved strawberry dessert for the next day's dinner—meringue nests that would later be filled with frosty pink strawberry ice cream, flecked with bits of red berries, adorned with spoonfuls of halved, sweetened strawberries, and drenched in torrents of their sweet red juice.

Now that was a dessert to anticipate! I could predict that my father would say, in his fashion, "Now there's a dainty dish to set before the king!"

Mother's making of the meringues was no less than a queenly favor bestowed upon us. Surely she was ready to rest after making our supper as well as the sparkling jars of strawberry jam that stood cooling on the table, which were soon to be added to our winter's supply of sweet spreads. But, nevertheless, she sat on a straight-backed kitchen chair with the large egg-white pan on her lap. She beat the egg whites with a whisk, using great circular motions that made them voluminous and airy, and her arms seemed never to tire. Every so often she stopped for a moment and, at her direction, I sprinkled sugar, a little at a time, over the rising mound of egg whites. Finally, when the cupful of sugar had all disappeared into the soft white mass and the peaks held their shape like miniature snow-capped mountaintops, Mother dipped out mounds of the beaten egg whites and put them on baking tins. She shaped a nestlike cavity in the center of each, using the back of a spoon, to later hold a mound of frosty pink ice cream and the luscious red strawberries. Then she slid the baking tins into the oven, where they would be left to bake slowly overnight. The fire in the range was at last dying down, after the day's cooking and preserving, but there was still just enough heat held in the oven to make the meringues crisp and dry and delicious by morning.

Summer fruits ripened in rapid succession. Following the acre of strawberries, there were red cherries, apricots, raspberries, gooseberries, plums, peaches, pears, quinces, grapes, and apples. In addition to the cultivated fruits, we had an abundance of wild fruits in the fields and fencerows around the farm. We gathered "wild goose" plums, mulberries, elderberries, "sarvis" berries, crab apples and wildings, red haws, pawpaws, persimmons, wild fox grapes, tiny wild strawberries, and wild blackberries.

BLACKBERRYING

Every summer without fail, Mother canned at least a hundred quarts of blackberries and fifty small jars of blackberry jam and jelly. In addition, she put up blackberry juice in half-gallon jars to make into fresh jelly later in winter if the supply dwindled.

I picked berries all summer to help Mother can her quota, beginning when I was about school age. We never considered blackberry picking a chore because such outings had the air of a holiday. Sometimes relatives from the city came to join us in picking blackberries, and they brought grand picnic lunches that were spread out on the ground under the maple trees in Grandpa's front yard, across the road from our house.

When blackberries ripened in July, we got up earlier than usual—usual was daybreak for Mother, six o'clock for slugabeds like me.

"Rise and shine!" was Mother's wake-up call. "It's a beautiful day! Get up! Get up! You spend a third of your life in bed. Don't sleep it away."

That was always Mother's philosophy. She did not believe in frittering time away. There was a sense of urgency about her approach to routine work, an eagerness to get it out of the way so she could do something extra. She looked on blackberrying and being outdoors, where she loved to be, as a respite from ordinary housework. But the chores had to be done before we could be away from the farmhouse all morning. Mother would pack a midmorning lunch for us in one of the berry pails.

"Step lively," Mother encouraged. "Someone will beat us to the best berries."

Nothing was more disheartening than finding the briars of the best berry thickets in the pasture tramped down and picked over. Very little land in our community was posted. Folks out berrying would pick wherever they could find fruit.

Getting dressed for blackberry picking was no small chore. A special outfit was called for to protect the picker from snags and scratches, chigger bites, and sunstroke during a day in the briar patch. For berrying, or whenever Mother helped with haying or at the barn with the milking, she borrowed a pair of bib overalls from Grandpa, which fit her neatly. These she wore over a faded blue denim work shirt with long buttoned sleeves and a high buttoned collar. In addition, she pulled a pair of cotton stockings, with the feet cut out, over her arms. Thin cotton gloves with just the fingertips cut off helped to protect her hands further. Mother always tried to keep her hands "nice," remembering her appearance as a schoolteacher for most of the year. Her standard berry-picking gear was completed by oxford shoes, heavy stockings, and a wide-brimmed calico sunbonnet with a deep ruffle that covered her neck.

Around her ankles, wrists, and waist she tied cords soaked in coal oil to ward off chiggers. I rebelled at being decked out similarly.

"I would rather have chiggers," I said. And I did.

My outfit consisted of straw hat, jeans, and a long-sleeved shirt. I took chiggers in stride, dabbing rubbing alcohol and bacon grease mixed with salt on the itching welts. Scratches were a condition of summer, too, and Mercurochrome stripes

on arms and legs were the red badges of courage.

When we reached the blackberry patch, the sun had barely begun its climb above the line of green woods surrounding the pasture. The morning stretched out before us, the very essence of summer freedom. Here was time to savor the choicest berries, to pick a bouquet of black-eyed susans, to watch sunfish glinting in a shallow pool of creek water. Now there was time to talk quietly—and so much time that, for long periods, it wasn't necessary to talk at all.

Again and again we filled the bright lard pails that hung from ropes tied about our waists with juicy, tart-sweet purple berries. As the smaller pails filled, they were emptied into the three-gallon milk buckets. With both hands free for picking, the buckets filled quickly. At midmorning, when the level of dark, glistening berries in our buckets reached the two-gallon mark, we stopped to rest under a spreading beech tree on the second rise of the hill in the woods.

This was a tree with many initials, names, and dates carved in its trunk, and it compelled us to pause in its shade whenever we were near. It was a ritual to read out from among the many anonymous initials those we recognized, and those that belonged to that infinite void of years before we were born. Mother's initials were there: "L. B. 1920," which stood for Laura Buse, a name I found in schoolbooks and college textbooks and written in albums below the face of a beautiful young woman with deep-set, soulful eyes looking shyly out of the photograph. I could recognize those same blue-green eyes now, with their happy look of contentment, as Mother took off her bonnet and fanned herself with its starched brim.

I explored the contents of the lunch, wrapped up in a newspaper, which Mother had packed for us at breakfast time.

Mine was a jelly sandwich: tangy red-plum jelly and freshly churned butter on Mother's good "light bread." Hers was a breakfast biscuit, split, with a cold hard-fried egg and a slice of bacon between the halves. The morning sun had warmed the wrapping; when opened, it released a richness of fra-

grance, created from the intermingling of several aromas closed
in together, that rises from all lunch boxes, sack lunches, and
picnic hampers. We carried drinking water in a canning jar
with the raised letters on its side spelling out BALL IDEAL.
The water looked cool and limpid in the blue-green jar, but
it was always lukewarm by the time we let ourselves drink
it.

We ate our lunch—the sandwiches, some oatmeal cookies,
bananas—and cooled off in the dappled shade cast by the big
beech tree, then started picking again with renewed vigor.
The last third of the berry bucket always seemed to fill more
slowly than the larger portion we had picked before lunch,
an illusion I often contemplated during the last interminable
hour in a berry patch. Then the sun is hottest, the last trek
up the hill to the woods is steepest, and the bucket is not
quite full.

"Don't let your eyes deceive you," Mother warned when I
grew restless and said my bucket was full. "Your bucket is a
long way from full."

"Full," by Mother's definition, meant a berry bucket not
only full to the brim but rising high above it to a lofty dark
peak on top of which not one additional blackberry could be
balanced without the whole mound spilling down.

Not until the last enormous gallon of blackberries gleamed
high above the rim of the bucket—full to the utmost—did
we head for home. Even then Mother couldn't resist picking
berries along the way. Every so often we stopped to take still
another handful of berries, too large and beautiful to pass by,
hanging within arm's reach along a fencerow like black jew-
eled pendants.

"It always seems," Mother mused, "that we find the best
berries after our buckets are full."

When we reached the barn lot, even the lard pails we wore
at our waists were filled with glistening dark berries. We felt
well satisfied with the morning's picking.

And so the peaceful interlude of blackberrying came to an

end. We reached the farmhouse kitchen at noon—faces heat-flushed, fingers scratched and stained, berry pails full. The tranquil morning slipped beyond reach, as unattainable as a cluster of huge blackberries hanging high over Yellow Banks Creek. The serious business of canning was now at hand.

CABBAGES AND KRAUT

During the canning season, all efforts centered around tending the garden, picking the fruits and vegetables, and preserving them for winter use. The food-preservation chores had a sameness about them for days at a time, and there was a feeling of accomplishment when we finished up with one fruit or vegetable and were ready to move on to "putting up" the next one in its season.

I liked the variations in the regular canning chores. Making sauerkraut and pickles offered a change in routine in the middle of the canning season, just when everyone was getting tired of berrying and huge steaming kettles filled with jars.

Sometime in July the cabbages in the garden would reach their optimum size—all at the same time.

"We have to make sauerkraut *today!*" Mother would announce.

It was urgent to work up the cabbages before the heads grew too large and burst. If it rained, the heads could sour and be wasted. Or the cracks would be invaded by voracious cabbage worms. Even the sight of the small white cabbage butterflies, which precede the invasion of the caterpillars, was enough to incite my mother to action.

The sauerkraut was fermented in a dark brown earthenware crock that held ten gallons. There was a round wooden board that fit inside the neck of the crock, especially to hold the kraut down under its liquid. This was weighted with a rock my grandfather had selected at some time or other, making

sure it was not limestone. These items were carried out of the smokehouse anteroom into the sunshine, where they were scrubbed, scalded, and aired. The kraut cutter, too, had to be brought out of storage in the attic, and it was washed and the diagonally positioned blades carefully dried. The kraut cutter was set over a washtub, which was also carefully scoured and scalded for the occasion.

When all the equipment was ready, Mother took a sharp knife and a bushel peach basket, and we went into the garden to cut the cabbage heads. The outside leaves were stripped off and left lying in the row, and the heads were washed clean under the stream of water from the pump over the backyard cistern. The cabbage was quartered and trimmed and then shredded on the kraut cutter until the tub was almost full to the brim with crisp, thin, uniform shreds no thicker than a dime.

The whole process of shredding, salting, and packing the cabbage into the large crock captured my interest. It was fun, a change from the hot, steamy kitchen activities, and Grandpa always helped. But, later, when the crock of cabbage began to ferment and the smell of souring juices filled the cellar, I only went down there upon command. I would dash down the steps, holding my nose, and fill the pan with potatoes or get the jar of tomatoes, as requested, then dash back up again, with no time wasted.

How could anything smell so bad in the making and taste so good later on when cooked with potatoes or used as stuffing for a fat baked hen or a Christmas goose?

A GOOD GARDEN

My father's habit was to walk out to the barn every morning by way of the garden. When he came in to breakfast, he always had something or other to report that would pique our curiosity.

"The corn grew three inches last night," he would comment. Or, "There is a big tomato about halfway down the center row that will be ripe by noon today." Or, "That big watermelon is beginning to sound hollow."

Hearing such observations made the oatmeal and eggs and biscuits fairly vanish off our plates. My brothers and I wished to be first out to the garden to make the morning discoveries.

"Whoever finds the ripe tomato gets it!"

"Watch out for that mean bumblebee! He's working on the pumpkin blooms."

"The beans are almost ready! Look! Look!"

Green bean bushes match tomato plants in their generosity, but they are more enthusiastic in their giving. A row of green beans is ready all at once, by the bushelful. Then, no sooner than the crop has been canned or pickled or cooked for the table, tender new green beans again appear on the bushes. By July, two long rows of beans in a garden can wear out the enthusiasm of even the most dedicated food preserver and bring an ache to the backs of even the youngest bean pickers.

"I can't look at another bean!" my mother would say when she had reached that point, when still another basket of beans was lugged in from the garden.

But the basket of green beans would sit on the porch table just long enough for Mother to get the kitchen in order for another round of canning. She was never one to let good food go to waste. She would pick up the basket of beans, not without a sigh, and take it to the porch swing, where she sat with a commodious pan in her lap, swinging gently while she broke the beans.

It took five deft motions to snap each bean, two to break off each end, followed by three crisp snaps to break the bean into pieces. That was a lot of work for each bean! But I think Mother welcomed the chance to sit in the wide swing and snap green beans. It was a relaxing activity compared to other work, something her hands could do without the help of her mind. I liked to be there on the shady porch when she was swinging gently and snapping beans, or shelling peas, or stemming strawberries. Those were the times when Mother could really listen to me, when she sang hymns and old songs, when she told funny stories about teaching school. It was cool and breezy and pleasant on the porch. There were always flower boxes on the ledges with drifts of purple and pink and white petunias blooming in them. Sometimes when we were very quiet, ruby-throated hummingbirds came to the flower boxes and hovered over the petunias, sipping nectar.

Many of the golden hours of summers gone by were spent on that vine-covered porch. Sometimes when I remember us sitting there together, snapping beans, stemming grapes, seeding cherries, I can recall the gentle squeaking of the white porch swing blending with the soft, soothing harmonies of Mother's hymns, as clearly as if it were yesterday. Those flashes of memory are as brilliant as the plumage of the hummingbirds that came to the porch and as sweet and fleeting as the fragrance of the petunias spilling over the flower boxes.

While the front porch with its swing was the site of much peeling and seeding and sorting in preparing the garden's bounty for table use and for canning, the back porch was nearer the kitchen and became its necessary extension in summertime. When the wood-and-coal-burning range was fired up full force on canning days, the kitchen was too hot for comfort. So we moved almost all our kitchen-centered activities, except cooking, to the screened-in back porch for the duration of the canning season. We ate our meals, prepared foods, and washed the dishes in the open air, as it were, because three sides of the porch were screened. It was cool and pleasant, with summer breezes blowing across the porch, and an ideal arrangement except when rains came from the north or east. Then we would push the table and chairs toward the innermost wall to keep them from getting wet, and we would return to the kitchen to do our work until the rain stopped.

THE ICEBOX

The icebox was always kept on the back porch. It was made of oak with a top-opening compartment that held a fifty-pound chunk of ice. Ice was delivered twice each week by Harless Tuley (Jewel's husband), who picked up the ice after he delivered the milk cans filled with our milk (and that of others on his route) to the cheese factory in Dale. The food was kept in a three-shelved compartment below the ice. It had a door that was latched with a brass catch. Under the icebox was a space to place a dishpan to catch the dripping water as the ice melted and cooled the insulated food compartment below it. The water ran down a long pipe at the back of the icebox into the pan. The trick was to remember to slide the pan out from under the icebox before it filled to the very top. It was concealed under the icebox by a hinged panel, and it was often forgotten until the pool of over-flowing water spread out onto the linoleum in front of the icebox.

The icebox was a fine improvement to our kitchen, and we did not have one until toward the end of the thirties. In the wintertime, we never bothered to keep ice in it at all. Those foods that required refrigeration were simply put into the icebox sans ice, with the door left ajar or closed, according to the temperature. In winter, the whole porch was an icebox, in effect, cold as the outdoors. The food could be placed where it would keep cold, or even be frozen, if we chose. We actually kept very little on hand that needed refrigeration. We had a daily supply of fresh milk and eggs. When we were to have chicken for dinner, one was butchered on the spot. Perishable prepared foods were never kept from one day to the next. If something was not eaten that same day, it was given to the bird dogs. Leftovers were not our style.

In summer, the icebox was used to chill the milk, cream, and butter, to keep the eggs and meat fresh and safe, to chill the watermelons, and to set gelatin desserts and salads. Having the big block of crystal-clear ice in the top of the icebox meant that we could chip off chunks to cool iced tea and lemonade and, best of all, that we could make ice cream in the hand-turned freezer.

HOMEMADE ICE CREAM

Mother's ice cream was rich and smooth because it contained lots of cream from our best Jersey cow. Sometimes she used Junket rennet tablets or a cooked custard base in making ice cream, but usually it was just a simple mixture of cream, eggs, sugar, and Rawleigh's vanilla extract. When peaches or other fruits were in season, she added those mashed ripe fruits to the mixture.

Mother seemed always to know just when we would most appreciate a freezerful of homemade ice cream. When my brothers and I came in for our noontime dinner after a long morning of picking peaches under a blazing summer sun, we spied the extra fifty-pound block of ice slowly melting and making a puddle of water near the basement drain, and the rest of the day took wings and sped by. The afternoon was miraculously shortened by the promise of the treat awaiting us. Suddenly we were quicker and nimble-fingered as we picked the remaining bushels of ripe fruit. Now there was a cooling mirage in the midst of the sweltering peach grove to inspire us onward—the image of a glass dessert dish mounded high with soft, delicate, tongue-frosting, homemade ice cream. No prospect was more stimulating to contemplate than that of making and joyfully consuming a freezerful of ice cream. Our eager anticipation of the summer evening to come all but banished the discomfort of the humid July weather and the aggravation of our itching skin irritated by peach fuzz.

When we finally gathered under the spreading branches of the Red Delicious apple tree at the side of the house, ready to take our turns cranking the handle of the White Mountain ice cream freezer—with dusk falling and the katydids and crickets beginning their rasping chorus, with the moon on the rise and the giant bullfrog tuning up in the barn lot pond, with the shy whippoorwills calling softly in the distance—our appetites, and indeed all our senses, were pitched to their highest peaks.

I was first to crank the wooden ice cream freezer because the handle rotated easiest before the creamy vanilla-flavored and peach-enriched custard began to thicken. When the liquid contents of the gallon-sized canister began to solidify and freeze, turning the handle required the strength of my brothers' arms.

Finally, after a time that seemed as endless as had the morning in the orchard, the handle of the ice cream freezer would hardly turn at all. It was then that my older brother sat firmly on top of the freezer, with a burlap sack between his seat and the crushed ice, to hold the ice tub down firmly while my father gave it the last few strong turns that ensured the proper consistency of the ice cream. When the dasher was at last drawn out, with a delectable firm mass of rich, smooth ice cream clinging to its wooden ribs, the moment was to be savored along with the peachy flavor of the frosty blend.

Of all the good foods we ate on the farm, none was more memorable than the irresistible ripe-peach ice cream that we made at the end of a day spent on top of the ladder picking the peach crop.

Mother's Chess Pie

$\frac{1}{2}$ cup butter
1 cup sugar
4 eggs
1 tablespoon yellow
    cornmeal

1 tablespoon lemon juice
1 teaspoon vanilla
1 9" pie shell, unbaked

Preheat oven to 350°F. In a bowl, cream the butter and sugar until fluffy. Beat in the eggs one at a time. Add the cornmeal, lemon juice, and vanilla, and mix well. Pour into the unbaked pie shell and bake in the lower third of the oven for 15 minutes. Reduce the heat to 350°F, and bake for 25 minutes more, or until the filling is set. Transfer the pie to a rack to cool.

This is how Grandma Marshall cooked dried beans, as remembered by Aunt Grace. A recipe for cooking beans was not one that was written down.

Grandma Marshall's Navy Beans

"It took about two teacupfuls of dried beans to feed all of us. Mom would soak the beans overnight in cold water. The next morning she poured that water off and covered the beans with fresh water. Then she would lift off one of the caps of the kitchen stove and set the black iron pot directly on the fire, if she wanted to hurry up the beans. When the beans boiled hard, she drained the water off and covered them with fresh water. Sometimes she parboiled the beans twice. Then, when the beans came to the boil again, she slid the pot to the back of the stove or wherever she wanted it, and let them cook slowly all morning. That was what made the beans so good, the slow cooking. If she had salt pork, she would put that in. Sometimes she cut peeled Irish potatoes into large cubes and cooked them with the beans during the last half hour of cooking."

Baked Sweet Potatoes

Scrub medium-size sweet potatoes. Rub skins with butter. Bake at 400°F for 35 to 40 minutes, or until tender. Split and serve with butter.

On washday, sweet potatoes with unbuttered skins were buried in the ashes under the wash kettle.

Mother's Forgotten Meringue Nests

6 egg whites
$\frac{1}{2}$ teaspoon cream of tartar
$\frac{1}{4}$ teaspoon salt

2 cups sugar
$1\frac{1}{2}$ teaspoons vanilla

Preheat oven to 400°F. Beat the egg whites by hand in a copper bowl, or in the bowl of an electric mixer, until they are foamy. Add the cream of tartar and the salt, and continue to beat the whites until they hold soft peaks. Sprinkle in the sugar, 2 tablespoons at a time, and the vanilla, and continue to beat the meringue until it holds very stiff peaks. Spoon the meringue in mounds onto parchment paper set on baking sheets, and with the back of a spoon make 3″ meringue nests. Place the meringue nests in the oven and immediately turn off the heat. Do not open the door for at least 12 hours. Fill the meringues with a scoop of strawberry ice cream and top with sliced strawberries and whipped cream.

MAKES 20 MERINGUES.

Fresh Strawberry Pie

1 9″ baked pie shell
2 pints whole strawberries
$1\frac{1}{2}$ cups crushed strawberries
1 cup sugar

3 tablespoons cornstarch
1 tablespoon lemon juice
Red food coloring
  (optional)
Whipped cream

Fill the pie crust with the whole strawberries. Combine crushed berries with sugar, cornstarch, and lemon juice. Bring to a boil and cook, stirring constantly, until mixture thickens and clears. When cool, add a few drops of red food coloring, if desired, and pour the mixture over the strawberries in the pie crust. Chill. Serve with whipped cream.

Oatmeal Raisin Cookies

1 cup shortening	$\frac{1}{2}$ teaspoon salt
1 cup sugar	1 teaspoon cinnamon
2 eggs, well beaten	2 cups rolled oats
4 tablespoons milk	$\frac{1}{2}$ cup chopped nuts
2 cups flour	1 cup raisins
$\frac{3}{4}$ teaspoon baking soda	

Cream the shortening. Gradually add the sugar, and blend together. Add the eggs and milk, and mix well. Sift together the flour, soda, salt, and cinnamon, and mix with the oats. Add to the creamed mixture a little at a time. Add the nuts and raisins. Drop by teaspoons onto a greased cookie sheet. Bake at 375°F for 12 minutes.   MAKES ABOUT 3 DOZEN.

Mother's Blackberry Cobbler

5 cups fresh blackberries	$\frac{1}{2}$ teaspoon salt
1 cup sugar	$\frac{1}{2}$ teaspoon cream of tartar
3 tablespoons flour	2 tablespoons sugar
2 tablespoons butter	$\frac{1}{2}$ cup butter
2 cups flour	$\frac{2}{3}$ cup milk (approx.)
4 teaspoons baking powder	

Butter an oblong baking dish (about 8″ x 10″) and fill it almost to the rim with ripe blackberries sweetened with 1 cup of sugar (more to taste). Sprinkle the 3 tablespoons flour over the sweetened berries and dot with butter. Set aside.

Sift together flour, baking powder, salt, cream of tartar, and sugar. Cut in butter until mixture resembles coarse meal. With a fork, stir in enough milk (slightly *less* than $\frac{2}{3}$ cup) to form a ball of dough. Turn out onto a floured board and roll dough to $\frac{1}{4}$″ thickness. Cover the blackberries with the dough and trim the edges. Cut a vent in the top to allow steam to escape during baking. Sprinkle the top of the dough generously with additional sugar and bake at 400°F for about 45 minutes, or until the crust is browned and the juices bubbling. Serve warm with rich cream.   SERVES 6 TO 8.

You can substitute other fruits for the blackberries: apple, peach, dewberry, mulberry, raspberry, blueberry, or huckleberry. Sweeten each fresh fruit to taste and add appropriate spices, if desired, such as cinnamon with apples and nutmeg with peaches.

Blackberry Pie

2 cups flour, sifted	4 cups fresh blackberries
1 teaspoon salt	1 cup sugar
⅔ cup shortening	3 tablespoons tapioca
6 tablespoons cold milk (approx.)	2 tablespoons butter

Sift together the flour and salt. Cut in the shortening until the mixture resembles coarse cornmeal. Sprinkle the milk, a tablespoon at a time, over the mixture, gently mixing with a fork until mixture is moist. Form the pastry into a ball, divide in half, and roll out two circles on a floured board to fit a 9″ pie tin.

Combine the blackberries, sugar, and tapioca. Pour into the pastry-lined pie tin and dot the top with butter. Cover berries with crust, cut a vent, and crimp the edges together. Brush the top of the pastry with a small amount of milk and sprinkle sugar on top of the dough.

Bake at 400°F for 10 minutes, then lower temperature to 350°F and bake for 40 minutes more, or until the crust is browned and the berry juices thickened and bubbling. Serve warm, with cream, if desired.

Homemade Ice Cream, Country-Style

4 to 6 eggs
2½ cups sugar
4 cups light cream
½ teaspoon salt

2 tablespoons vanilla
2 to 4 cups light cream
2 cups fresh fruit, pureed
    and sweetened to taste
    (optional)

Beat the eggs until light and fluffy. Add sugar gradually, beating well after each addition. Stir in the 4 cups of light cream, salt, and vanilla extract. Pour the ice cream mixture into the chilled one-gallon canister of an ice cream freezer. Add enough additional cream to fill the canister three-fourths full, (about 4 cups).* Add fruit if desired.

Position the dasher inside the canister, cover, and place the assembled canister inside the freezer tub. Pack the tub with alternate layers of crushed ice and salt, using about 1 pound of ice cream salt to 6 to 8 pounds of crushed ice.

* If fresh fruit is to be added, use only 2 cups of additional cream.

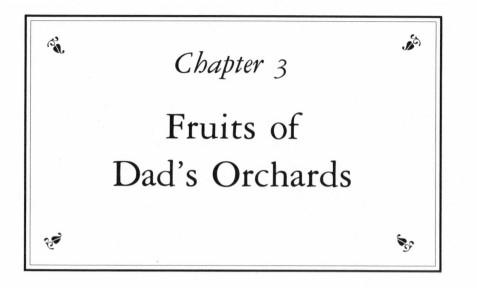

Chapter 3

Fruits of Dad's Orchards

GOLDEN PEACHES OF SAMARKAND

I N SUMMER, we ate on the screened back porch, a shady bower covered with vining morning glories, whose blue and white trumpets of bloom opened to the morning sun rising over the peach trees east of the porch.

Mother sometimes complained that Dad had planted peach and apple trees too close to the house. When the fruit was ripening, it was a daily chore to pick up the dropped fruit and so keep flies from gathering around the house. Fallen fruit lying on the ground for even a single day during hot weather brought the flies out of nowhere.

The battle against houseflies was a constant one. Mother simply couldn't abide them. Before meals we opened a door and chased them out. A pair of us walked together through the house, swinging dish towels through the air in a wind-mill-like motion, one in each hand, driving the flies before us. It was a method that worked remarkably well. In addition to driving them out and trying to keep them out ("Don't hold the door open!" Mother would call out, almost before we got inside the door itself), Mother had other methods of eradicating flies.

"Kill a fly in May, keep a million away," she would say as she used the wire fly swatter.

As the summer deepened, uncurling sticky fly strips hung from the ceiling of the kitchen and back porch. Old plates were set around with pieces of flypaper exuding their poison into a puddle of water to lure the unwelcome insects. If all else failed, Mother tied a red kerchief over her nose and sprayed the "fly dope" around the closed-up house with a hand-pumped sprayer, and we all stayed out of the house until the flies were dead and the ill-smelling fumes dissipated.

Because Dad had a fine orchard of 250 peach trees, we had peaches on our table almost daily year round. From the time the first delicately flavored Belle of Georgia peaches ripened in July, to the last yellow-fleshed Hale Havens in September after school had begun, there was a steady procession of fresh peach dishes across our table. Sugared sliced peaches with rich cream, peach cobblers, peach pies, peach ice cream, peach upside down cake, peach custard pie; these were the usual peach-season favorites.

All during peach season, Mother canned the fruits for winter use, as many as 200 quarts, and she made lots of peach butter as well.

Mother's canned peaches were choice, and our family never tired of them. A canned peach half covered with rich cream was in itself a dessert par excellence. Her jars of canned fruits were beautiful to behold in their perfection, and they were worthy of blue ribbons at the county fair. Mother was a skillful, painstaking canner with the advantage of a wealth of fresh fruit right outside our kitchen door. She used only peaches of the best quality and the fullest flavor at their ultimate stage of ripeness, and she literally hand picked them at the last minute for her jars. Peaches for canning remained on the tree until she was ready to can them. Every particle of peach flavor, enhanced by ripening on the tree in the summer sun to the moment of golden perfection, was captured in each canning jar.

We didn't know the riches we had in our cellar at the end of those summers. They seem as priceless as the golden peaches of Samarkand when I think of them today.

PICKLED INDIAN PEACHES

One of the last canning projects was the preserving of pickled peaches from a prized Indian peach tree that grew next to the driveway. It was a wild seedling tree Dad had found growing on the creek bank. A firm, clingstone variety with red-tinged flesh, the peaches were no larger than good-sized plums.

Mother canned the small fruits whole, on the seed, in a sweet-tangy syrup judiciously spiced with cinnamon and clove. Her pickled peaches lacked the strong twang of vinegar of those canned by certain of my aunts, and their milder flavor suited our family's tastes better.

Pickled peaches were not garnishes. They were often served as a side dish with our meals, like applesauce, or even as a spicy fruit accompaniment to bland sponge cake or sugar cookies, which called for something to go with them. Garnishes did not have much importance at our meals. There was no room for them on the plates and the fresh garden and orchard foods were beautiful in themselves.

The only way to eat a pickled Indian peach was to put it whole into one's mouth—a perfect mouthful for a child—and carefully work the soft, flavorful peach flesh away from the small kernel without biting down into it, or, heaven forbid, swallowing it. Then there was the matter of getting rid of the peach seed with decorum. The only place we were allowed to spit out seeds of fruits (watermelon in particular) crudely was outdoors. Mother had high standards for everything from manners to canning.

"You can take it out of your mouth the same way you put it in." Mother's tone of voice could be very schoolteachery at times, even at home. "Your teaspoon works both ways."

MAKING PEACH BUTTER

Mother also made large amounts of peach butter, one of the sweet spreads for the hot biscuits and breads that appeared daily on our table. Very ripe, juicy peaches, those too soft for canning, were required for peach butter. Peeled and cut into small pieces, mashed slightly to start their juices flowing, they became tender very quickly when cooked in a kettle on top of the stove. Then, after mashing or sieving, the juicy peach puree was put into a large, deep, heavy enamelware dishpan that was reserved only for cooking. Sugar stirred in, a stick of cinnamon added—and the uncovered pan went into the oven, where the peach butter baked, very slowly, for several hours.

Every half hour or so, Mother drew out the rack burdened with the heavy pan and stirred the fragrant, thickening puree. Toward the end of its baking period, she stirred more often and attended closely so that the butter would not stick to the bottom of the pan and scorch. When a mound of peach butter spooned onto a saucer did not make a puddle of juice, it was "done." Mother would then pack the golden peach butter into steaming hot canning jars and process them in a boiling-water bath.

One summer she tried canning peach butter by placing the filled jars in the oven for the final processing, a method fraught with dangers, which Aunt Blanche had nevertheless praised. Mother was very nervous about the whole thing, but she wanted to try it. She handled the jars gingerly when she placed them in the oven, for fear one would explode and endanger anyone nearby with flying glass and spattered, boiling-hot peaches.

"Keep out of the kitchen!" she warned, even as she risked herself.

The calm and peace of the kitchen was shattered by the new method of oven canning. Every time a jar exploded inside the closed oven, accompanied by the crack and tinkle of glass falling on the oven rack, Mother cringed.

"There's another one lost!" she exclaimed, regretting the wasted peach butter. "What a mess!"

And the oven *was* a mess when she finally let the stove cool down and opened the door to survey the damage. Most of the jars withstood the process, but they were bespattered with exploded peach butter. The spilled peach butter stuck onto the sides and bottom of the oven, and little fires burned on the oven floor, smoking up the kitchen. An unpleasant smell of burnt peaches replaced the usual pleasant spicy fragrance of baking peach butter.

When the oven was clean once again, the broken glass removed, and the surviving jars stored away on the cellar shelves, Mother abandoned the oven method and returned happily to the old faithful boiling-water bath method of canning peaches.

DRYING PEACHES ON A HOT TIN ROOF

Putting by our supply of dried peaches for use in winter was a small chore compared with canning two hundred jars of peaches, but it was one that varied the regular canning chores and provided the makings for dried peach pie.

"Fit for a king!" Dad pronounced peach pie (as he did all of his other favorite dishes) when it appeared on the table.

Those fruits that Mother dried for winter use—peaches, apples, apricots—were spread out on the low sloping tin roof of a shed attached to Grandpa's chicken house. That was the hottest place to be found on either farm in summertime. On the roof, the temperature must have reached over 100°F on the hot, sunny, dry days that were ideal for drying fruits.

One day my cousin Annabelle said the tin roof was hot enough to fry eggs at noontime, and she swiped some out of the nests and broke them on the roof to prove it. But the eggs slid off before we could see if they really would cook, and we had to endure the awful suspense of waiting to see if Aunt Helen would miss the wasted eggs we had gathered in from the nests—all for nothing.

The roof was a favorite playing place for me and my cousins, a hideaway that could be reached easily without a ladder by climbing the top of the fence to a nearby limb of a tall cedar. From there we could step down onto a lower roof, and then climb to the upper level of the chicken house roof. From there we could get into the tops of the red plum trees on the other side, a good perch for picking sour-sweet fruits to eat, or to gather for Mother's best blackberry and red plum jelly.

That was how *we* gained access to the rooftops of the chicken house. When Mother was ready to carry the prepared peaches up to the roof for drying, she leaned a small ladder against the side of the building.

The peaches were prepared in two ways: some were peeled and sliced, the rest went unpeeled and were halved. The peaches were arranged in a single layer on a clean, discarded lace window curtain, then covered with another sheer curtain to keep the insects off.

It took several days of hot sunshine to dry the fruit slices or halves until they were as pliable and leathery as Dad's belt. Meanwhile, Annabelle and I kept an eye on the peaches to make sure the covering did not blow out from under the bricks that weighted down the edges. Several times a day we were sent up to the roof to turn the fruit, and in the second day of drying, we pushed the center of the halves inward to speed the process. Every afternoon, when the sun went down behind the trees and shade crept up the roof toward the drying fruit, we gathered it up and took it inside so that the evening dew would not dampen the partially dried fruit, and to keep it safe from field mice, who might steal it during the night.

There were lots of little chores connected with the slow process of drying fruit. But we did not care to stay around when Mother burned flowers of sulfur under an overturned box covering the slices that were to be dried. The fumes made the fruit insect-proof and kept its color bright, but they made a stink worse than rotten eggs.

MAKING APPLE CIDER

My father was always generous. If he had a surplus of apples, peaches, sweet corn, or strawberries, he sent word to relatives and neighbors that we had more than we could use.

"If you folks want peaches, you are welcome to come out and help yourselves. Nice peaches are going to waste. I would like to see someone use them."

When the orchard was yielding its maximum, during the Depression of the 1930s, Dad extended gleaning privileges to families of our community, who picked up the windfall fruits. Peaches were bringing only seventy-five cents a bushel, but many families did not have seventy-five cents. So Dad gave the fruits away rather than have them rot on the ground and go to waste.

One time Dad took a truckload of peaches to Huntingburg to peddle them along the streets.

"Folks don't have money for gas to drive over here," he said.

Apples brought "all the way from give-away to a dollar fifty to two dollars a bushel." But we had apples by the wagonload! Since there were only a "precious few" paying customers to buy them and choice apples to spare, we used only the best apples from the trees, not the windfalls, for making cider. That was Dad's practice in good times as well as in hard times.

Dad instructed the pickers: "I don't want any scrub stuff in my cider. We have apples a-plenty, so pick the best."

Early in autumn, when the spreading apple trees were bending with fruit, Dad and Grandpa moved the huge cider mill out of the storage shed and placed it near the front well by the house so it could be cleaned up before use.

We had a heavy, old-style cider mill that stood as tall as a man, and it took two men to move it around. Mother scrubbed it with soap and water and Dad greased the cogs and wheels so that they would turn easily without binding and squeaking.

Then, on a perfect Indian summer day late in September or early in October, when there had been a change in the weather that brought a nip to the air, but before the first frost, Dad would send my brothers to the apple shed to haul in several bushels of apples.

"Take whatever comes handy—Romes, Weinsaps, Golden Delicious." Dad did not swear by any particular variety of apple, as each added its delicate flavor to the blend, but he did insist that all the apples be perfect and washed clean. My brothers and I sorted and washed the apples before they went into the hopper of the cider mill, and it took about six bushels to make a barrel of cider.

While Dad considered cider made of windfalls imperfect, or overripe, mealy apples unfit to drink, he did not think it necessary to take time to cut and core the apples and remove the seeds, which, when crushed, some purists thought possibly added a trace of bitterness to cider.

When the first bushel was filled with clean, perfect, firm apples, Dad hoisted the basket up, dumped it into the hopper of the cider mill, and began to grind the apples to make the pomace from which the apple juice was pressed with the cider press.

A handle on the outside of the cider mill was turned by hand to operate the grinder that produced the pomace. When the hopper was filled with apples, turning the handle was a job for a strong man, like Dad. When the hopper was almost empty and Dad took a rest, we children tested our muscle.

Turning the handle of a cider mill was a different matter than turning the grindstone or the sausage mill or the ice cream freezer, but just as compelling to children.

Every now and then, the big apples in the hopper had to be pushed into the grinders with the end of a stick. The finer the apples were ground, the harder the handle turned.

When the slatted basket beneath the hopper was filled with ground apples, or pomace, it was removed from the mill and placed under the cider press. To press the apple juice from the pomace, Dad turned the handle of a large jackscrew, which pressed a wooden disc down on the ground apples with enough pressure to make their juice—the cider—run out between the slats of the basket into a trough, and out a spout into the tub below the cider press.

When the first stream of cider ran out of the spout, all the children of the farm were standing ready with tin cups to catch it, each vying to have the first taste of the apple nectar, to quench the exquisite thirst for it that had grown almost unbearable with waiting.

Dad said our squeals reminded him of the pigs at the trough when they were given the "pummies" after cider making. One time the pomace was fermented before it was fed to the hogs. Fermented pomace has a considerable alcoholic content. Consequently, the hogs went on a jag and got drunk. They ran and squealed and carried on for hours, fighting and biting and chasing each other, until finally they laid down, one by one, and slept it off. It was funny to watch, and we spent a long time laughing at the shenanigans of fat, drunken porkers. But Grandpa was quite worried about the hogs, for fear that some would die. None did, but it was costly nonetheless, because the hogs ran off a lot of fat.

Dad liked pigs. He spent a lot of time watching them and concluded that they had a lot of intelligence.

"Pigs are the smartest animals on the farm," he always said. "I've seen them figure out some things, just like people do."

When the hogs got drunk on fermented pomace, Dad found a human comparison.

"Look at those damned fools," he said. "They act just like that bunch at the saloon in Holland on Saturday night."

Dad was basically a teetotaler. There was no liquor in our house. But he made a small keg of wine every summer or two, which he kept in the cellar to dispense during the winter for gifts or for "medicinal purposes." The wine might be made of grapes, blackberries, peaches, or elderberries.

Dad's standard treatment for a winter cold, especially one that had settled in the chest, was a hot toddy made with wine.

When a hot toddy was called for, Dad drew off some wine, squeezed the juice of some lemons and oranges into it, and sweetened it with a spoonful of honey or sugar. If the toddy was for any of us children, it was weakened considerably with a dip of well water. Sometimes the toddy was heated on the stove, and sometimes Dad made an entertainment out of heating the toddy. It depended upon whom it was for. When *he* was sick, he skipped the entertainment part.

He would put a clean poker into the hot coals of the kitchen stove and heat it until the end was fiery red. Then he would put the end of the red hot poker, with a great sizzling, directly into the pitcher of sweetened wine and juice. The ailing one was put to bed with the hot toddy and an extra comforter, cozily warmed inside and out by Dad's ministrations.

SWEET APPLE CIDER SPREE

Sometimes we used rye straws to drink the sweet apple cider through, bringing up small sips to savor fully on our tongues. We became so sticky with apple juice that the pesky yellow jackets hovering around the cider mill tried to land on us! Our apple cider spree continued all afternoon. The cider still tasted good even when we were full. We swilled until our stomachs were tight as ticks and we were commanded to stop.

"Stop, or you will be doing a two-step tonight."

The apple smell surrounded us but a sharp nose could pick out the varying scents when a new batch of apples was added to the blend. Some varieties were perfumed strongly of apple scent: McIntosh, Banana, Golden Delicious and Red Delicious.

The addition of a few crab apples when the cider was too sweet brought a piquant sharpness to the cider—and to the very air around us. The essence of apple clung to our clothes and hair and hands and breath. Mother said we were flavored with apple, inside and out, just like worms inside apples.

The days were growing shorter when we made cider in the early autumn, and sunset was a signal to stop grinding apples and finish pressing those that were already in the mill. Daylight seemed to run out too soon when we were involved in a special task. We always seemed to be finishing up in the dusky shadows, lighted by the afterglow of spectacular autumn sunsets, which occur during apple harvest time.

One of the rewards of living on a farm is the necessity of being out and about at sunset, doing daily chores or finishing up the work, when long streaks of sunset colors—red, orange, salmon pink, pale yellow, mauve—merge into each other and briefly ebb upward on the horizon, illuminating the sky.

Farmers and farm children take notice of sunsets. They mark the ending of the work day, foretell the coming weather, inspire awe of heavenly glories, and lift the spirits of those who work on after sunset.

"Red sky in morning, shepherd's warning; red sky at night, shepherd's delight."

When there was a red sky at night, we could plan to make apple butter the next day. Good weather was needed because apple butter was cooked outdoors over a wood fire.

MAKING BOILED CIDER

Making apple butter followed making apple cider almost immediately. Sweet apple cider was needed for making apple butter and cider did not stay "sweet" very long. When the weather is warm, apple cider begins to ferment almost at once, and makes "hard" cider. In cool weather it takes a little longer for the sugar in the apple juice to turn to alcohol.

We children had about a week's grace during which we could go down the steps into the dark, cool cellar, turn the spigot on the cider barrel, and draw a cup of sweet cider to drink after school. After that, when the taste began to change and take on a zing and a snap, my brothers and I were forbidden to go near the barrel.

In the meantime, we continued our sweet cider binge without ill effects while Mother and Grandma busily cooked down kettles full of cider until it became a dark, sweet-tart syrupy liquid. For days the large kettles boiled gently on the back of their kitchen ranges. It took hours to reduce the cider to the right consistency before it was canned in glass canning jars.

This was Mother's way of making boiled cider:

"Boil four quarts of sweet cider over a low fire till two quarts are left. Use a heavy kettle and watch or it will burn.

Seal in glass jars while hot, the same as canned fruit. Will keep until used."

The apple-scented steam rising from the kettles carried promises of richly flavored mincemeat, apple pies, moist fruitcakes, Mother's delicious boiled cider pies, and apple butter.

In preparation for the family event of making apple butter outdoors over a wood fire, Mother and Grandma drew off a tubful of sweet apple cider from the barrel and carried it outdoors to the cast-iron kettle, which stood on its own tripod over a bed of ashes in Grandma's backyard.

This same kettle was the washday boiling kettle, in which both of our families heated wash water or boiled white sheets in lye water. Though Aunt Blanche firmly stated her opinion that the apple butter kettle should be copper because an iron one darkens the butter, Grandma did not see the need for an expensive copper kettle.

"Fiddlesticks!" she would say. "A little iron is good for you."

The chore of peeling, coring, and quartering the apples began early in the morning of the day apple butter was to be made. Anyone who could peel apples with any skill at all helped with the bushel of Golden Delicious apples—Dad, Grandpa, the hired girl. Even I was given a short-bladed paring knife. It did not matter if my peelings were thick. There were plenty of apples.

"She has to learn sometime," Grandma said.

Peeling apples was fun for a while. I tried to take thin peelings because peeling was a skill children all wanted to be trusted to learn. But a long, unbroken, curling strand of apple peeling, thrown over the right shoulder, was one of Jewel's kitchen fortune-telling devices. The letter formed by the peeling foretold some future good luck at home or at school.

Once my curiosity about my fortune was satisfied, I pre-

ferred making peelings with Grandma's old black apple peeler, which clamped onto the edge of a table. It had a two-tined prong on which an apple was impaled. When the handle of the wobbly gadget was turned, it rotated the apple around and around under a stationary blade that cut the peeling off the apple in a long curl. The peeled apple was then trimmed by hand of bits of remaining peel, then quartered and cored.

Using the apple peeler helped speed up the process of peeling. Still, with so many people pitching in to help, the bushel basket emptied in a hurry.

"Many hands make light work," Grandpa said. "We're finished."

Since apples turn brown quickly, Grandma whisked away the big crocks as soon as they filled with apples. She carried the peeled apples out to the iron kettle in the backyard. A lively fire had brought the apple cider in the kettle to a boil, and cooked it down to about one-half kettle.

After the apples were dumped into the boiling cider, they floated on top of the seething, steaming liquid, momentarily stilling its roiling motion. Grandma gave the apples in the cider a few stirs, pushed some slabs of maple wood farther in under the kettle to feed the fire, and soon the cider and apples together in the kettle came back to the boil.

When the apples were stewed quite soft, Grandma lifted them out of the boiling cider with a long-handled skimmer with holes in it to allow the juice to drain away from the cooked apples. She placed the stewed apples in a tub at the side of the kettle while she stewed the next crockful of peeled apples. When the tub was almost filled with stewed apples, there were enough to make a kettle of apple butter. Then they were put back into the boiling cider all at once. There was about half as much cider in the kettle as apples.

From then on, stirring was done with a long-handled apple butter paddle that looked like a hoe held horizontally. The blade was made of wood and was long enough to reach the bottom of the kettle. There were several round holes in the blade to allow apple butter to pass through, making stirring easier. The handle was long enough to allow the stirrer to stand back from the hot kettle a few feet, out of the smoke and away from the heat.

Grandpa made this unique tool himself and stirring the apple butter was his job. The butter had to be stirred constantly to keep it from sticking to the bottom of the kettle. A moment's carelessness could result in a scorched taste to the butter, so Grandpa kept a watchful eye on the stirring if he relinquished the paddle for a few minutes to an eager grandchild who wanted to take a turn on the end of the apple butter paddle.

In the beginning, the stewed apples cooked to the appearance and consistency of pale green applesauce. More boiled cider from a reserve pot was added if the sauce in the kettle became too thick as it cooked slowly, bubbling and sputtering over the wood fire, and gradually it changed in color to reddish brown.

There was a festive air to the apple butter–making that masked its complexities and plain hard work. Taking turns at the apple butter kettle with Grandpa—stirring, stirring, stirring—had the feeling of a game to the children of the farm. For our parents and grandparents, the day provided a change from the everyday routine.

The fragrances wafting over the backyard were captivating: the odor of wood smoke rising from the warming fire; the tangy, spicy scent of boiling cider mingling with the fruity fragrance of apples. Then, when the glistening brown mass began to thicken, along about an hour before the butter finished cooking, Mother stirred in sugar, pouring it directly from the ten-pound sugar sack without measuring. She knew from experience about how much it took, approximately four cups of sugar to every gallon of apple butter. And every bushel yielded about two gallons of apple butter. Anyway, the sweetness of the apples had a lot to do with how much sugar was added, as well as the opinions of the tasters around the apple butter kettle. The apple butter simply had to taste "right," a condition determined after much tasting and discussion and stirring in of a "little more" sugar or spices.

The spicing of the apple butter required a light touch to suit our family's taste. We like mostly cinnamon, with just a hint of nutmeg, cloves, allspice, and ginger. The spices were stirred in shortly before the end of the cooking time, when the apple butter was beginning to sputter and plop thickly in the kettle. Then Grandma spooned out a large spoonful onto a plate and called for another round of tasting.

"Looks done," Grandma said when no water seeped out around the edges of the russet blend.

"Best way to tell is to taste it," Mother said, passing out spoons.

"Enough ginger!" stated Grandpa, who was not overly fond of ginger.

"Needs to be sweeter," Dad was sure to say, because he had a sweet tooth.

Mother and Grandma made the final adjustments, stirring in a little more cinnamon and sugar, and stirring the butter carefully to mix it all in evenly during the last few minutes' cooking.

It would be late in the afternoon, when big bubbles plopped on the surface of the spicy dark butter, when the menfolk were thinking once again about starting the evening milking, that Mother would finally declare the apple butter "done."

"Let the fire die, Charles," she would say. "It's ready to be canned."

Before Dad headed toward his barn, and Grandpa to his, they pulled most of the fire out from under the kettle and raked it off to one side. Only enough embers were left under the kettle to keep it warm while Mother and Grandma canned the apple butter.

The jars, which had been made ready to receive the butter,

were standing on a wash bench moved close to the apple butter kettle. Mother canned her share in one-quart mason jars and sealed them with rubber rings and zinc caps turned with a canning wrench. But Grandma ladled her apple butter into old-fashioned apple butter crocks. These pottery jars were shaped almost like mason jars, with a narrowed top and an opening with a lip. A tin cap was placed on the lip, then sealed down with sealing wax poured around its edge. Grandma thought apple butter tasted better when kept in dark crocks because they kept the light away and somehow a certain virtue was imparted to the flavor.

By sundown, the squat apple butter crocks and the glass mason jars were filled with reddish-brown apple butter, and ready to be stored in the cellar. There was a big bowlful left over to spread on our biscuits at suppertime.

Apple butter never tastes better than when it is made over a wood fire in an open kettle on a choice October day.

Peach Upside Down Cake

$1\frac{1}{4}$ cup flour, sifted

$1\frac{1}{4}$ teaspoon baking powder

$\frac{1}{4}$ teaspoon salt

$\frac{3}{4}$ cup sugar

4 tablespoons butter, softened

1 egg, well-beaten

$\frac{1}{2}$ cup milk

1 teaspoon vanilla

4 tablespoons butter, melted

$\frac{1}{2}$ cup brown sugar

2 cups sliced peaches, fresh or canned

Sift together flour, baking powder, salt, and sugar. Add to softened butter. Add egg, milk, and vanilla; mix together and beat for two minutes. Pour over remaining ingredients arranged evenly in the bottom of an 8″ x 8″ x 2″ baking pan, or an 8″ iron skillet. Bake at 350°F for 45 to 50 minutes. Let stand 5 minutes, then turn cake upside down on a plate.

You may substitute pineapple, cooked apricots, or apples

for the peaches. Marischino cherries may be put inside the pineapple rings, or hickory nuts or pecans put in the bottom of the pan with the peaches. Serve with whipped cream.

Peach Custard Pie

2 cups sliced fresh peaches
¾ cup sugar
4 tablespoons flour
1 tablespoon grated lemon
   rind

1 cup cream or canned milk
Sprinkling of mace or
   grated nutmeg
1 8″ pastry shell, unbaked

Mix together peaches, sugar, flour, lemon rind, cream, and spice. Pour the mixture into a chilled, unbaked pastry shell. Bake until firm at 400°F, about 45 minutes.

Pickled Peaches

6 pounds clingstone peaches
   Whole cloves
6 cups sugar

2 cups cider vinegar
3 cinnamon sticks

Plunge peaches into a kettle of boiling water for 1 minute. Drain and peel, and insert 2 cloves in each peach. In an enamel kettle, combine sugar, vinegar, and cinnamon sticks. Bring the liquid to a boil, stirring and washing down any sugar crystals clinging to the sides of the pan with a brush dipped in cold water. Add the peaches. Simmer the peaches for 5 minutes, or until they are just tender, and transfer them with a slotted spoon to three sterilized one-quart mason-type jars, packing them tightly. Put 1 cinnamon stick in each jar, pour the hot syrup over the peaches, and seal the jars with the lids. MAKES 3 QUARTS.

Peach Butter

Scald and peel very ripe peaches and remove the pits. Cook the peaches until tender, using only enough water to start the cooking. Press the pulp through a food mill or puree in a blender or food processor.

To each cup of pulp, add $\frac{1}{2}$ cup sugar. Add ground or stick cinnamon, $\frac{1}{2}$ to 1 teaspoon (or one 4-inch stick) to each 4 cups of pulp. Cook the peach butter slowly on top of the stove, stirring frequently, until thick, or about 1 hour. Or bake at 325°F in an uncovered shallow pan until thick, stirring two or three times an hour, for about 2 hours.

Pack the boiling-hot butter into sterilized jars, leaving $\frac{1}{4}$-inch space at the top, and adjust the lids. Process in a boiling-water bath for 10 minutes.

Peach butter is done when only a tiny rim of liquid forms around a spoonful dropped onto a cold saucer.

Half-Moon Pies

4 cups dried apples or dried peaches
$\frac{3}{4}$ cup sugar
3 cups sifted flour
1 teaspoon salt
1 cup lard or shortening
$\frac{1}{3}$ cup water
Fat for frying

Cook the dried apples or peaches in water to cover until they are tender. Add the sugar and set aside.

Make a pastry of the remaining ingredients. Sift together the flour and salt. Cut in the shortening until the mixture resembles coarse cornmeal. Sprinkle the water, one tablespoon at a time, over the mixture, gently mixing with a fork until it is all moist. Form the pastry into a ball, divide into six portions, and roll out and cut each portion into a circle around a medium-size plate. Put a portion of dried cooked fruit onto each round of dough, moisten the edges with water, and fold over to make a half-moon shape. Press the edges together with the tines of a fork. Fry the pies in hot fat ($\frac{1}{2}''$ deep) for about 5 minutes on each side, taking care not to crowd the pies and keeping heat low enough to keep from burning the pies.

Dried Apple Stack Cake

4 cups dried apples
$\frac{1}{2}$ cup sugar
1 cup lard or shortening, at room temperature
1 cup sugar
1 egg

1 cup sorghum syrup
1 cup buttermilk
1 teaspoon baking soda
3 cups sifted flour
$\frac{1}{2}$ teaspoon salt

Cook the dried apples in water to cover until they are tender. Sweeten with the $\frac{1}{2}$ cup sugar and set aside.

In a mixing bowl, combine the shortening and the 1 cup sugar and cream well. Add egg and beat, then add sorghum, buttermilk, baking soda, flour, and salt. Mix well.

Grease and flour two iron skillets (9″ x $2\frac{1}{2}''$) and pour the batter into the pans. Bake at 375°F for 35 minutes, or until a tester inserted in the center of the cakes comes out clean. Cool cakes and split each one in half crosswise. Spread the dried apples between the layers and on top of the cake. Reassemble.

Boiled Cider Pie

1 cup boiled cider
3 egg yolks, beaten
1 cup sugar
$1\frac{1}{2}$ tablespoons flour

1 cup milk
2 tablespoons melted butter
3 egg whites, stiffly beaten
1 8″ pie shell, unbaked

Mix together cider, egg yolks, sugar, flour, milk, and melted butter. Fold in egg whites. Pour mixture into unbaked pie shell. Bake at 450°F for 10 minutes. Lower oven temperature to 325°F and bake for about 30 minutes longer, or until center of pie is set.

Open Kettle Apple Butter

Bring 10 gallons of sweet apple cider to a boil in a large kettle hung over an outdoor open fire. Cook the cider down to about half its original volume. Gradually add 4 bushels of Winesap apples, Turley, or Stayman, which have been peeled, cored, and quartered. Stir and cook for about 3 hours before adding sugar and spices. Sweeten with about 5 pounds sugar for each bushel of apples. Add spices to taste, using about $\frac{1}{2}$ cup spices, consisting primarily of cinnamon, with some nutmeg, cloves, ginger, and allspice. Cinnamon sticks can be used (6 to 10) to keep the apple butter lighter in color. Cook for about 1 hour after adding the sugar and spices, or until no liquid separates from a spoonful of the butter when it is placed on a saucer.   MAKES ABOUT 25 QUARTS.

Ham in Cider

6 pounds of cook-before-
    eating smoked ham,
    bone-in
2 large carrots, sliced
1 medium onion, sliced
4 stalks celery, diced

12 whole cloves
6 black peppercorns
1 bay leaf
2 to 3 quarts cider

Place the ham in a large kettle with remaining ingredients, using enough cider to cover the ham. Bring to a boil, cover, and simmer for 2 hours, or until tender. Serve hot, or let cool in the broth, remove, and refrigerate before serving.

Oven-Baked Apple Butter with "Red Hots"

16 cups applesauce
8 cups sugar
½ cup cider vinegar

1 package (approx. ½ cup)
  "red-hots" (cinnamon
  imperials)

Combine all ingredients and bring to a boil in a heavy kettle on top of the stove. Pour into a flat-bottomed baking pan and bake at 350°F for about 2 hours, stirring often. Ladle into hot sterilized jars, leaving ¼-inch head space. Adjust lids. Process in a boiling-water bath for 10 minutes.

MAKES ABOUT 8 PINTS.

Mulled Cider

2 quarts apple cider
½ cup brown sugar or honey
1 stick cinnamon

6 whole cloves
6 whole allspice

Place apple cider and sweetening in a kettle. Tie the spices in a piece of cheesecloth and crush slightly with a heavy object. Add to the cider. Bring to boil over medium-high heat. Reduce heat and simmer for 10 minutes. Remove spices. Serve hot.

SERVES 10 TO 12.

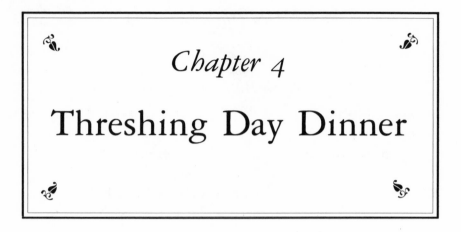

Chapter 4

Threshing Day Dinner

FIRST HARVEST OF THE FARM SEASON

WHEN WE WERE ON Havill Hill at the back of Grandpa's farm or in the hill pasture next to his woods, we could look out over Grandpa's entire farm, and Dad's just beyond. We could see where the creek, outlined by small trees and bushes along its banks, wound across the fields. Grandpa's green-shuttered white house looked small and far away, and the tall old cedar trees forming the windbreak west and north of it looked like the miniature trees in the village under our Christmas tree. Our white bungalow, across the road and just east of Grandpa's house, nestled at the edge of Dad's orchard, its red tin roof a bright patch on the scene spread out in front of us.

The pond in Grandpa's pasture was like a mirror flashing in the sun. Behind our house was a small woods—Dad called it a thicket—and near it, Dad's second orchard, which was always referred to as "the other orchard."

Along the back of Dad's farm, rooftops and buildings on neighboring farms, belonging to the Barrs, Taylors, and Lindseys, stood out on the tree-ringed horizon. It was as if our family's farms and those of our nearest neighbors were in the center of a world encircled by woods. The only hint of the world outside seen from the hilltop was the church steeple at Dale, which could be seen on clear days even though it was five miles distant.

We went to the hilltops almost daily in summertime. We had no purpose in going other than getting to the highest place, turning around, looking out over the farm, looking for the steeple, and going home. That seemed enough. And well it might. The entire territory of our childhoods, my brothers', my cousins', and mine, lay at our feet, and we could see it all in one sweeping view from the very top of our world.

But we were not looking for symbolic meanings in such everyday experiences. What we saw were neat cornfields and grainfields and pastures, marked off by fencerows, in geometric patterns below us. We watched the movements of shadows sweeping across sunlit fields when the clouds rolled across the sky, hiding the sun. When the sun "came out" again, we saw fields of grain waving in the breezes.

When the longest summer days came, the dancing fields of oats and wheat gradually ripened and turned from green to pale, tannish-yellow. Then Uncle Roy, Grandpa, and Dad and his hired hand went into the grainfields with the strong-muscled horses and the reaper to cut the grain. By the Fourth of July, the landscape of our world changed and shocks of wheat stood in the fields, waiting for the threshing machine to come to our farms to thresh the grain from the sheaves of wheat, rye, and oats.

Excitement mounted. Threshing was a major event in every farm community. It was the first harvest of the farm season.

ARRIVAL OF THE THRESHING MACHINE

The steam engine and separator belonged to Fred Bochstahler, from Dale, five miles to the east of us. Whenever the threshing crew began to proceed from farm to farm of the threshing ring (comprised of eight or ten farms), Grandpa, Uncle Roy, and Dad took their wagons and horses and joined the other farmers gathering at each farm in turn to help bring the bundled grain from the fields. They then hauled the separated grain to the granary for storage. It was a cooperative effort that brought neighbors together to help each other get their harvesting done in a spirit of communal effort and sociability.

The crew worked its way around the ring until all the grain was threshed and in the granaries and every barn had a big strawstack standing beside it. The size of a farmer's strawstack was important to us children, but Dad and Grandpa spoke of bushels per acre when they talked about how the crops turned out.

The threshing machine usually came the night before our threshing day, so that the big black steam engine could be set up by the barn in readiness. We could hear the steam engine huffing and puffing as it came through the lane from "Lish" Barr's farm, where they had just finished threshing, but when it reached the crossroads, Mr. Bochstahler pulled the whistle anyway, just to let us know he was coming.

With cries of excitement, we children clustered out by the road to await the arrival of the great smoking, chugging machine, which spewed sparks like a mechanical dragon as it turned into the barn lot in front of us.

We kept an eye on Mr. Bochstahler. He was a very fat, roly-poly man. He was too fat to climb through a barbed wire fence like everyone else did, by pushing down the middle wire, bending over it sideways, lifting one leg over the wire and through to the ground on the other side, shifting weight to that foot, and following along through the wires with the other leg and the rest of the body—without getting scratched.

Mr. Bochstahler hooked the bottom wire of the fence over

the middle wire, wherever he could find a wire loose enough. Then he laid down on the ground and *rolled* under the fence! It was always a moment of shared hilarity between us cousins—only we had to hold back our laughter until we could run away from the scene—behind the woodshed or a tree— where we could let it out in wild haw-haws. We knew what "splitting with laughter" meant, when we couldn't laugh at Mr. Bochstahler to his face.

"You kids be careful!" my father warned as we followed the great mechanical monster into the barn lot. "Stand over there by the woodpile, out of the way."

So we watched from a safe distance while the men dug holes to hold the wheels of the engine, and positioned the separator so that the belts were lined up properly, and the straw spout aimed at the spot where the strawstack was to be built.

THRESHING DAY

The next morning, the milking was finished early and the cows hustled out to pasture at the crack of dawn. Breakfast was barely over when the teams and wagons and hayracks began to pull into the barn lot. At sunup, the barn lot was a hubbub of noise, with harnesses jingling, wagons creaking and rattling, and loose pitchforks bouncing around in the wagon beds. Horses whinnied to one another and stamped nervously because of strange surroundings and presence of unfamiliar animals. Sometimes a nervous animal threatened to rear in harness, and a runaway seemed imminent. Men's voices called out commands to high-strung horses: "Whoa! Whoa, now." There was cussing and kidding and laughing. It was a scene to watch from a swing under the maple tree or from a perch on the split rail fence.

The steam engine had been fired up and a head of steam

was building to rotate the engine's drive wheel. Puffs of steam billowed upward from the smokestacks. The hay wagons clattered down the lanes toward the grainfields as soon as the farmers had all gathered. Soon the loaded wagons began to return, piled high with shaggy loads of grain bundles, lumbering like giant mammoths toward the threshing machine.

"Here's the first load! The first load is here!"

Each wagon pulled up beside the separator, and men standing on top of the load of grain pitched the sheaves into the maw of the machine, one at a time. Soon the separator began to spew out golden blasts of straw onto an ever-growing pile on the ground. At the same time, a steady stream of grain flowed out of a side spout into a wagon below it, and whirlwinds of chaff blew around the threshing machine.

When the first wagon was filled with threshed grain, it was pulled over to a granary, where two men with scoop shovels loaded the grain through the wide window into bins inside.

Meanwhile, the wagons were going to the fields and returning with loads of wheat, rye, and oat sheaves. And at the house, Mother, Grandma, Aunt Helen, and the hired girl had been cooking all morning to prepare a delicious dinner for the threshing "hands."

THRESHING DINNER

For several days before the threshers' arrival, every able body was put to work baking, gathering and preparing fruits and vegetables, borrowing china and chairs, setting up extra tables, and cleaning house in anticipation of the cooking event of the year. A washtub and a wash basin, along with a new bar of gray, gritty Lava soap, were set on a bench outdoors near the cistern where the sweat-drenched threshing crew, itching with chaff and dust, would wash up before dinner. A water bucket for fresh drinking water stood near the cistern, with a water dipper hung on a nearby peach tree limb. A small mirror, a communal comb, and a number of heavy white blue-bordered towels hung on limbs of the Georgia Belle peach tree, as well.

Inside, furniture in the dining and living rooms, which were two open rooms connected by an arch, was rearranged to make way for chairs and an extra table borrowed from Grandma. Three tables placed end to end and covered with overlapping tablecloths made one enormous table that extended out of the dining room through the wide arch and into the living room. Twenty men could sit down to eat at one time.

The threshing crew and the men who worked around the separator came in for the first sitting. Twelve o'clock was always dinnertime for farmers, and on threshing days they were ravenous and appeared almost before the pealing of the dinner bell faded away. The first group gathered at the cistern, getting a drink of water and waiting for a turn at the washpan to scrub off the dirt, sweat, and chaff. They hung their hats about on the towel-hung peach tree, further ornamenting it.

First they washed their hands and arms, making a white lather with Lava soap, then they bent over the washpan and dipped and splashed water over their faces with their hands. Some of them dunked their heads and splashed water over the back of their necks to get rid of the scratchy chaff that had worked its way under the red handkerchief tied inside a buttoned shirt collar. Then a few swipes with a towel and big-toothed comb, and the first crew trooped through the kitchen to the dining room.

Threshing was hard work, but long days of hot, dirty work had rewards. For at least two weeks, men in a threshing ring feasted at two meals a day at the most bountiful tables of the year. The men enjoyed the communal aspect of working to-

gether as a change from solitary labor, and a holiday spirit prevailed at the table. There was a lot of good-natured kidding and joking, reminiscing, and earthy humor, as well as serious farming talk when the men tilted back their chairs, gargantuan appetites and thirsts satisfied.

The cooks in the kitchen modestly accepted their compliments as the men filed back outdoors through the kitchen, fortified for the afternoon's labor.

Mother had a reputation for being a good cook, and never did she live up to it better than she did with threshing dinners. The long table was overflowing with food, ample and varied, when the men sat down at the table. The desserts had to be placed on the library table. Plates of fried chicken at each end of the table, as well as salmon cakes and meat loaf, gave the men a choice. Some men chose to eat all three. There was potato salad and mashed potatoes and scalloped potatoes. It took a dishpan full of new potatoes that had been peeled and cooked. Cole slaw with the first heads of cabbage from the garden; green beans; summer succotash; fresh corn, cut off the cob and fried; macaroni and cheese; freshly made applesauce; sliced tomatoes; pickled peaches; bread and butter pickles; pickled beets; chow chow; and "perfection salad," made of lemon gelatin, shredded cabbage, celery, and green pepper. There was plenty of milk gravy made with the chicken drippings to go with the mashed potatoes and hot biscuits.

Mother's biscuits were made with clabbered (sour) milk, and they were light, tender, and delicious. She made two large pans of biscuits, in pans the size of the oven racks, before the men sat down, and then she filled the pans again and baked another batch. The biscuits were "man-sized," cut out of the rolled-out dough with the rim of a water glass. They were almost as light as bread. Their tops and bottoms were lightly browned and delicate as only an old-fashioned kitchen range could bake them.

When the biscuits were split in half, spread with home-made butter to melt in their tender insides, and then spread with freshly made blackberry-red plum jelly, they were irresistible. Every man at the table put away his share and there were none left on the plate when the table was cleared.

"They cleaned them *all* up!" Mother whispered to Grandma in surprise. "Four pans of biscuits! I never saw men eat so many biscuits."

No matter how many biscuits the threshing crew put away, they always had room for dessert. There were always twice as many desserts as needed. Neighboring women often brought over desserts as a friendly gesture. Cakes and pies could not be made on threshing day because the oven was needed for biscuits and oven-frying the chicken, so they were made the day before. Extra pies and cakes were made because there was a possibility the threshers might not finish in half a day, and they could be on hand for supper as well as dinner.

The library table was a sight to behold. There were juicy fresh peach pies, and cream pies with delicately browned, two-inch-high meringues. There was a butter cake iced with Seven-Minute Frosting, and peach upside-down cake. There was blackberry cobbler and fresh sweetened peaches from the orchard. There was banana pudding and angel food cake. And to wash it all down we made a canning kettle full of iced lemonade, gallons of iced tea, and a large pot of coffee.

After dinner, some of the men napped on the grass under the oak tree in the front yard. ("They're sleeping off the biscuits," Mother said.) Others pitched horseshoes or knocked croquet balls through the wickets. Some smoked and chewed and joked. When the last man had eaten, it was time to head back toward the barn and continue threshing.

"We'll finish along about mid-afternoon, Laura," Dad announced. To Mother and her helpers, that was welcome news. They could leave the unfinished dishes in the kitchen, and at last sit down and have their own meal. They were tired to the bone, but already planning for next year.

"Guess I'll have to make five pans of biscuits," Mother said.

Baking Powder Biscuits

2 tablespoons vinegar	$\frac{1}{2}$ teaspoon salt
$\frac{3}{4}$ cup milk, less 2 tablespoons	$\frac{1}{4}$ cup lard
2 cups unbleached flour	$\frac{1}{4}$ teaspoon baking soda
2 teaspoons double-acting baking powder	2 teaspoons lard

Preheat oven to 400°F.

In a measuring cup, pour vinegar and milk. Put aside and let stand until thickened.

Sift together flour, baking powder, and salt. Add the $\frac{1}{4}$ cup lard and blend with a pastry blender or fingers until the mixture resembles meal. Add the baking soda to the soured milk and stir with a fork. Stir the soured milk into the flour mixture. Turn the dough out on a lightly floured surface and knead briefly. Roll out the dough to a $\frac{1}{2}''$ thickness, and with a 2″ cutter, cut out rounds, dipping the cutter each time into flour to prevent sticking.

In a 9″ round cake tin, melt the 2 teaspoons lard. Allow to cool slightly. Dip the biscuit rounds in the lard, coating both sides, arrange them close together in the tin, and bake for about 20 minutes, or until golden. MAKES ABOUT 12.

Mother made these biscuits with clabbered sour milk. Milk soured with vinegar approximates clabbered milk. Sour cream can also be used, although the biscuits will be heavier than those made with sour milk. Substitute approximately 1 cup sour cream for the $\frac{3}{4}$ cup soured milk, if desired.

Salmon Cakes

1 can (16 ounces) pink
   salmon
3 eggs, beaten

Cracker crumbs
Fat for frying
Salt and pepper

Drain salmon, remove dark skin and large bones (or crush bones), and flake with a fork. Add eggs and enough cracker crumbs to make salmon mixture hold shape when pressed into patties. Shape mixture into six or seven patties and brown on both sides in hot fat over medium heat. Season with salt and pepper to taste.

Cold mashed potatoes may be used instead of crackers. A small amount of onion may be added also.   SERVES 4 TO 6.

Country-Fried Chicken

Cut chicken into serving pieces. For each $2\frac{1}{2}$ to 3 pound chicken, blend 1 cup flour, 1 teaspoon salt, and $\frac{1}{4}$ teaspoon pepper. Dredge the chicken pieces in the flour mixture. (Chicken may be dipped in milk before dipping in flour for frying, if desired.) Heat shortening (lard, vegetable shortening, or vegetable oil) in a cast iron or heavy skillet, to a depth of one-half inch, until sizzling hot. Place well-floured pieces skin side down in the frying pan. Cook about 8 to 10 minutes per side, turning to brown all over, or until golden brown. Drain off excess fat, reduce heat, and loosely cover the skillet and cook for about 20 minutes longer, or until tender. Uncover the skillet to recrisp skin. Drain on paper towels. Serve hot on hot platter. Make gravy using the pan drippings.

Oven-Fried Chicken

Prepare the chicken as for Country-Fried Chicken. Brown the chicken for a few minutes on each side in the skillet on top of the stove, then place the pan in a oven preheated to 400°F and bake for 30 minutes, turning once, until tender and browned.

German Coleslaw

8 cups shredded cabbage
½ sweet green pepper, minced

1 medium onion, chopped fine, or ⅓ cup minced green onions

Dressing

3 tablespoons sugar
3 tablespoons hot water
3 tablespoons cider vinegar
½ teaspoon celery seed

½ teaspoon salt
¼ teaspoon pepper
¼ cup vegetable oil

Combine cabbage, green pepper, and onion in a large bowl and toss to mix well.

To prepare dressing: Combine sugar and hot water, stirring to dissolve sugar. Stir in vinegar, celery seed, salt, and pepper. Pour vinegar mixture over slaw and toss well. Drizzle in oil and toss well.

Cover and keep in a cool place for about two hours before serving.

Scalloped Potatoes with Ham and Cheese

2 quarts peeled, sliced potatoes
$\frac{1}{3}$ cup butter
$\frac{1}{3}$ cup flour
1 quart milk
Salt

$\frac{1}{4}$ teaspoon pepper
3 tablespoons chopped onion or 1 tablespoon chopped chives
1 cup chopped ham
2 cups mild cheddar cheese

Place the peeled sliced potatoes in a large greased baking dish, about 12″ x 14″ x 2¼″. Make a white sauce of the butter, flour, and milk. Season with salt, according to the saltiness of the ham, and pepper. Add onion or chives, ham, and cheese. Pour over potatoes in the baking dish and mix. Bake at 375°F for about 1 hour. Reduce heat to 350°F if the top of the potatoes brown too much before the potatoes are tender. Serve with a green vegetable or salad.

SERVES 8 TO 10.

VARIATION

Both the ham and cheese may be omitted if the potatoes are to be served as a side dish instead of a main course.

Summer Succotash

Cut enough fresh sweet corn from the cob to make 2 cups. In a kettle, cover the cobs with water and boil gently for 30 minutes. Remove the cobs from the water and add 2 cups of "shellie" beans *or* two cups of fresh lima beans. ("Shellie" beans are shelled-out, mature green beans that have gone past the snap stage.) Cook until the beans are tender. Add the corn and cook for several minutes more, or until the corn is tender. Drain. Add salt and pepper to taste, butter, and a little cream.

Fried Corn

6 ears fresh sweet corn
¼ cup butter
¾ teaspoon salt

⅛ teaspoon pepper
2 teaspoons sugar

Cut the corn from the cobs and scrape the cobs with the edge of a knife to get the corn "milk" from the cob. Heat the butter in a skillet, and add the corn and milky juice from the kernels. Season with salt, pepper, and sugar. Cover and simmer for 5 to 10 minutes, stirring occasionally, until the corn is tender.   SERVES 6.

String Beans and Bacon

¼ pound bacon, diced
1 small onion, chopped
1 quart fresh string beans, snapped into 1" to 1½" lengths

2 medium potatoes, peeled and cut into ½" cubes
1 teaspoon salt
2 cups water (approx.)

Brown the bacon. Add the onion and sauté briefly. Add the rest of the ingredients. Cover pan loosely, and cook over low heat for about 30 minutes, or until the potatoes are soft.   SERVES 4.

Fruit Cobbler

¼ cup butter
1 cup sugar
1 cup flour
⅛ teaspoon salt

2 teaspoons baking powder
½ cup milk
2 cups fruit* sweetened
　 with ½ cup sugar

Cream butter and sugar. Sift together flour, salt, and baking powder, and add alternately with milk to the creamed mixture. Pour batter into a greased 9″ x 9″ x 2″ pan.

Drain fruit, reserving 1 cup of juice. Place drained fruit over batter. Over this pour 1 cup of juice. If too little juice drains from fruit to make 1 cup, extend it by adding water or appropriate fruit juice.

Bake at 375°F for 45 minutes. Batter will rise to the top and fruit will settle to the bottom. Serve warm with cream, ice cream, or whipped cream.   SERVES 6.

Potato Salad

5 pounds peeled boiled
　 potatoes
6 hard-cooked eggs, sliced
1 cup sweet pickle relish
2 cups salad dressing or
　 mayonnaise †
1 tablespoon celery seed
　 Salt and pepper

¼ cup chopped green onions
　 (optional)
¼ cup minced fresh parsley
　 (optional)
¼ cup finely chopped celery
　 (optional)

---

*Blackberries, dewberries, cherries, peaches, plums, blueberries, huckleberries, raspberries, apples, or other fresh fruit. Fruit may also be lightly spiced. Suggested spices to add to the fruit with the sugar are: cinnamon and nutmeg with apples, nutmeg or mace with peaches; almond flavoring with cherries; lemon juice with blackberries, blueberries, and huckleberries.

†The taste and consistency of this potato salad is greatly affected by the salad dressing or mayonnaise used. Miracle Whip or homemade mayonnaise may be used. If the homemade mayonnaise is thin, add only enough to moisten the salad.

Slice the cooled boiled potatoes to about $\frac{1}{8}''$ thickness. Layer the potatoes and other ingredients in a large bowl, then gently toss to combine them, taking care not to break up the potatoes. Mix just until the salad dressing moistens all of the potatoes. Makes one large mixing bowlful, and tastes even better the next day. Keep refrigerated. Garnish with one of the boiled sliced eggs. Prepare several hours before serving.

Perfection Salad

1 3-ounce package lemon-
   flavored gelatin
1 cup boiling water
$\frac{1}{2}$ cup cold water
2 tablespoons white vinegar
1 tablespoon lemon juice

$\frac{1}{2}$ teaspoon salt
1 cup cabbage, finely
   shredded
$\frac{1}{4}$ cup diced celery
$\frac{1}{4}$ cup diced green pepper
1 tablespoon pimiento,
   minced

Combine gelatin and boiling water; stir until dissolved. Add cold water, vinegar, lemon juice, and salt. Chill until partially congealed. Fold remaining ingredients into gelatin. Turn into lightly oiled individual molds, or a 3-cup salad mold. Refrigerate until firm. Unmold onto bed of lettuce. Serve with salad dressing or mayonnaise.   SERVES 6 TO 8.

Chow Chow

1   2½-pound cabbage,
      shredded
6   red bell peppers,
      chopped
6   green bell peppers,
      chopped
1½ pounds green tomatoes,
      cut into ¼" cubes
6   onions, chopped
 ¼ cup pickling salt
6   cups apple cider vinegar

2½ cups sugar
2   tablespoons mustard
      seeds
2   tablespoons prepared
      mustard
1   tablespoon mixed
      pickling spice
1   tablespoon celery salt
1½ teaspoon turmeric
1½ teaspoon ground ginger

In a large earthenware crock, combine cabbage, bell peppers,
green tomatoes, onions, and pickling salt. Toss the mixture
and let stand overnight in a cool place. Drain.

In a kettle, combine vinegar, sugar, and spices. Bring the
liquid to a boil, then stir in the drained vegetables. Simmer
for 10 minutes. Pack the chow chow into jars, leaving ¼"
head space. Adjust the lids. Process for 10 minutes in a boiling-water bath.   MAKES ABOUT 8 PINTS.

Bread-and-Butter Pickles

25 to 30 medium-size
      pickling cucumbers
 8 large onions, thinly
      sliced
 2 large green bell peppers,
      thinly sliced
 ½ cup pure salt

5 cups sugar
5 cups apple cider vinegar
2 tablespoons mustard seeds
1 teaspoon turmeric
 ½ teaspoon ground cloves

Wash cucumbers and cut a ⅛" slice off each end, but do not
pare. Slice cucumbers crosswise as thinly as possible, using a

slicer to insure uniform slices. Combine cucumbers, onions, bell peppers, and salt. Let stand for 3 hours in a cool place. Drain thoroughly.

In a large pickling kettle, combine sugar, vinegar, and spices. Bring the mixture to a boil, then add the drained sliced vegetables. Carefully heat the vegetables to scalding, stirring frequently, but do not boil. Pack while hot into hot canning jars, leaving $\frac{1}{4}''$ head space. Adjust lids. Process 5 minutes in a boiling-water bath. To avoid overcooking, start counting the processing time as soon as the water in the canner returns to boiling.

Banana Pudding

4 eggs, separated	1 teaspoon vanilla
$1\frac{1}{4}$ cups sugar	Crushed graham crackers
$\frac{1}{8}$ teaspoon salt	(approx. 16)
2 tablespoons cornstarch	5 bananas
4 cups milk, scalded	

Beat the egg yolks lightly. Combine with $\frac{3}{4}$ cup of the sugar mixed with the salt and cornstarch. Slowly add the scalded milk. Stir and heat the mixture in the top of a double boiler (or use a heavy pan placed on a grid over low heat), stirring constantly, until the mixture will coat a silver spoon. Remove from the heat and stir in the vanilla.

Place a layer of graham cracker crumbs in the bottom of a large ovenproof bowl. Slice a layer of bananas over the crumbs, then add a layer of custard. Repeat layers until the bowl is three-fourths full.

Beat the egg whites until stiff. Gradually beat in the remaining sugar to make a meringue. Spread the meringue on top of the banana pudding. Bake at 325°F for 12 to 15 minutes, or until lightly browned. SERVES 8.

VARIATION

Cook the custard using whole eggs and omit the meringue on top of the pudding. Or, use vanilla wafers instead of graham crackers.

Homemade Lemonade

6 lemons $2\frac{1}{2}$ quarts water
$1\frac{1}{2}$ cups sugar

Roll the lemons on a table, pressing them with the palm of the hand. Slice lemons in thin rings and place in the bottom of a heavy pottery pitcher. Add the sugar and mash with a wooden mallet (we used the potato masher) to extract juice. Let stand for up to 20 minutes, then add cold water and ice. Stir until well blended.   MAKES 3 QUARTS.

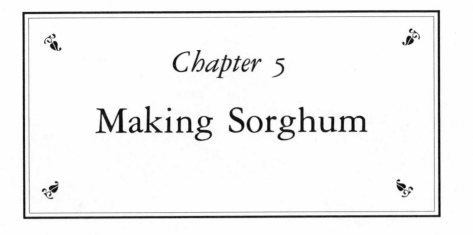

Chapter 5
Making Sorghum

DAD'S SORGHUM CANE PATCH

I REMEMBER WELL my father's fondness for sorghum on hot biscuits—his own sorghum made from his own cane. No other met his requirements for flavor, color, and consistency. Every spring he planted a quarter of an acre of sweet sorghum, using seed he saved from one year to the next. The original seed was given to my father by my grandfather, and it was a strain that had withstood drought and produced juice of just the right sweetness.

Much like corn, the sorghum cane grew to a height of eight feet or so. When the tasseled seed head at the top of the stalk became rust colored and the tiny grains in the tassel hardened so they could not be crushed between the fingers, the cane was ripe. Then my father and brothers would go to the sorghum patch to "strip" the cane, pulling the leaves off the plant while it was still standing in the field. Some farmers would not bother to remove the leaves from the cane stalks before pressing out the juice; this omission was one of the points of making sorghum that my father argued made the difference between "good" sorghum and that which he considered not fit to eat.

After the cane was stripped, the stalks were cut off near the ground with a sharp, long-bladed corn knife that my father wielded like a machete. My brothers cut off the sorghum seed tops, bundled the cut cane together, and gathered up the fallen leaves for fodder and the seed heads for chicken feed.

Next, the sorghum was cut and bundled and taken to a shed near the house, where it was stored in the shade until our turn came to have the crop made into syrup at Uncle Emmett's sorghum mill. Until then, my brothers and I routed our chores and errands by way of the shed, where the pleasant scent of the cut stalks drifted to our noses and stirred an appetite for the taste of the sweet sap contained in the stalks. All during sorghum season we walked about chewing on cane "suckers," short lengths of peeled cane stalks. Cane suckers were a sweet snack we could forage between meals, as we might a twig of sassafras, a sip of honeysuckle nectar, or a handful of wild berries.

DINNER AT AUNT BESSIE'S

When the day came for our crop to be made into syrup, it meant an end to cane suckers but the beginning of a whole season of delicious foods made with fresh sorghum syrup—beginning with the midday meal prepared by Aunt Bessie on the day of sorghum making. The table would be loaded with food, much of it from Aunt Bessie's garden and cellar: green beans, mashed potatoes, fried green tomatoes, piccalilli, corn salad. There was also the usual crisp and golden fried chicken and its accompaniments—baking powder biscuits and milk gravy made in the frying skillet. We never tired of a fried chicken dinner, but it seemed less ordinary when the sorghum pitcher stood ready in the middle of the table for anyone who wanted to sample fresh syrup on hot buttery biscuits. For dessert there would be warm sorghum cake studded with black walnuts and capped with a dome of whipped cream.

Sorghum cake was one of Dad's favorites, and from the moment Aunt Bessie placed it on the table until the last crumb was devoured, talk of weather and crops and politics ceased. All attention focused on the dark, rich cake.

"Oh, *oh!*" my father would exclaim, drawing out the sound of the last "Oh!" with great emphasis. "Sorghum molasses cake!" (In our locality sorghum and molasses were synonymous, although the two are not the same, true molasses being a by-product of sugar refining. The colloquialism was extended further by using "sorghum" and "molasses" together—but everyone understood what was meant.)

From around the table would come a chorus of accolades, clinking dinner forks, and soft, monosyllabic sounds of appreciation.

Spending the entire day making sorghum syrup heightened our enthusiasm. During the morning, Dad fed our cane into the rollers of the sorghum mill, three or four stalks at a time. A good-natured mule named Jack, hitched by a rig on his collar to the end of a long pole sweep, walked in a neverending circle around the mill, pulling the sweep that turned the rollers. Keeping old Jack moving was a problem. He was lazy, and, if not prodded or otherwise encouraged, he would plod slower and slower and finally stop walking altogether.

"Wake up, Jack!" Dad would yell. "Giddap!" And old Jack would plod on for another round or so before he again slowed down. We children recognized opportunity.

"Let us ride him," we pleaded. "We'll keep Jack going."

We were not often allowed to ride the work animals, but this time Dad gave in, making the day even more exciting for us. Squeezing the juice from the cane was a slow job, but if old Jack kept plodding and the raw green juice kept running out of the spout of the mill in a small, steady stream, the barrel would gradually fill.

Under the sorghum shed, Uncle Emmett strained the barrels of juice into another container, from which it would be piped into the boiling pan as he needed it. (Eight to ten gallons of sorghum juice were required to make one gallon of sorghum syrup.) When Uncle Emmett was ready to begin cooking sorghum, he turned on the spigot to allow the first of the juice to trickle into the pan.

"Look, now," he'd say. "That green juice will be sorghum on your biscuits by suppertime."

The juice entering the pan was a cloudy, pale green with a sweet, saplike taste. As it boiled in the first section of the pan, a green scum foamed to the surface. Uncle Emmett used a long-handled, shovel-shaped utensil to skim it off, collecting the sweet skimmings in a bucket so they could be fed to the farm animals that evening.

"Just wait," said Uncle Emmett when he saw doubt on our faces. "This old green water will turn into larruping good sweetening by the time I'm through with it."

And sure enough the boiling liquid in the pan began gradually to change appearance. Before long the unattractive greenish-brown sap became darker and thicker, and gold highlights glistened when bubbles burst on top. After a while the steam hovering above the pan began to smell a lot like Mother's kitchen when popcorn balls were in the making. The aroma drew us to the pan time after time for sample tastes. We bravely shooed away the pesky yellow jackets that were also attracted to the bucket of "skimmins" taken from the end of the pan near the spigot where the finished sorghum would be drawn off. These skimmings were caramellike and delicious, and we dipped pieces of cane into the foamy mass and tasted the sorghum again and again until we were tired of its new flavor.

When Dad had finished extracting sorghum juice with old Jack at the sorghum mill, he would join Uncle Emmett at the sorghum shed, and they would swap stories—as they always did when they were together—about the days of their own childhood in their family of sixteen children.

"Do you remember, Emmett," my father began, "one year when we had sorghum cane down on the creek on the homeplace? Walter Marshall was working for us, helping us get the sorghum ready by cutting and stripping the leaves off by hand, and he rousted a great big water moccasin. It was right by his feet when he saw it, and he cut it to pieces with his corn knife."

"Yes," Uncle Emmett continued the chronicle, "our sister Blanche was down there helping us strip the cane that morning, and the mosquitoes nearly ate her up. Dad had to take her to the doctor."

"She didn't have any business being down there; she was only seven or eight years old," Dad commented. "But every child had to work in those days. Think of the food it took to feed us! Dad had to make two barrels of sorghum to last us through a winter."

"Dad had those barrels made just for sorghum," Uncle Emmett remembered. "They held sixty gallons apiece."

"Yes, and one time we had a whole barrel of that sorghum molasses go to sugar. Do you recall that, Emmett?" Dad asked. "It was so hard that Mother had to cut it out of the barrel with a hammer and chisel. It was just as pretty and yellow and firm as any candy you could buy, and it was *good*. We took it to school in our dinner buckets. Sometimes we would trade it to a classmate for a piece of cake or pie. It was a treat."

"Mom didn't think so," Uncle Emmett said. "She would have to recook that sorghum to turn it back to syrup before we could use it on the table."

And so the reminiscences would continue, while Uncle Emmett stirred and skimmed and tended the cooking sorghum. When the bubbles in the last compartment of the pan began to plop noisily and the syrup looked dark and glossy and thick, the damper of the furnace would be partly closed to slow the fire and prevent scorching the syrup in the final stage of cooking. A spoonful of hot syrup was dipped up for one last approving taste.

"Come here, children," Uncle Emmett called. "Tell me if this is not the larruping good sorghum I promised you it would be."

LARRUPING GOOD SORGHUM FLAVORS

Only children brought up on sorghum syrup or adults accustomed to the nuances of its flavor could have rendered a discriminating judgment. The uninitiated palate might well mistake sorghum syrup for light molasses or wild honey. Although sorghum syrup has a unique flavor—rich, tangy, strong, and sweet—it is definitely more like light molasses than anything else.

When I was a child, New Orleans molasses was expensive and uncommon, whereas sorghum syrup was plentiful. In addition to the standard molasses recipes in which we substituted sorghum, local cooks had special recipes using sorghum that took full advantage of its sweetening power and flavor.

The sorghum pitcher, a regular fixture at every meal, was a heavy glass container with a special metal spout designed to be drip-proof. The spout had a hinged lid that was opened by depressing a lever with the thumb to allow a slow dark ribbon of the syrup to dribble out when the pitcher was tilted. When the thumb was released, the hinged lid snapped shut to cut off the stream of sorghum without leaving a sticky drip on the lip of the spout. The sorghum pitcher was passed around the table whenever oatmeal, pancakes, biscuits, and cornbread were served. To be at the far end of the table when the sorghum pitcher was en route, or when the sorghum was *cold,* was to understand the expression "as slow as molasses."

One of my favorite afterschool snacks was a slice of home-baked bread spread with butter creamed with sorghum. The mixture was combined in a saucer, using enough sorghum with the butter to make it spread smoothly but not so much that it became thin enough to drip off the edges of the bread.

I never carried sorghum to school in my dinner bucket, but some of my classmates brought small jars of it to pour into holes poked with a finger into cold, leftover breakfast biscuits. Because I did not regard cold biscuits (or cold bacon or cold fried eggs) as edible, this was a sorghum peculiarity that I never learned to appreciate. Another sorghum combination I did not find tolerable as a child was a concoction relished by Grandpa Buse at breakfast: a small stream of sizzling hot bacon grease was beaten vigorously into a saucer of sorghum, using a fork; then the mixture, which was almost an emulsion, was poured over hot biscuits or buckwheat pancakes.

Another local sorghum eccentricity, one that I always found delicious, was sorghum egg jelly, also known as egg jam, egg butter, and molasses egg jelly. Recipes differed slightly from house to house in the community, but basically all consisted of eggs, sorghum, and cream beaten together and cooked until thick and spreadable. Sorghum egg jelly was a spread for hot bread and toast, a thick sauce for warm cake, pudding, or gingerbread, or a filling between cake layers.

Not all culinary creations using sorghum were as unusual as sorghum egg jelly or sorghum and bacon grease spread. Sorghum flavored our baked beans, sweet potatoes, pumpkin pies, whole-wheat bread, and gingerbread. Certain cakes, especially dried apple cakes, and sorghum pie, made in the fashion of pecan pie or shoofly pie, could not be made without sorghum. And then there was the cookie jar's reliable offering—giant spicy sorghum cookies, their soft centers studded with raisins and black walnuts.

Aunt Bessie's Sorghum Molasses Cake

4 tablespoons butter

$\frac{1}{2}$ cup sugar

2 eggs

1 cup sorghum

$\frac{1}{2}$ cup buttermilk

1 teaspoon baking soda

2 cups flour

1 teaspoon baking powder

1 teaspoon cinnamon

1 teaspoon cloves

$\frac{1}{2}$ teaspoon salt

$\frac{1}{2}$ cup black walnuts

Cream butter and sugar until fluffy. Add eggs and beat well. Add sorghum and blend. Combine buttermilk and soda. Sift together flour, baking powder, spices, and salt. Add flour mixture to the sorghum mixture in several portions, alternating with buttermilk mixture. Add walnuts.

Bake in a greased and floured 8″ square cake pan, at 350°F for about 45 minutes, or until a tester inserted in the center comes out clean.

Ice with caramel frosting or serve with whipped cream.

Sorghum Applesauce-Raisin Cookies

2 cups flour

1 teaspoon baking soda

1 teaspoon salt

2 teaspoons cinnamon

$\frac{1}{2}$ teaspoon ground cloves

$\frac{1}{2}$ cup (1 stick) unsalted
butter, softened

$\frac{1}{2}$ cup light brown sugar,
firmly packed

1 large egg, beaten lightly

$\frac{1}{2}$ cup sorghum syrup

1 cup applesauce

$\frac{1}{2}$ cup black walnuts or
coarsely chopped
English walnuts

$\frac{1}{2}$ cup raisins

Into a bowl, sift together flour, baking soda, salt, cinnamon, and cloves. In a large bowl, cream the butter with an electric mixer. Add the sugar, beating until mixture is fluffy. Add the egg, beat the mixture well, and beat in the sorghum syrup and the applesauce alternately with the flour mixture. Add the walnuts and raisins and blend batter well.

Drop batter by rounded teaspoonfuls two inches apart onto lightly buttered baking sheets. Bake at 350°F for 10 minutes. Let the cookies cool on the baking sheets for 2 minutes, then transfer them with a metal spatula to a rack. Let cool completely. The cookies will be soft. MAKES ABOUT 72.

Pork Chops with Sweet Potatoes and Apples

4 pork chops
3 tablespoons shortening
  Salt
2 large sweet potatoes,
    cooked and cut into
    pieces
2 large cooking apples,
    peeled and sliced

$\frac{1}{2}$ cup light brown sugar or
    sorghum
$\frac{1}{4}$ teaspoon cinnamon
$\frac{1}{4}$ teaspoon nutmeg

In a large iron skillet, brown pork chops in hot shortening. Add salt to taste. Move the chops over to one side of the skillet to make room for the sweet potatoes. Add the apples to the top of the sweet potatoes. Sprinkle brown sugar or add sorghum to the top of apples and potatoes, and sprinkle them with cinnamon and nutmeg. Turn the heat to low, put a lid on the skillet, and heat slowly until the apples are steamed tender and the sweet potatoes are glazed, about 30 minutes. Baste the sweet potatoes, apples, and pork chops with the syrup in the bottom of the skillet several times while cooking. Serve with a green vegetable, cooked or raw, and spoon bread. SERVES 4

VARIATION
Instead of apples, use 6 canned peach halves.

Spoon Bread

1¼ cups yellow cornmeal
3 cups milk
1 teaspoon salt

2 tablespoons butter
3 eggs, well beaten
2 teaspoons baking powder

Heat milk in a saucepan. Gradually stir in the cornmeal. Let the mixture come to a boil, stirring constantly, and cook until the mixture thickens. Remove from heat, add salt, butter, and eggs, and stir well. Stir in the baking powder. Pour into a greased 1½-quart baking dish, and bake at 350°F for 30 minutes. Top with butter. Serve directly from the baking dish or spoon into warmed dishes. Serve in the place of potatoes, rice, or bread. SERVES 4 TO 6.

Dried Apple Sorghum Cake

2 cups dried apple slices
1 cup sorghum syrup
1 teaspoon baking soda
  dissolved in ¼ cup hot
  water
⅔ cup (1 stick plus 2⅔
  tablespoons) unsalted
  butter, softened
1 cup sugar
2 large eggs
3 cups flour

2 teaspoons double-acting
  baking powder
½ teaspoon freshly grated
  nutmeg
1 teaspoon cinnamon
1 cup milk
1 cup raisins
½ cup coarsely chopped
  pecans
Confectioners' sugar

Preheat oven to 325°F. Let the apple slices soak in hot water to cover for 15 minutes. Drain, then chop coarsely. In a saucepan, combine the apple with the sorghum syrup. Bring the mixture to a boil, stirring occasionally, and boil for 15 minutes, stirring occasionally. Transfer the mixture to a bowl, let cool for 10 minutes, and stir in the baking soda mixture.

Line a buttered baking pan, 13" x 9" x 2", with wax paper, butter the paper, dust the pan with flour.

Cream the butter with an electric mixer, add the sugar, a little at a time, beating, and beat the mixture until it is fluffy. Add the eggs, one at a time, beating well after each addition. Sift together flour, baking powder, nutmeg, and cinnamon, and stir into the butter mixture alternately with the milk. Stir in raisins, pecans, and apple mixture, pour the batter into the baking pan, and bake for 50 to 55 minutes, or until a cake tester inserted in the center comes out clean. Let cool in the pan on a rack for 15 minutes, invert onto the rack, and peel off the wax paper. Let the cake cool completely, invert it onto a serving plate, and sift the confectioners' sugar over it.

Sorghum Egg Jelly (Sorghum Custard Sauce)

3 large eggs

1 cup sorghum syrup

1 cup heavy cream

$\frac{1}{4}$ teaspoon freshly grated nutmeg

In the top of a double boiler set over simmering water, beat the eggs until they are light and lemon colored. Add the sorghum syrup, cream, and nutmeg. Beat until well blended, and cook, stirring, until mixture coats the spoon. Do not allow mixture to boil. Serve the sauce over cake. This sauce keeps, covered and chilled, for up to three days.

MAKES ABOUT $2\frac{1}{2}$ CUPS.

Whole-Wheat Sorghum Bread

2 tablespoons active dry
    yeast
1 cup warm water
1 teaspoon sugar
1 cup milk
½ cup unsalted butter, cut
    into bits
1 cup sorghum syrup

¼ teaspoon ground ginger
1 tablespoon salt
2 cups whole-wheat flour
5 to 6 cups all-purpose flour
2 tablespoons unsalted
    butter, softened

In a small bowl, proof the yeast in the warm water with the sugar for 15 minutes, or until it is foamy. In a saucepan, heat the milk over low heat until it is steaming but not scalded. Remove the pan from the heat, add the butter, and stir the mixture until the butter is melted. Stir in sorghum syrup, ginger, and salt. Transfer mixture to a large bowl and let it cool until it is lukewarm. Add the yeast mixture and the whole-wheat flour and beat until smooth. Add 5 cups of the all-purpose flour, 1 cup at a time, stirring well after each addition, and stir the dough until it leaves the sides of the bowl. Knead the dough on a floured surface for 10 minutes, until it is smooth and elastic but still slightly sticky, adding more all-purpose flour as necessary to keep the dough from sticking. Transfer dough to a lightly oiled bowl, turn to coat with oil, and let it rise, covered tightly with plastic wrap, in a warm place for 1½ to 2 hours, or until double in volume. Punch down the dough and let it rise, covered loosely, for 1 hour more, or until it is double in volume.

Punch down the dough and divide into halves. Knead each half on a floured surface for 30 seconds, form it into a loaf, and fit it into a buttered loaf pan, 8½″ x 4½″ x 2¾″. Rub the tops of the loaves with 1 tablespoon of the softened butter and let them rise, covered loosely, in a warm place for 1 hour, or until they are double in volume. Preheat oven to 350°F. Bake in the middle of the oven for 45 to 50 minutes, or until the loaves sound hollow when the bottoms are tapped. Turn out onto racks, brush with the remaining 1 tablespoon melted butter, and let cool.   MAKES 2 LOAVES.

Sorghum Nut Pie

3 large eggs	1¼ cups pecan halves
1 cup sugar	1 unbaked 9″ pie shell,
1 cup sorghum syrup, or ½	chilled
cup sorghum syrup and	
½ cup light corn syrup	

Preheat oven to 300°F. Beat the eggs until they are light and lemon colored. Add the sugar, and beat until the mixture is well blended. Stir in the sorghum syrup and 1 cup of the pecans and pour the mixture into the chilled, unbaked pie shell. Arrange the remaining pecans decoratively on the top of the pie and bake on a preheated baking sheet in the lower third of the oven for 1 hour, or until a knife inserted in the center comes out clean.

Gingerbread

½ cup butter, margarine, or	1½ teaspoons baking soda
solid vegetable	½ teaspoon salt
shortening	1 teaspoon ginger
½ cup sugar	1 teaspoon cinnamon
1 egg	1 teaspoon cloves
1 cup sorghum or molasses	1 cup hot water
2½ cups sifted flour	

Cream shortening and sugar. Add the egg and beat well. Add sorghum and beat to blend. Sift together the flour, soda, salt, and spices. Add the sifted dry ingredients to the creamed mixture alternately with the hot water, a small amount at a time. Beat after each addition until mixture is smooth.

Pour into a greased pan (10″ x 14″) that has been dusted with flour. Bake at 375°F for 40 to 45 minutes, or until a cake tester inserted in center comes out clean. Serve hot or cold.

Baked-on Topping for Gingerbread

$\frac{1}{4}$ cup butter or margarine
$\frac{1}{2}$ cup brown sugar, firmly packed
$\frac{1}{4}$ cup flour

1 teaspoon cinnamon
$\frac{1}{2}$ teaspoon grated lemon rind
$\frac{1}{2}$ cup chopped nuts

Combine all ingredients and spread on gingerbread ten minutes before it has finished baking. Serve gingerbread hot or cold, as usual, with whipped cream or ice cream.

Chapter 6

A Country Kitchen Thanksgiving

THANKSGIVING DAY

T HANKSGIVING DAY on our Indiana farm always meant an epic of cookery for the women, a day of quail hunting for the men, and unstinted feasting for all who sat at our table to partake of the bountiful meal that symbolized the end of another growing season and the gathering in of the year's crops. In my childhood, the Thanksgiving feast was not an occasion for a full-scale reunion with our many relatives, although we were never without company for dinner. Extra places were laid at the table for my maternal grandparents and perhaps for an aunt and uncle, some cousins, or visiting hunters. And usually among our guests were the hired hands who worked steadily, sometimes even on Thanksgiving Day, to complete my father's harvest before the end of Indian summer and the advent of bad weather.

It was my parents' custom year round to rise before dawn, as soon as the roosters began their crowing. On ordinary days, I was only dreamily aware of the henhouse cacophony and the muffled sounds of morning activity that drifted up to my

bedroom under the eaves. But on such a special day as Thanksgiving, the sounds arising from below the stairway were different from the everyday sounds of breakfast preparation. It was not a day when Mother tiptoed in the kitchen so the rest of the household could sleep. Was that the rattling of the turkey roaster? Would the enormous bird vanish into the oven while I drowsed? The impending activities of the day and the lure of the kitchen were enough to rouse even the most incurable sleepyhead from a featherbed.

On the last Thursday in November, I could stay in bed only until the night chill left the house, hearing first the clash of the heavy grates in the huge black iron range, with its flowery scrolls and nickeled decorations, as Mother shook down the ashes. Then, in their proper sequence, came the sounds of the fire being made—the rustle of newspaper, the snap of kindling, the rush of smoke up the chimney when Mother opened the damper, slid the regulator wide open, and struck a match to the kerosene-soaked corncobs that started a quick hot fire. I listened for the bang of the cast iron lid dropping back into place and for the tick of the stovepipe as fierce flames sent up their first heat, then the sound of the lid being lifted again as Mother fed more dry wood and lumps of coal to the greedy new fire. The duties of the kitchen on Thanksgiving were a thousandfold, and I could tell that Mother was bustling about with a quicker step than usual.

Outside, beneath my window, my father whistled for Queen, our English setter. At the sound of his whistle, my brothers, who were sleeping in the next room, would begin to mumble and stir. Their ears were as acutely attuned to my father's whistle as mine were to the kitchen noises. Jim and Harold did not want to be left behind, tardily finishing their chores, when Dad strode out across the fields with the gun on his shoulder and Queen at his side. And I did not want to miss the goings-on in the kitchen, where Mother, Grandma, and Aunt Emma would cook and visit all morning, telling interesting stories and creating delicious foods for the harvest feast.

As soon as the sweet after-scent of smoke and heat drifted upstairs and I was certain that the kitchen was warm, just moments after my brothers' heavy shoes clattered on the steps and the back door slammed, I would throw off my comforter, seize my clothing, and dash downstairs to dress beside the warming stove.

BREAKFAST ON THANKSGIVING MORNING

The kitchen would already be redolent of biscuits baking and coffee perking. The teakettle sizzled on the back of the stove, sending a thin ribbon of steam from its crooked spout, and hot fat crackled in a covered skillet from which arose a delicate meaty aroma that teased my appetite almost beyond endurance. One sniff was enough to tell me were were having our traditional Thanksgiving breakfast of crisp fried quail, clabbered-milk biscuits, and milk gravy made from the pan drippings and the crusty morsels left in the pan after the quail were cooked. There would be oatmeal (as there was every morning, regardless of the rest of the menu), and no baked apple for me, its center stuffed with raisins and black walnuts, until I had eaten a small bowl of it. But that was a delicious ultimatum, because Mother's oatmeal was hot and hearty, and it was sweetened with honey and doused with cream.

On Thanksgiving morning, my parents' routine was different from that of other days. While Mother cooked breakfast, she kept returning to the preparations for our afternoon feast, which she had begun the night before; and as soon as the biscuits came out of the oven the turkey would go in.

My father did not go to the barn as usual. Instead he would head out across the frost-crusted grass to listen for the soft whistling of the quail as they called to each other in the chilly dawn. Then, after breakfast, he would take Queen and return to the areas where he knew the quail had huddled together for the night, and the keen-nosed dog would locate the birds in their coverts and stand at point until they took flight.

Quail hunting season opened about two weeks before Thanksgiving, and within its short duration my father went shooting as often as he could. He was an excellent shot and an avid quail hunter, and we always had an abundance of the birds for our table. Those were the golden days of quail hunting on our farm and its environs. There were twelve to fifteen coveys on the farm itself, and Dad made the birds welcome by leaving a few cornstalks standing in the fields and by letting small shrubs and trees grow along his fencerows. During severe winters he scattered buckets of grain in the fencerows so the birds would not starve. He hunted a dozen or more times each season, but, by never reducing the number of birds to a point that allowed no margin for natural predators, he practiced game management long before it was recommended by conservation agencies.

By Thanksgiving Day, Dad and Queen would have brought home the bag limit several times, and we ate quail regularly throughout November. During the first decade of my life I did not regard quail as a delicacy any more than I did any of those foods that we enjoyed in their seasons, such as wild strawberries or sweet garden peas or the more fleeting summer berries. They were simply familiar fresh foods that we took for granted.

My father always gathered wild persimmons from a certain tree late in November when he was out shooting quail. I remember the late autumn day when he appeared at the kitchen door after the day's hunting, with the happy English setter swirling at his heels and the pockets of his khaki coat bulging with the day's bag. After he unloaded his shotgun and returned it to its place behind the kitchen door, he laid out the limp, beautiful birds, one by one, for us to count and admire. Then, promising us a surprise, he unbuttoned the flap of the roomy game bag and revealed the wild bounty of which he was almost as proud as he was of the quail—the frosty persimmons harvested from the late-ripening tree at the back of the farm.

These Mother stirred into a spicy persimmon pudding, which sent fragrant messages to our noses from behind the oven door, while the quail spattered and crackled in the frying pan on top of the stove.

The dark, rich pudding cooled on the lowered oven door while we ate the hunter's feast—the platter of golden-fried quail and the delectable milk gravy made of the crusty morsels and drippings left in the frying pan, the mound of fluffy mashed potatoes with rivulets of melting butter coursing down its peak, the feather-light biscuits made with clabbered milk, the savory bowlful of green beans from our summer's garden—celestial dishes, all! But none so heavenly as the persimmon pudding, which Mother portioned out at the table and served, still warm, with a snowy coverlet of sweet whipped cream.

Every such meal was an occasion of thankfulness and a reminder of the plenty we enjoyed from the farm's wild crops, as well as the cultivated harvest that we celebrated at a traditional Thanksgiving feast.

PREPARATIONS FOR THANKSGIVING DINNER

The bird regarded as a delicacy in our house was the plump turkey that Mother was preparing to stuff with a savory mixture of crumbled homemade bread bound with eggs and seasoned with sage and onion. Our usual fowl was chicken, and it appeared on the table all year long, at least once a week, beginning with the first small tender fryers of spring and ending with the last fat stewing hens of winter. Mother had a henhouse full of chickens to supply us with meat and eggs for the table, but she did not have good luck raising turkeys. Although she set a clutch of eggs to hatch nearly every spring, some mishap or other always seemed to befall her flock. Either the eggs hatched poorly, or the brooding hen left her nest too long and let the eggs grow cold, or the brooding house was invaded by night marauders. There were seldom more than a few black and gray speckled turkey hens following the grand old gobbler who ruled our poultry yard.

What a fierce, magnificent bird he was! He dominated the hennery, bringing to it an exoticness that the placid Plymouth Rock and Rhode Island Red chickens lacked, and he regularly intimidated all intruders in the chicken yard, especially the dogs and me. When he walked to and fro along the chicken wire fence, patrolling his borders, his bare head and red wattled neck bobbed up and down between his shoulders, and he walked with a strange swinging gait like a lady in a hoopskirt. His plumage was beautiful, and he could ruffle and smooth his feathers at will. When he strutted and spread his beautiful fan tail, resplendent with dark iridescent white-banded feathers, it looked like the headdress of an American Indian warrior.

He commanded the attention of the entire chicken yard whenever he called *"Turk, turk, turk"* and made the gutteral, chortling sound of his gobble. And he was definitely warlike when he lowered his wing feathers, stretched out his neck, pointed his sharp yellow beak, and gave me chase, hissing and gobbling, when I arrived to gather eggs. But I could clear the fence in seconds. My father once observed that Old Tom was getting mean and offered to put the bully on the Thanksgiving platter; but I was accustomed to the tyrant and regarded our fierce encounters as great fun—as long as I escaped the yellow beak—and I made my father promise not to touch a single one of Old Tom's feathers.

Sitting behind the stove on one particular Thanksgiving morning, cozy in a warm cubicle where I could stroke Queen's silky head, I could see the deplumed turkey on the counter awaiting its savory stuffing. Although it was at least a twenty-pound bird, it looked remarkably small without its feather camouflage, and I realized that I would not have been so terrified of Old Tom had I known his actual body was no larger than that. But it occurred to me that it was *not* Old Tom resting in the roasting pan—at least, I thought it was not.

Suddenly I was gripped by a desire to visit the chicken house. "I'll go see if there are enough fresh eggs in the nests for Dad's breakfast," I volunteered.

When I returned several minutes later, three brown-shelled eggs in hand, I had been reassured, because, once more, I had barely escaped the wicked beak. That turkey in the roaster was indeed the young hen turkey that had been penned near the corncrib and fed extra portions of corn to fatten her for the feast.

Often, Dad would lean back in his chair during a particularly satisfying meal and take inventory of the foods on the table. Frequently he could attribute all of them to our own efforts and acres, and from the walnut table in the kitchen we could actually see where much of our food grew. The garden lay along the south side of the house, separated from it by a double row of fruit trees, including the Georgia Belle peach, which bore white-fleshed fruits, and the Red Delicious apple. From the same window we could see the barn beyond the garden where the cows and steers were stabled; and behind the barn was the feedlot where the pigs were kept. The kitchen's east window faced the poultry house against the background of more fruit trees, for our house touched the edge of a large orchard. The fencerow beside the orchard was lined with blackberry brambles, and the strawberry patch ran alongside the road. Beyond the fence lay fields that yielded quail and small game, and bordering them were the wild plum, crab apple, and persimmon trees, a wild orchard from which we gathered fruits from trees Dad had not tended. In the woods were the tall shagbark hickories and the majestic black walnuts that showered down nuts in the autumn, and wild grapevines twined over smaller trees nearby.

We actually sat in the midst of our fields of plenty. The kitchen table was a veritable cornucopia for the harvest from our acres. In the center, piled in a crunchy mound on the ironstone meat platter, were the quail Dad had hunted. The biscuits keeping warm on the lowered oven door had been made with flour ground from our own wheat, and the short-ening was white-leaf lard rendered from hogs we had butch-ered. The clabbered milk in the biscuits and the sweet milk in the gravy came from our Jersey cows. The butter was from our own churn, and the deep golden sorghum was the prod-uct of cane grown in a small plot down by the creek. The Stayman Winesaps had been grown in the orchard, and the walnuts were from our woods. Honey from my grandmother's hives, eggs from our hens, and tart wild plum jelly from the cache of home-canned foods in the cellar completed the array.

A considerable amount of our meat came to us through Dad's skill as a small-game hunter. He and my brothers hunted and fished for whatever was in season, and enriched our table with the variety and wild flavors provided by quail, deer, ducks, rabbits, squirrels, fish, frogs, and, less frequently, snapping turtles.

After breakfast on Thanksgiving, Dad would button his khaki hunting vest and take his red cap from the hook be-hind the kitchen door. At the moment he began getting his gear together, even before he picked up the shotgun, Queen would flash out from under the stove and station herself at the door, whining and yipping, tail wagging, excited and ready to go hunting. I can still remember how they looked from the window as I watched them receding into the landscape until only the red spot of Dad's cap was distinguishable from the autumn fields.

Our Thanksgiving dinner was always in the afternoon, never earlier than two o'clock, and sometimes later if the men came home late from hunting. Mother never complained about the hour, for she needed plenty of time in the kitchen.

The bread sponge had been set to rise the night before. In a deep blue-and-white crock, Mother would combine the yeast starter, a part of which she saved from one baking to another, with scalded milk and hot potato water, salt, honey, lard, and flour. She would then wrap the crock in a towel and set it in the warming closet above the stove. And in the morning, when the turkey was in the oven, Mother would pull out the breadboard, tilt open the flour bin, and sift a white pyramid of flour into the bubbling bowl of yeast-fragrant batter. As soon as she had stirred in enough flour to make the dough, she would turn it out onto the board and knead and pummel it until it was smooth and elastic. The glossy mound of dough then went into the greased crock and was covered with the towel and set on the back of the stove to rise. When it had doubled in bulk Mother would punch it down and let it blossom once more before kneading it the last time and shaping it into fat buns. These she arranged in a large, shallow black pan that had been greased with lard, and when they had risen she touched their plump cheeks with melted butter and popped them into an oven so hot it brought a rosy glow to her face as she bent before the open door. Almost at once the heavenly smell of baking bread filled the house so temptingly that it could hardly be borne until the pan of buns, as golden as wheat fields in July, was drawn from the oven at dinnertime.

In between the sifting and kneading and rising, Mother smoothly dovetailed all the other preparations for dinner. It seemed that no endeavor proceeded uninterrupted from beginning to end. Early in the day I would doubt that the various parts of our dinner could ever be finished at the same time; but Thanksgiving was a day for two cooks in the kitchen, and Grandma always came to help.

The making of the Thanksgiving mincemeat was among Grandma's projects. She made delectable mincemeat pies. As thin and delicate as her piecrusts, Grandma was as energetic and spirited as the brandy-laced mincemeat that she made each autumn. When Grandma arrived on Thanksgiving morning and tied her apron with those quick, deft motions that characterized all of her movements, I knew that the mountain of work would begin to disappear.

The preparation of the turkey stuffing was the most urgent task once breakfast was over, so while Mother cleaned onions and celery, Grandma's fingers flew over the pan of bread, pinching and crumbling it into small pieces. I was summoned again to assemble and turn the food chopper as Mother fed into it the turkey neck and giblets. In went the slices of onion—I stood at arm's length to keep my eyes from tearing—and finally the more amicable celery and parsley. As soon as the flat pan was filled, Grandma would sweep it away and add its contents to the crumbled bread. Next, Mother brought out chicken broth saved from cooking the giblets, and several lightly beaten eggs, and these, too, were added to the growing mound of stuffing, along with salt, pepper, and dried sage from our summer garden. Grandma tossed the fragrant mixture until it was well blended, and then both women alternately deposited handful after handful of stuffing in the cavities of the bird. Together they sewed up the openings; the bird was covered with pieces of buttered muslin; and finally it went into the oven to roast for at least eight hours, being all the while annointed with bastings of butter and juices until the skin turned a rich deep brown.

After the turkey was in the oven, I was called to fill the teakettle, wash and dry dishes, pick chrysanthemums, fill the water bucket, make the beds, feed the chickens, polish silver, fetch the pickles, bring in dry wood, fill the coal bucket—

all chores I was eager to perform in preparation for our Thanksgiving feast.

While Grandma and Mother put the kitchen in order, there was a sociable flow of gossip, recipes, and stories. A wealth of knowledge could be picked up by keen ears listening to the chatter of the two women working in the kitchen.

"Emma's coming after church," Mother announced on her way to the pantry. The pans rattled and clanged in the adjoining room. "Oh, my! Better churn tomorrow or this cream will go bad."

"Child, run and get the sweet potatoes out of the attic." Grandma's hands moved deftly in the bowl of pastry ingredients. "There's not a pie worth eating, save mince, that was baked the day before."

"This boiled cider is nice—could you taste it in the baked apples?" Mother scraped the last syrupy remnants of the pan as she cleared away more dishes.

"The Staymans are baking better than the Rome Beauties this year." Grandma brushed milk on a round of dough. "Blanche uses egg yolk to glaze the top of her crust."

"How much apple butter did she put up, did she say?" Mother scrubbed potatoes in a pan in the sink.

"Pa wouldn't give her a nickel for any of it; she puts in too much clove." Grandma came out of the pantry carrying the stewed pumpkin. "We'd better beat the egg whites for this pie." Grandma separated the eggs, dropping the whites onto a shallow platter and the yolks into the pumpkin. "Pa simply can't abide a solid pumpkin pie." With great gusto she whisked the whites into soft, fluffy peaks right on the meat platter, using a flat wire beater, and even though she held the platter at an angle not a drop of egg white slid off.

Mother peeled the tawny sweet potatoes, cut them into sections, and into the kettle they went. She next prepared onions for creaming, green beans, Brussels sprouts—dinner was well underway.

The oven was always overburdened on Thanksgiving, for

the sweet potatoes and dried corn pudding demanded baking, as did the pies and rolls. But Mother had a long-legged kerosene reserve stove on the screened-in back porch, which she used in the summer when it was too hot to have a fire in the kitchen stove, or for holiday meals and threshing dinners, or to can fruits and vegetables and make jelly—and this she put to use on Thanksgiving Day.

THE BOUNTIFUL TABLE

Setting the table and readying the dining room were my realm. The day before Thanksgiving, my brothers and I would move two large square tables together and extend them to their ultimate length with extra leaves. The tables, covered with white damask cloths that matched so closely you could scarcely tell they were not one, stretched from the dining room through the wide arch into the living room. I gathered straight-backed chairs from all over the house and borrowed some of Grandma's as well, and although they didn't match they were all Victorian with fancy designs carved in their wide top slats. Bouquets of chrysanthemums graced each end of the table and in the center the cornucopia basket overflowed with samples of autumn's bounty. Mounded in front of the horn and extending down toward the flowers trailed an assortment of nuts, apples, gourds, small pumpkins, bittersweet, sprays of wheat, colored leaves, ears of Indian corn, and strawberry popcorn; and arrayed along the length of the table were numerous sparkling pressed glass and china bowls awaiting jellies, pickles, relishes, olives, celery, and sauces. Reigning over this company of dishes, as usual, was the queenly old "Starburst Spooner."

"Use the gold-banded dinner plates today," Mother suggested when she brought in a cut-glass bowl filled with rosy, cinnamon-flavored applesauce that had been tinted and flavored with "red hots."

When I wanted to bring in shocks of corn to place about the room Mother put her foot down, however, and I had to be content with standing them beside the front door. I arranged pumpkins on the steps, a swag of bittersweet on the door, and branches of bright leaves and Indian corn in any empty corner I could find.

One by one the diners would begin to straggle into the house. My brothers returned from their hunting and listened to football games on the radio until dinnertime. Grandpa, who usually spent the morning shucking corn, would invariably appear at the kitchen door bearing a jug of sweet cider. The hired hands came up from the granary and washed up on the back porch, using strong, clean-smelling soap. Then, shirts tucked in and hair combed, they joined Grandpa by the stove in the living room. Aunt Emma would arrive after church, bringing a jar of pickled peaches and a bowl of tart-sweet cranberry sauce.

In the kitchen, everything was nearly ready. We awaited only Dad's return from his morning hunt, and I was stationed at the dining room window to watch for his approach. His longstanding habit of hunting on Thanksgiving was as true to the precedent of that historical feast as cooking the turkey.

The first flash of his cap attracted my eye, and soon I could pick out his khaki-colored form against the landscape. "He's coming now!" I'd call, and by the time Dad appeared at the back door the dishes were being carried to the table.

In the dining room, the magnificent turkey, ringed with a garland of parsley, spiced crab apples, and pickled peaches, rested on the platter in front of my father's place. We took our chairs and bowed our heads while Grandpa gave our Thanksgiving blessing.

When I lifted my eyes there was a vision of plenty, and sometime later, in her beautiful schoolmarm's script, Mother recorded it on a page of looseleaf notebook that served as her diary, cookbook, and farmwife's record.

Thanksgiving 1939: For breakfast, fried the quail Charles
had shot and used boiled cider on the baked apples for breakfast, with good results. For Thanksgiving dinner, Mother and
Father sat down with us, also Emma and the hired men. We
had a good meal with more than plenty for all. The turkey,
about twenty pounds in weight, roasted done by the time
Charles came in from hunting and the stuffing was well received. But maybe next year we will have oysters in the stuffing, for a change. Also cooked, with Ma's help, dried corn
pudding, mashed potatoes and brown gravy, candied sweet
potatoes (with marshmallows for the children), green beans,
creamed onions, Brussels sprouts, and baked cushaw. Emma
brought pickled peaches and a cranberry sauce. We used pickles, relishes, and jellies from the cellar, as usual. One of the
hired men had never tasted damson plum preserves or peach
butter. Ma baked mince, pumpkin, and squash pies. We also
had a nice persimmon pudding for Charles, and a good laugh
as well, because the pudding was made with juicy-ripe persimmons he carried in his hunting cap last week—and ruined
it! The good weather still holds and we are thankful to have
the harvest home. It is a year of plenty.

Baked Apples with Boiled Cider

6 large apples
$\frac{1}{2}$ cup light brown sugar,
   firmly packed
$\frac{1}{3}$ cup raisins
$\frac{1}{3}$ cup chopped walnuts or
   pecans

1 tablespoon boiled cider
4 tablespoons butter
$\frac{1}{2}$ cup boiled cider

Peel the top third of the apples and core them. Place in a
buttered baking dish.

Combine brown sugar, raisins, nuts, and the tablespoon of
boiled cider. Stuff apples with the mixture. Pour the $\frac{1}{2}$ cup
boiled cider over the apples and bake, covered, at 375°F, for
1 hour or until they are tender, basting every 10 minutes.
Spoon the juices over the apples, and serve warm with heavy
cream, if desired.

Baked Turkey with Mother's Turkey Stuffing

1½ pounds firm white bread, torn into small pieces

2 cups (approx.) ground, cooked giblets and neck meat

1 cup ground celery

6 sprigs celery, minced

½ cup ground onion

1 teaspoon salt

½ teaspoon freshly ground black pepper

8 dried sage leaves, crumbled, or 1½ teaspoon powdered sage

1 cup turkey broth

4 beaten eggs

1 12-pound turkey

1 tablespoon salt

½ pound butter, melted

In a large bowl, combine all of the ingredients except the last three and mix together lightly until stuffing is evenly moistened.

Rub the cavity of the turkey with the 1 tablespoon of salt. Stuff the bread mixture into the body cavity and also the neck cavity of the turkey. Fasten the cavity openings with skewers and string. A heel of bread may be placed in the body cavity opening to keep the stuffing from falling out. Truss the legs together and fold the wing tips under the turkey's back.

Place the turkey on a rack in a roaster and pour the melted butter over it. Roast the turkey, uncovered, at 325°F for 4 hours, basting with butter every half hour, or until a meat thermometer inserted in the turkey's thigh registers 185°F. If the breast and drumsticks begin to burn, cover them with muslin that has been dipped into melted butter, or shield the turkey with a tent of aluminum foil.

My mother made a plain bread stuffing. It was not especially moist, as my grandmother's was, and it was not always served with turkey. Sometimes the stuffing, more often called "dressing" in southern Indiana, was baked in a casserole and served with baked chicken, fried chicken, or roasted meats. The giblets and sage could be left out if the dressing was served with something other than fowl, and the dressing was then inundated with brown gravy made from the roast meat drippings.

Dried Corn Pudding

1 cup dried corn	3 tablespoons brown sugar
2 cups scalded milk	½ teaspoon salt
2 eggs, lightly beaten	1 tablespoon butter
½ cup heavy cream	

With an electric blender, food processor, or grain mill, grind the dried corn. Pour the scalded milk over the corn and let the mixture stand for 1½ hours. Stir in eggs, cream, brown sugar, and salt. Pour into a buttered baking dish, 10″ x 6″ x 2″, and dot the top with butter. Bake the pudding at 350°F for 30 minutes, or until it is puffed and golden.

Drying Corn Cut the kernels from ears of sweet corn and spread them in one layer on jelly-roll pans. Heat the corn in a very slow oven, 150°F, with the oven door ajar, for 6 to 8 hours, or until it is completely dry. (Or use a food dehydrator, following the manufacturer's directions.) Transfer the dried, cooled corn to paper bags and tie the bags closed. Store the corn in a cool, dry place.

Baked Cushaw

Cut off a piece of cushaw squash large enough to make the desired number of servings. Refrigerate the rest until needed.

Scoop out the seeds and membranes of the cushaw, but do not peel. Place the squash, rind side up, on a greased cookie sheet. Bake at 350°F until done (about one hour), when a knife will pierce the rind easily. Remove the squash from the oven, scoop out the pulp and use, when cooled, for making pie. Or serve hot, seasoned with salt, pepper, and butter, as a side dish.

Cushaw Pie

2 cups cooked cushaw squash, mashed or pureed
1 cup cream
2 egg yolks, beaten
$\frac{3}{4}$ cup sugar (more to taste)
$\frac{1}{2}$ teaspoon salt
1 teaspoon cinnamon
$\frac{1}{4}$ teaspoon nutmeg
$\frac{1}{8}$ teaspoon ginger
$\frac{1}{8}$ teaspoon cloves
2 egg whites, stiffly beaten
1 9" pie shell, unbaked

Combine squash, cream, egg yolks, sugar, salt, and spices. Fold in stiffly beaten egg whites. Pour mixture into the pie shell. Bake at 425°F for ten minutes, then reduce heat to 350°F and bake until the center of the pie is set (about 45 minutes). Serve with whipped cream.

Damson Plum Conserve

3 cups unpeeled damson
    plums, seeded and
    halved
3 cups sugar
1 cup raisins

Juice of 1 lemon
2 seeded oranges, chopped
    with the rind
1 cup walnuts

In a heavy pan, combine plums, sugar, raisins, lemon juice, and chopped oranges and rind. Cook slowly until the mixture is thick and clear, stirring constantly, about 30 minutes. Stir in walnuts. Pack in sterilized jelly jars and cover with paraffin.   FILLS 6 1-CUP JELLY JARS.

Mother's Wild Persimmon Pudding

2 cups sugar
2 cups persimmon pulp
2 eggs
1 teaspoon baking soda
$1\frac{1}{2}$ cups buttermilk
$1\frac{1}{2}$ cups flour

$\frac{1}{8}$ teaspoon salt
1 teaspoon baking powder
1 teaspoon cinnamon
1 teaspoon vanilla extract
$\frac{1}{4}$ cup cream
2 tablespoons butter

In the bowl of an electric mixer, combine sugar and persimmon pulp. Add eggs and beat well. Add baking soda to buttermilk and stir until mixture stops foaming. Add the buttermilk mixture to the persimmon mixture.

Sift together the flour, salt, baking powder, and cinnamon. Add to the persimmon mixture gradually and beat well. Stir in vanilla and cream.

Melt butter in a large baking pan, 9" x 13" x 2". Pour the melted butter into the pudding batter, leaving just enough in the baking pan to grease the bottom and sides. Beat the melted butter into the batter, pour the batter into the baking pan, and bake the pudding at 350°F for about 45 minutes. The pudding is done when it pulls away from the sides of the pan and the center is set. It will fall after being taken from the oven. Serve the persimmon pudding with whipped cream.   SERVES 8 TO 12.

Chapter 7

A Country Christmas

A CEDAR CHRISTMAS TREE

OUR CHRISTMAS TREE was always a red cedar tree cut down somewhere on Grandpa Buse's farm. Dad would not allow cedars to grow on his land because they were host to cedar-apple rust, which was a threat to his apple orchard. So we always located a pretty cone-shaped cedar that would make a good Christmas tree at some distance from the house. About two weeks before Christmas on a beautifully bright Sunday afternoon, we would all walk across the farm to bring home the chosen tree.

The cedar tree was selected long before the glorious season of Christmas was at hand. I remember one particular summer day when my brother Harold announced that he had found our next Christmas tree. We all trooped to the back of Grandpa's woods to see the cedar tree, which was ceiling-tall, much taller than our usual four- or five-foot-high Christmas tree. That year we needed a horse and sled to bring in the tree.

We started in right after Thanksgiving making decorations for the tree. With scissors and flour paste, we cut and stuck together colored construction paper loops to make yards and yards of red and green garlands. We made popcorn strings and cut out lacy white paper snowflakes.

The tree was placed in front of the double front windows of the living room, its trunk braced in a tub of wet sand and swaddled in Mother's cotton quilt batting. Our homemade decorations, along with a few fragile treasured glass ornaments, and long icicles of silver tinsel dripped over fragrant evergreen boughs, were the tree's simple adornments.

There it stood, in the same place every year, the most beloved and essential decoration of the joyous season. It was a colorful magnet, drawing us toward its fragrance and centering our imaginations upon the approaching day.

Our family tradition was to "have Christmas" when we returned from the Christmas Eve program at the Lutheran church at Holland. The house would be dark when we came into the wood-scented living room because kerosene lamps were always blown out when we left home. For a few minutes we had to stand waiting, just inside the front door, in breathless anticipation, while Mother went to the kitchen in darkness to light a lamp.

As she walked toward us, returning, the lighted lamp held aloft cast soft, dancing shadows across the walls. Light gradually reached the Christmas tree and illuminated the mysterious mound of ribboned packages under it.

All too quickly, secrets were revealed and the brief magic time when wishes come true was gone for another year. It was time for bed and a contented snuggle in the feather beds without the delicious torment of Christmas-coming staving off sleep. And there was still Christmas dinner to come, before someone would sigh loudly and say: "Well, Christmas is over."

CHRISTMAS DINNER

Christmas dinner was a sumptuous meal following in the tradition of our Thanksgiving feast. We ate the home-grown garden vegetables that Mother had canned: green beans, corn, beets. There were sweet potatoes, relishes, pickles, Waldorf salad, whole cranberry sauce, homemade rolls, and pies— cushaw, fresh coconut, and mince. When we butchered at Christmastime, our holiday dinner centered around a crisply crusted pork roast with sage dressing. And instead of fruit-cake, we had an old-fashioned pork cake made with fresh sausage.

BUTCHERING

When the weather turned crisp and cold after Thanksgiving, preparations began for butchering a fat hog for the winter's supply of pork. With Mother and Dad both teaching, hog butchering ideally coincided with their Christmas vacation from school.

When Christmas fell toward the middle or end of the week, butchering was out of the way before Christmas, weather permitting, and we had a luxury of fresh pork. Some of it had to be eaten immediately or given away, especially the organ meats. Supper on the first day of butchering always centered around a generous platter of *fresh* pork liver that had been dipped in well-seasoned flour and browned quickly in bacon fat in the heavy iron skillet. For Dad, there was the added treat of fried onion rings to accompany the meat. Fresh pork liver has a mild, delicate flavor that has an evanescent quality, like that of new peas and sweet corn, which changes to a completely different flavor in a very short time.

There are gaps in my memory of butchering day. Not only was hog-killing day in competition with Christmas-coming, but it was a day that I longed for and dreaded at the same time. It was one of those farm events that inspired both pain and pleasure.

Before sunup, the fires were crackling under two erstwhile wash kettles filled with water. The butchering site was located in the barn lot, not far from the pigpen. From my upstairs bedroom window, I could see Dad, the hired hand, Grandpa, and the neighbor who had come to stick the hog. They were busily finishing up chores near the hoist and scraping table, against which the scalding barrel was tilted at a 45-degree angle. It was a scene to watch until the men converged toward the pigpen. Then I dived back into the feather bed to muffle the appalling outcries and terrorizing squealing that carried clearly to my upstairs sanctuary.

The silence returned and, eventually, courage, and I crept down the stairs and toward the comfort of the kitchen.

But Mother and Jewel were bustling about with white dishpans and stewing pots filled with all manner of innards removed from the slaughtered hog (which could be plainly seen from the kitchen windows, hanging upside down by his hind legs above the scraping table, white and steaming and headless).

The bacons and hams were piled on the back porch table to cool and be trimmed before Grandpa started curing them with a mixture of sugar, salt, saltpeter, and pepper. Later he would smoke them in his smokehouse, along with some of the long sausages, over fragrant fires of hickory wood.

The scent of hickory smoke evokes a memory of Christmas in a country kitchen just as certainly as does the fragrance of cedar or sausage crackling in a frying pan on a winter's morning.

One of the chores of butchering was making sausage. Meat trimmed from hams, shoulders, middlings, head, and jowls of the slaughtered hog is run through a sausage grinder, then seasoned with salt, pepper, and sometimes sage.

Our sausage grinder was mounted on a board about the length and width of an extra table leaf. It was a large, heavy-duty version of an ordinary food chopper. Turning it to grind the meat was a heavy job, and it fell in Grandpa's province.

The sausage grinder was placed between two chairs with the ends of the board resting on the chair seats. A tub was placed on the floor under the grinder to catch the ground meat as it came through. Grandpa sat on one chair, straddling an end of the board upon which the grinder was mounted. He fed the meat chunks into the hopper with one hand while turning the handle of the sausage grinder with the other. Sometimes another person sat on the other chair, feeding in the chunks of meat and holding down the other end of the grinder mount. Sometimes I was that other person.

We stayed up late on nights after slaughtering, as Grandpa referred to it. There were several steps in making sausage, and it was important to get the meat worked up quickly. After grinding the sausage meat, it was stuffed into casings, which were simply the cleaned, washed, and scraped intestines of the hog.

Butchering the Christmas hog was a shared family event for many years. The related chores—making sausage, rendering lard, smoking hams—were as traditional to the holidays as the Christmas dinner and the Christmas program at church.

Essences of Christmas From the Rawleigh Drummer

At Christmas, the breath of our kitchen was exalted with the sweet fragrances of candy-making and holiday baking. Vapors of almond and lemon and peppermint replaced the scent of everyday vanilla. We could look forward to almond-flavored cherry pies and angel food cakes. There would be lemon-flavored sponge cakes and Christmas cookies shaped like Christmas trees, Santas, angels, and stars, sprinkled with colored sugar and iced with tinted frostings. There would be fondant stuffed dates, fudge, and peanut brittle. We would pull peppermint taffy and beat big bowls of divinity. The hearty smells of butchering were replaced by the delicate essences of Christmas flavoring extracts, which we always bought from the Rawleigh drummer.

The Rawleigh drummer represented an old reliable company, "a friend of the family since 1889." He was a summer regular among a horde of traveling salesmen who traversed our rural area during the Depression.

On the Rawleigh salesman's last round of the season, in August, Mother always bought small bottles of flavoring to use in holiday baking and candy-making. I always looked forward to that visit because I knew Mother would be laying in the Christmas flavorings.

The Rawleigh drummer came around only during the summer. He never called on us after school started because Mother was away during the day teaching at the township school in Selvin, one-half mile away. Most traveling salesmen and unusual visitors to the farmhouse disappeared once school started, anyway. Only an intrepid few kept up their rounds in winter because our road was a narrow, unpaved dirt road until the WPA came through building new roads. In rainy weather and during the spring thaw, a dirt road became a mud road, impassable by automobile for periods of time because of mud holes or a covering of snow.

The Rawleigh drummer carried his merchandise in a brown leather case that looked like a suitcase. He always placed it on the seat of the porch swing, and opened it so that the top and bottom lay flat, displaying the wares inside. The drummer's case was made to fit the items he carried. Elastic bands or pockets inside the case secured each bottle or item on a display board. When the case was open, the merchandise displayed on the inside cover could be seen, along with that fastened to the first display board on top of a number of other such display boards. The display boards were turned like pages of a book; after we had seen the merchandise on the top layer, he turned the first display board to the top of the case, revealing a new array of items in the next layer.

There were shaving knives and soap, whetstones, shoe polish, linaments, cough syrups, patent medicines, tonics, and potassium permanganate—the "purple salt" we put into the baby chicks' drinking water. And finally there was the collection of flavoring extracts and spices from which Mother always made a selection. While she usually bought only vanilla extract, the Rawleigh drummer carried at least a dozen other flavors that were purely irresistible. Black walnut, almond, lemon, orange, banana, rum, maple, peppermint, pineapple, cherry—the visions invoked by the very names of those flavors rose like Christmas genies from their bottles, and I always wished Mother would buy them all.

I knew that Christmas wishes *could* come true because it had happened to me.

THE GIFT OF SNOW

The first Christmas that I can remember, I asked for a doll with curly hair and long eyelashes to replace a loved, but outgrown, baby doll. My brother, Harold, wanted a red sled and recklessly asked for "lots of snow to go with it." We listed these wishes and many others and sent them off to Santa at the North Pole via the rural mail carrier.

The gift of snow arrived a few days before Christmas. Snowflakes swirling lightly in the air were proof that the important letter had reached its destination, and we felt assured that our Christmas wishes were coming true. We failed to see the falling snow as a dire portent.

Overnight, the countryside was transformed into the most beautiful snowscape my brothers and I had ever seen, and still the snow was falling. It was a day when we needed no urging to eat steaming bowlfuls of hot oatmeal, no admonishments to hurry about our morning chores.

Even the chicken yard and barn lot were enchanted places, and the pristine hillside beyond the barn invited us to make footprints and trails in the unmarked snow. All day we tumbled and slid down the steep slope, made angel wings on every snowbank, and built forts and snowmen until we looked like snowmen ourselves. But gradually the drifts deepened, and we began to wish the snowfall would stop.

For several days, we had expected Dad to come home from the school in central Indiana where he taught, but he did not arrive. Mother worried that he might not be able to drive home if it kept snowing. Grandpa had cleared away snowdrifts blocking our road to town with the work horses hitched to a sled, but the highways beyond were still impassable by automobile.

By Christmas Eve the prospects were gloomy—Dad would not arrive home in time for Christmas, Santa might possibly be delayed by the deep snow, and we could not drive to our church in a town five miles away for the traditional Christmas program.

We were stricken with disappointment. We children had never known a Christmas without Dad at home, without Santa's visit, without the Christmas program at the Lutheran church in Holland. We simply could not imagine it.

Dad always brought armloads of presents, baskets of Florida fruits, sacks of peanuts in the shell, English walnuts, almonds, and store-bought candies we had only at Christmas—orange slices, chocolate drops, coconut bonbons, peppermint sticks, and hard, clear candies shaped like animals. For weeks we had practiced and memorized our verses and songs in preparation for the pageant. And on the eve of eves, Santa always left our presents under the Christmas tree in the living room. We were crestfallen.

"I wish I had never wished for snow," my brother moaned.

But our mother had an idea that rescued us from dejection.

"We will visit the Christmas program in town at the Methodist church. We can walk that far on the path Grandpa made in the road."

THE CHRISTMAS PROGRAM

So we pulled on our boots and, muffled and mittened, waded the half mile through the snow to the church in town. At last the snow had stopped and the night was cold and clear. The stars glittered and sparkled and seemed brighter than ever before. One star, brighter than all the others, seemed to stand still, and the enchantment of Christmas returned. Snow crunched underfoot, and I felt that something magical could happen after all.

At first the unfamiliar surroundings felt strange, but the church was warm and fragrant with the scents of burning candles and of the cedar tree beside the stage. The angels in bedsheet robes were my classmates, and Joseph was our neighbor. Christmas seemed the same here as in our own church, perhaps even more exciting. After the familiar carols and pageant, I stopped regretting the snowstorm and the changes it brought to our Christmas. It was as nice a Christmas Eve as ever before.

As the program ended, there was a jingle of sleigh bells, a commotion at the back of the church, and a jolly, red-clad figure appeared in the aisle amid a burst of frenzied squeals of surprise. Then, in the hush that followed, one name after another was called out to receive the beribboned packages, and finally, to our gasps of surprise, my own name and those of my brothers. It was a thrill to receive a coloring book from Santa when I had not even asked for one!

When we stepped out into the cold, sparkling night, there was my father waiting by the door. Not only had he arrived safely, but at the very moment Santa alighted. This was truly a night for surprises. For convenience, Santa had arranged to leave our presents in the back seat of Dad's car, where we could barely see their intriguing dark shapes by the reflected light of the snow and the brightly shining stars.

Two Dolls From Santa

The next morning, when the presents were at last spread out under the Christmas tree, we saw that all our wishes had come true, and more. My brother had his red sled (and lots of snow) and I had a raven-haired doll with dreamy eyes that opened and closed. The doll had her own bed and a patchwork quilt made out of scraps left over from my dresses. And to my wonderment, she had a red-haired sister just as beautiful as she—and with her was a doll's tea set! It was the best Christmas ever.

I was puzzled by Santa's unusual generosity. No one ever received two dolls on one Christmas! But I relished my good fortune and happily sewed dolls' dresses and had a tea party with my new set of dolls' dishes when my school chum, Doris, arrived via horse and sledge to visit while "Uncle" Dave went to town.

The tea set was lustrous ochre-colored porcelain with decorations of delicate pink asters, green leaves, and blue rims. It was so fragile that one's fingers could be seen through a saucer held up to the light. Red letters on the bottom of the teapot spelled out: MADE IN JAPAN. Mother brewed cambric tea, made by weakening sweet tea with milk until it was white, and placed coconut macaroons and fondant-stuffed dates

on the little plates. The piano bench, covered with a cro-
cheted doily, made a tea table of just the right height.

THE JOY OF GIVING

A few days later, Grandpa came home from a visit to Uncle Ollie's house with news that placed me on the horns of
dilemma. A cousin, Betty Rose, who was about my age, had
also wished for a doll for Christmas, but Santa missed her
house on Christmas Eve because of the snow. My grandfather
told me how disappointed and tearful she was and suggested—firmly—that I give one of my dolls to my cousin.

Needless to say, it was difficult to give up one of the dolls.
Both were beautiful and loved. But I was finally able to make
the choice and decided to part with the red-haired doll. After
I had given it to my cousin, we spent the afternoon playing
with the dolls together. To my surprise, I found that giving
my doll away made me feel just as elated as I had felt when
I first found her under the Christmas tree.

Because of a Christmas made topsy-turvy by a calamitous
snowstorm, I was pressed into my first experience of giving
and began to learn something of the essence of Christmas and
the realities of life.

SNOW HOLIDAYS FROM SCHOOL

For once, we finally had our fill of outdoor fun in the snow.
We sledded, made snowmen, snow angels, and snow forts.
We had snowball fights and played "fox and geese" in the
snow. We warmed ourselves by eating hot vegetable soup
and drinking hot cocoa. And we made a treat we could have
only in wintertime when there was lots of clean, new-fallen
snow—snow ice cream. We gathered up fresh snow in a bowl,

added enough cream to make it the consistency of ice cream, flavored it with vanilla, and sweetened it with sugar. That is all there was to it, but the flavor of snow ice cream seemed a pure delight.

The gift of snow brought us a few extra days of Christmas holidays. School almost never let out for snow. For one thing, we seldom had as much snow as we had in 1936. For another, we had a school bus that could traverse our unimproved road in all but the worst of weather. Our school bus was horse drawn.

The school bus was an ingenious conveyance. It was home-built, a square wooden shelter built over the entire bed of a farm wagon. It had little windows in the sides to let in light and air, and a door at the rear. There were two hanging steps at the back below the door so we could step up to get into the bus. Inside there were benches for us to sit on along both sides of the covered wagon. There was a window in the front of the structure so the driver could see the road, and a small cut-out below it through which the reins to the horses passed. Heman Oxley, the driver, sat on a seat inside the school bus and drove the horses over the five-mile route of winding country roads without having to be outside, exposed to the weather. There was even a small coal-burning stove inside the wagon, with its stovepipe extending up through the roof, which kept the bus warm during cold weather. We rode to school in cozy comfort in a unique vehicle.

It took an impressive amount of snow in our community to interfere with school. Weather was taken in stride. Dad, who, as a boy, had a three-mile walk to school, thought we ought to be back in school.

"They never turned schools out for a little snow when I was a boy," Dad remembered. "Once we had a snow about two feet deep. We only had snow like that here once in my memory. That was the snow of 1918. We had six to eight inches before Christmas and it was almost melted off. On

Christmas Day it began to snow and it snowed every day until after the first of the year. It was knee deep. Then, come Monday morning, when we got ready to go back to school, there we were—with no galoshes, nothing. So I went to the barn and got two old gunnysacks and made myself some gunnysack leggings. Ed saw me do that, so he went and got himself some sacks and did the same thing; then Robert, and then John. We were ready to go back to school, so we started out. I was just up on Miller hill when I looked back and saw my sister Blanche coming. She taught school at Selvin then. All she had was galoshes, but she was walking in our tracks. That was a long walk, yes sir! And a hard one walking in snow that deep. I was hot as a firecracker when I got there."

When Dad told stories about long-ago snowstorms as we sat around the heating stove in the front room during those snowbound Christmas holidays, I sensed that those were once-in-a-lifetime days to be treasured and held in memory, for they were not likely to come again in so perfect a way.

MAKING ORANGE MARMALADE

At Christmas, when Dad came home for the holidays from the school where he taught, he always brought treats we did not usually have. Store-bought fruits and candy were novelties to us. We were like puppies digging for bones when we began to scratch through the bags of candies and nuts. In a bushel basket were fresh coconuts, tangerines, grapefruit, lemons, and oranges.

We enjoyed the Christmas fruits long after the holidays. Oranges and tangerines in our dinner buckets were a nice change from apples. Grapefruit for breakfast gave us a rest from stewed apples and canned peaches. Fresh coconut gave our cream pies a new holiday flavor. Even the citrus rinds brought new flavors to our table.

Mother was never one to waste anything. When the citrus rinds accumulated, she made something delicious out of them. She candied fruit peels to add to quick breads and fruit cakes. And she made jars of orange marmalade that tasted bitter and sweet at the same time, and seemed by far the most exotic of homemade sweets we spread on breakfast breads.

Making marmalade was another kitchen chore calling for the long-bladed, all-purpose knife that we called the "butcher knife." This knife was not actually a butcher's knife, according to today's classifications, but we called any sharp cutting knife with a long blade a *butcher* knife and any short-bladed knife a *paring* knife. And before every ambitious cooking project involving peeling and chopping, my father sharpened the knives.

At breakfast on the morning the marmalade was to be made, my mother brought the kitchen knives to my father at the table and laid them beside his plate. When Dad finished his breakfast, he pushed away his cup and saucer and cleared a place on the table to lay out the knives. Then he picked them up, one by one, and ran a cautious finger along the edge of each knife blade.

"Dull as a froe," he pronounced. "Sis, run and get my whetstones."

I welcomed the chance to rummage gently in the top drawer of his dresser—which was forbidden at other times because the shells for Dad's hunting gun were kept there. The satiny, dark, rectangular whetstone, the smoothing hone, and its companion, the cutting hone, a light gray gritty whetstone, were found easily enough among the interesting accumulation of special objects in the drawer. And when I had found them, there was just a moment to spare to finger the gold watch kept there, and Dad's military ribbons from the World War, and the old photographs—the seldom-seen contents of that small drawer always piqued my curiosity.

But the sharpening of the knives was a familiar ritual. My

father pushed his chair away from the table and placed the rough cutting whetstone on his knee. To provide the moisture necessary to soften the stone, he simply spit on it. Then he cut down the knife blade on the rough whetstone with a series of slow, deliberate motions. At first he would hone toward the front edge of the whetstone with regular, rhythmic movements; then he would whet the blade away from himself, toward the back edge of the stone, drawing first one side of the blade, then the other, over the gritty surface. When he thought the blade should be sharp enough, he wiped both sides of it across the knee of his whipcord trousers, then raised the knife and passed his thumb along its keen edge. If it was not sharp enough to suit him, he spit on the whetstone again and repeated the honing. When he had cut the blade down to a sharp edge on the surface of the cutting stone, he smoothed it down by the same method on the finer-grained dark whetstone, using a circular motion.

Finally he laid the smoothing whetstone on the table.

"There." He was satisfied with what he had done. "Now that blade is sharp enough to cut my whiskers."

When Dad felt in a playful mood, he would take the knife to the small mirror hung above the washstand on the back porch and demonstrate its sharpness by cutting away a tiny patch of his bristly beard.

He never handed the sharpened knives to my mother without a word of caution—"Careful, now. They're sharp as razors." And they were!

Mother chose a dozen Christmas oranges and washed them at the sink. Then they were cut into halves. It was my task to pry out the pips with the nutpick, gather them together, and tie them up in a muslin square. The pips were to be boiled in the kettle with the marmalade to give it flavor. As the oranges were seeded, Mother juiced each half on the ribs of the glass juice reamer and put the juice into the preserving kettle. Then, with the mound of rinds in front of her on the cutting board, she sat down at the kitchen table to cut the orange rinds carefully into slices as thin as the blade of the sharp butcher knife. If there were some orange rinds left from breakfast, she used those, too, along with several sliced lemons. Then the slivered rinds were placed in the kettle along with the pips in their muslin bag and a small amount of water, and the kettle was put onto the stove just long enough for the citrus juices to come to a gentle boil.

But that was only the first cooking. This was the beginning of a three-day process that made the kitchen as fragrant as a king's orangery, with pungent, fruity aromas arising from the kettle or escaping from the covered crock where the cooked orange rinds were put aside to stand in their juices until morning and the second cooking.

On the third morning, the rinds and the juice were measured and returned to the preserving kettle with an equal amount of sugar. All morning Mother attended the cooking mixture watchfully as it simmered on the kitchen range. With her long-handled wooden spoon, she stirred and tested, stirred and tested, until finally the tangy, sweet syrup began to thicken and the slivers of rind became translucent. When the mixture looked "about right," she quickly took a clean metal spoon, dipped it into the boiling marmalade, and held it up to see how the drops of amber jelly fell off the side of the spoon. When the twin drops at the edge of the spoon merged and dropped off the spoon as one, Mother pushed the kettle to the back of the stove.

"It's jelled," she stated.

On the kitchen table, rows of squat, sparkling jelly jars were waiting for their bittersweet contents. Mother ladled the marmalade, a thickened, pale orange, shimmering jelly with slivers of translucent rind suspended in the clear jell, into the jars. Then, from a discarded coffee percolator saved expressly for this purpose, she poured melted paraffin over the top of the marmalade in each jelly jar.

Later, when the thin layer of paraffin had hardened and the marmalade had set, we tied waxed paper over the tops of the jars—and the winter's supply of marmalade was made.

Holiday breakfasts had unusual variety, with the Christmas marmalade spread on toasted homemade bread; fresh sausage and sausage-flavored gravy made with the pan drippings; scrapple made with lean boiled pork and served with sorghum syrup; grapefruit halves with each sweetened segment cut around and loosened; and kuchen with chopped dates and white icing drizzled over its top. The flavors and fragrances and savory memories created in Mother's country kitchen at Christmas were richly melded of holiday foods, freshly butchered pork, and the good everyday food we enjoyed there in all seasons.

Old-Fashioned Pork Cake

1 pound fresh pork sausage
3 cups brown sugar, firmly packed
1 egg, lightly beaten
1 teaspoon baking soda
1 cup cold strong coffee
1 cup raisins

1 cup hickory nuts, walnuts, or pecans
1 teaspoon salt
3 cups sifted flour
1 teaspoon each cinnamon, nutmeg, and allspice

Mix sausage with sugar. Add the beaten egg and mix well. Add the soda to the coffee, then stir mixture into the sausage mixture. Add raisins, nuts, salt, flour, and spices, and mix well. The batter will be very stiff. Turn into a 9″ or 10″ tube pan with greased sides and a waxed-paper lining on the bottom. Bake at 350°F for one hour, or until cake shrinks from sides of pan and tests done when a cake tester is inserted in its center. Ice with caramel frosting.

Caramel Frosting

½ cup sugar
1 cup dark brown sugar,
    firmly packed

1 cup light cream
1 tablespoon butter

Combine all ingredients in a saucepan and boil to the soft-ball stage, or 234°F on a candy thermometer. Cool slightly, and beat until thick enough to spread.

Waldorf Salad

4 apples
2 tablespoons lemon juice
½ cup diced celery
½ cup seeded purple grapes,
    halved
½ cup walnuts or pecans

½ cup mayonnaise thinned
    with 2 tablespoons
    cream *or* ½ cup
    mayonnaise folded into
    1 cup of whipped
    cream

Core and dice the apples. Sprinkle lemon juice over apples and combine them with celery, grapes, and nuts. Toss mixture with thinned mayonnaise (or with mayonnaise and whipped cream combination), and chill before serving.

MAKES 8 TO 10 SERVINGS.

Homemade Sausage Meat

1½ pounds lean pork,
    ground
½ pound fat pork, ground
2 teaspoons salt
½ tablespoon sage

1 teaspoon ground black
    pepper
2 teaspoons brown sugar
¼ teaspoon cayenne
    (optional)

Mix all the ingredients together. Pack the mixture in a crock or any tightly covered container and store in the refrigerator overnight to absorb the seasonings. You may use the sausage meat the next day, or freeze it.

Shape the sausage in patties and brown in a skillet.

SERVES 4 TO 6.

Vegetable Soup

Every summer Mother canned mixed vegetables with which she made her delicious vegetable soup in the winter. Her combination was tomatoes, carrots, lima beans, corn, green beans, shellie beans, and cabbage. When she had cooked a tasty beef broth with a meaty soup bone, all she had to do was add a can of mixed vegetables and some cut-up potatoes, and perhaps some celery and onion. This recipe can be used when there are no home-canned mixed garden vegetables.

2–3 pounds of beef (arm or chuck roast) with bone
2 quarts cold water
1 teaspoon salt
2 quarts plain or seasoned tomato juice
small onion, diced
2 stalks celery, diced
1 cup sliced carrots
1 cup whole-kernel corn

1 cup lima beans or shellie beans
1 cup green beans
1 cup peas
1 cup shredded cabbage
4 medium-size potatoes, cubed
$\frac{1}{4}$ cup chopped parsley
1 tablespoon fresh basil or 1 teaspoon dried basil
Salt and pepper

Place the beef in a large, heavy soup kettle and cover with the cold water. Add salt, cover, bring to a boil, and simmer for about 3 hours, until the beef is tender. Skim during cooking. Remove the meat. Add the tomato juice and all of the vegetables except the potatoes to the broth. Cook the vegetables in the broth over medium to low heat for about 15 minutes, or until the carrots, lima beans, and green beans are beginning to get tender, then add the potatoes and seasonings. Cut the meat into serving-size pieces, remove the fat and bone, and return it to the soup. Cook for about 20 to 30 minutes longer, just until the potatoes are fork-tender.

MAKES OVER 1 GALLON.

Scrapple was made at butchering time using the hog's head meat and lean scraps of pork.

Scrapple (Ponhaus)

3 pounds lean, bony pork	2 teaspoons salt
2 quarts water	$\frac{1}{2}$ teaspoon pepper
2 cups white cornmeal	Powdered sage (optional)

In a kettle, cook the pork slowly in water until it falls apart. Set aside. When cool, discard the fat and take the meat from the bones, breaking it into small pieces and shreds.

Bring 1 quart of the broth to a boil. Sift in the cornmeal, stirring constantly. Cook and stir for about 5 minutes over lowered heat, then add the meat and seasonings, stirring well, using 1 to 2 cups of meat.

Continue to cook over very low heat for about 20 minutes. Pour into a greased oblong bread pan and store in a cool place until ready to use. Cut in thin slices, $\frac{1}{4}''$ to $\frac{3}{8}''$ thick, and fry in hot fat until crisp and brown. Serve for breakfast with hot sorghum or maple syrup.

Scrapple may also be made with turkey broth and turkey meat, a good way to use the turkey carcass and leftovers at Thanksgiving.

Fried Apples

6 tart apples
⅓ cup margarine
¼ cup water

⅓ cup sugar (granulated or
    brown)
Cinnamon

Wash, core, peel, and slice apples. Heat margarine in skillet, add apples, and sauté over medium heat. Add water as the margarine is absorbed by the apples. Turn apples to prevent sticking, and cook until they are barely tender. Sprinkle with sugar and cinnamon. Serve with pork chops, sausage, or ham.

Potato Pancakes

2 cups grated raw potatoes
1 tablespoon grated onion
2 eggs

4 tablespoons flour
1 teaspoon salt
⅓ cup fat

Combine all ingredients except fat. Heat fat in heavy skillet and drop potato mixture from tablespoon into the skillet. Flatten each cake with the back of a pan. Fry on each side until browned. Drain on paper towels. Serve hot. Serve with pork sausage or pork loaf and fried apples. A small amount of syrup poured over pancakes makes them part of a hearty breakfast. MAKES ABOUT 8 PANCAKES.

Taffy

2 cups light corn syrup
3 cups sugar
1 tablespoon butter
1 teaspoon plain gelatin
    softened in 1
    tablespoon cold water

3 tablespoons grated paraffin
1 pint cream
¼ teaspoon salt
1 teaspoon vanilla or ¾
    teaspoon peppermint
    extract

Combine all the ingredients except flavoring in a heavy saucepan and bring to a boil, stirring constantly. Then, stirring as little as possible, cook over medium-high heat until a small amount of the mixture, dropped in cold water, becomes hard or registers 248°F to 254°F on a candy thermometer, or when the ball rings when hit on the edge of a teacup. It will be tan and thick when ready. It may be necessary to lower the heat to medium near the end of the cooking time. Remove pan from the heat and add the flavoring.

Pour mixture onto a greased platter. Divide into several parts for pulling. With slightly greased fingers, pick up taffy as soon as it is cool enough to handle, roll into a ball, and pull until it is creamy white and holds its shape. This is a soft, chewy taffy. Wrap it in squares of waxed paper after cutting it into two-inch lengths and twist ends of papers.

Fondant

2 cups sugar $1\frac{1}{2}$ cups boiling water
$\frac{1}{4}$ teaspoon cream of tartar

Combine and cook all ingredients in a deep, 2-quart saucepan. Stir over low heat until the sugar dissolves, then allow to boil gently to the soft-ball stage. Cover the pan for the first 3 minutes, then uncover and wipe the sugar crystals from the side of the pan several times with a damp cloth wrapped around the tines of a fork.

When the soft-ball stage is reached (238°F on a candy thermometer), immediately pour on a platter without scraping the pan and cool until the hand can be held on the bottom of the platter without burning. Scrape the fondant from the edge of the platter toward the center using a spatula or wooden spoon. Work with the spatula until fondant is creamy and stiff, then knead until smooth and free from lumps. Wrap in waxed paper and allow to ripen in the refrigerator for 24 hours. It may be kept as long as 3 or 4 weeks in a covered jar.

When ready to use, knead the fondant, tint it with food coloring and flavor, if desired, then shape, decorate, or use it to stuff dried fruits. Melted over boiling water, it may be used to dip fruits and nuts, and to make Jordan almonds.

Fondant-Stuffed Dates

Remove stones from dates, if unstoned, and place a whole nut in each cavity. Stuff each piece with a small piece of vanilla-flavored fondant, then roll stuffed fruits in sugar.

Peanut Brittle

In a heavy saucepan, combine 2 cups sugar, $\frac{1}{2}$ cup water, and 1 cup white syrup and cook to 170°F on a candy thermometer. Add 2 cups shelled raw peanuts, with or without the red skins (blanched or unblanched). Cook to 300°F stirring constantly. Remove candy from heat, and add 2 tablespoons butter and 1 teaspoon baking soda. Beat until well blended and foamy. Pour candy onto a cookie sheet or ironstone platter greased with butter or onto a greased marble slab. Spread as thin as possible but handle carefully to avoid being burned by the hot syrup. Cool until the underside is set; check by running a spatula under the candy. When the sheet of candy is set enough to hold together, lift and turn the entire sheet. When cool, break into pieces and store in an airtight container.

Chapter 8

Grandma Buse's Old-Fashioned German Kitchens

GRANDMA'S WINTER KITCHEN: PLACE OF SEHNSUCHT

M Y MATERNAL GRANDPARENTS lived almost directly across the road from our house. In my earliest memories, I am running back and forth between our houses several times a day, keeping the path well worn and never missing out on anything interesting that might be going on at either place.

I always looked first for my grandmother—and expected to find her—in the kitchen. But if she wasn't there, I knew she was probably in the garden or somewhere close by, and she would be back before long. In the meantime, if I had not been sent to borrow a cup of sugar or to deliver an urgent message from my mother, I began looking for the sources of the enticing aromas that were always present in Grandma's kitchen.

Grandma Buse's kitchen smelled different from ours, although both were places of wonderful, heady aromas. Her kitchen smelled good even when the wood fire was not burning and nothing was cooking on top of the kitchen range. Its fragrant ambience changed from day to day, according to whatever Grandma was cooking for dinner. I could easily name the prevailing scents—coffee, cinnamon, dried apples, bacon fat, yeast, vinegar, lye soap, blackberry cobbler. But even after the dishes were washed and put away, after the fruity spirits of apple kuchen baking and the stench of cabbage boiling had dissipated, there still remained a characteristic smell that I could identify even today, with my eyes closed, as the vaporous atmosphere of Grandma's kitchen. It diffused its own subtle perfume of cookery, a mixture of will-o'-the-wisp fragrances distilled of the ghostly remnants of the thousands of meals my grandmother had prepared in that kitchen, which permeated every nook and cranny of the room and Grandma herself. Sometimes, when I sat close to her on the daybed where she took her rest after the noontime meal, when I leaned my head against her dark calico dress, I thought Grandma and the comforting aura of her kitchen smelled alike. Grandma's aproned self emanated a faint, invisible breath of her kitchen, just as surely as the butter churn bespoke the buttermilk.

THE PIE SAFE

When between-meal visitors to Grandma's kitchen were struck with pangs of hunger, as most were sure to be, they would open the doors of the pie safe. Inside on the wide shelves there would certainly be one kind of pie or another, still warm from the oven, perhaps, and ready for the next meal. Enticing aromas wafted through heart-shaped perforations in the punched-tin panels of the safe, which served to ventilate as well as to decorate.

The pie safe, which stood against the wall at the west end of the room, was the only storage space for perishable foods

in the kitchen. In that era, most foods were prepared and eaten on the same day. Leftovers from the previous meal might be saved until the next one, but never longer, and they were stored temporarily in the pie safe along with just-opened jars of preserves, pickles, jellies, pies, cakes, and the cookie tin. The only cool storage for prepared foods in the summer was a bucket hung down in the cistern with its bottom just above water. This is how we kept our butter and milk cool. In the wintertime, the unheated summer kitchen served as a cold pantry, and during the coldest months, even fresh meat could be kept safely for a few days.

Also stored in the yellow poplar pie safe were the standard items that were placed on the center of the table at every meal in all farmhouses thereabout: the lidded china sugar bowl, the dish of comb honey, the hinged-top pitcher of sorghum, the silver-plated caster set with its heavy glass cruets of vinegar and chili sauce, salt and pepper cellars, a jar of horseradish, and the very same pressed-glass spoon holder with its teaspoon supply that I have in my own kitchen today.

The safe was truly a repository of riches, all of Grandma's creation in the kitchen, and the place where I assuaged my youthful hunger with a crusty chicken drumstick, a hartshorn sugar cookie, or a piece of custard pie.

GRANDMA'S PIES

Since Grandma made better pies than anyone in our community, I never passed up the chance to eat at her house, whether it was between meals or for any meal of the day, including breakfast. Grandpa often polished off a modest wedge of fruit pie after a hearty breakfast of meat, eggs, biscuits, and gravy. After all, by the time he sat down to breakfast, he had been up for hours and had already done a good day's work at the barn. An ample breakfast was called for, and a piece of fruit pie with a thin, flaky crust was not at all outlandish for a farmer's breakfast.

Grandma could turn anything edible into a delectable pie. Fruits in season were predictable, as were dried and canned fruits in winter, and there were endless transformations of the basic milk-egg-sugar combination. But Grandma's inventiveness was most obvious when she lifted the everyday pie out of the ordinary by tucking unusual and unexpected ingredients into her crusts—cottage cheese, boiled cider, squash, oatmeal, buttermilk, and even vinegar.

No wonder the ladies of the church always put Grandma on the pie committee for the Thanksgiving and Fourth of July church dinners!

But most unusual and surprising of all to a youngster with a somewhat timid attitude toward tasting the unfamiliar was the revelation that Grandmother's hearty, brandy-laced mince pies contained *meat.*

As a child, I never liked mince pies, but I loved the annual ritual of making the mincemeat. Making mincemeat accompanied the butchering, which took place as soon as the animals were fattened for the slaughter and the weather was cold enough to preserve the meat safely. With equal measures of foresight and good fortune, the two conditions would come close enough together to ensure mince pies for holiday feasting, and throughout the winter when Grandma had to find fillings to take the place of the fresh fruits she used so lavishly in her summer pies. For the further improvement of Grandma's cookery, a fresh supply of newly rendered lard would be on hand after the hog was slaughtered to enrich her crusts.

Grandma's pastry was incredibly tender and flaky. If, in cutting the pie, a careless hand hurriedly drew the sharp knife through the delicate crust, it crumbled. To Grandma, the savory shells were not "pastry" but simply "pie crust." Her usual ingredients were only the essential ones—flour, short-ening, salt, and milk or water—and there was no secret to her recipe. Her measuring utensils were a cracked, handleless teacup and a tablespoon, but she had a practiced eye that judged the proper size of a lump of lard, and a light, deft hand that knew the feel of dough when it was right to roll out on a soft sprinkling of flour milled from the wheat of Grandpa's fields.

Grandma looked as light as a feather and as fragile as her pie crusts, but her appearance was misleading. She undertook the endless chores of each day with a steady flow of energy that seemed never to waver from the time she donned her starched, flower-printed apron in the morning and tied its sashes into a bow behind her back, until she took it off again and hung it on a hook behind the door after supper, when mountains of work were behind her. Interesting projects were always in progress in Grandma's kitchen, but the crescendo of activity was far more compelling when it centered around a special task, such as making mincemeat.

MAKING MINCEMEAT

Grandma's mincemeat recipe was one of the few she wrote down. She copied the recipe in her lacy old-fashioned hand-writing on a slip of paper that today is foxed by age and shows faded stains made by her fingers. It was kept in a latticework wall pocket along with a few other special rec-ipes, the *Old Farmer's Almanac,* the weekly church publica-tion, *The Lutheran Standard,* greeting cards, letters, and ac-cumulated household and farm receipts. I remember Grandma rummaging in that fascinating collection of papers, looking for the recipe, when we were making ready for mincemeat making. But after the preliminary review of the recipe, it was stuck into the papers at the front of the cache and seemed thereafter not to be all-important to the actual concoction of the mixture. Grandma proceeded with the ingredients she had at hand and improvised on her written recipe if she felt inclined to do so.

This is the recipe Grandma used as a guide when she was making mincemeat:

"Finely mince 2 pounds lean boiled beef; half as much clear white suet; twice as much firm, tart apples; Baldwins, Yorks, or Winesaps. Use $\frac{1}{2}$ pound preserved citron melon or pickled watermelon rind, nicely chopped; 1 pound sugar, or more; 2 cups boiled cider; 1 pint canned pie cherries; 1 pound seeded raisins, picked over, or currants; 2 jars good tart jelly, currant or damson. Spice well with 1 grated nutmeg, cinnamon, mace, cloves, and salt. Use beef broth or cider for cooking mincemeat. Keep a slow fire until done. Cover with apple brandy in a stone crock. Keeps all winter in a cold pantry."

Tireless as she was, Grandma welcomed helpers in the kitchen when preparations for making mincemeat were under way. My brother kept the woodbox and the coal bucket filled, and my grandfather lifted the heavy kettles. (Mother would always help with the chores that accompanied butchering because the project was a cooperative one between our two families.) And a granddaughter could feed morsels of boiled beef through the meat grinder and impale red Baldwins on the prongs of the apple peeler while the suet, the pared apples, and the dried fruits were being minced by more skilled hands.

When the kettle was simmering on the stove, filling the air with spicy scents, it was my chore to stand on a stool and wash the canning jars in a dishpan of sudsy hot water. My small hands fit easily into the mouths of the jars and I could reach down inside and swab them clean.

Grandma kept mincemeat for immediate use in a stoneware crock with a layer of brandy poured over it. The rest was canned in aqua-colored mason jars and stored in the dark cellar until it was needed.

When the jars of mincemeat had been lidded and put into the canning kettle, the kitchen activity slowed down to the less frenetic pace of cleaning up, after which my mother went back across the road to our house. But I always stayed around while the jars of mincemeat boiled on the black range. They were boiled for hours, and the steam fogged the kitchen windows so densely that the starched white curtains went limp and my initials traced on the panes would last only momentarily before little streams of water ran down the glass and erased them. There was something more than marking initials on the windowpanes that kept me from going home before the jars were removed from their bath and sealed, however. No sooner had Grandma cleared the kitchen table of the chopping knives and bowls and utensils, and wiped the oilcloth cover with a damp dishcloth, than out would come the rolling pin, the handleless teacup, the tablespoon, the lard tin, and the worn breadboard.

"Time to get supper started," she would say as she dipped the teacup into the flour bin—three times to make the mound in the mixing bowl and once for the white drift of flour strewn in the center of the breadboard. And there I would happily stay, perched on a hospitable bench behind the kitchen table in that plain country room where handwoven rag rugs covered the floor and the windowsill was filled with red geraniums grown from the same cuttings as those that now bloomed in Mother's kitchen. I watched my grandmother make the mixture of flour, lard, salt, and milk. With the sweeping gestures and majestic strokes of an artist, she would roll the dough into a perfect circle, fit it into a pie tin, and fill it with fragrant, newly made mincemeat. Another crust laid on top was embellished with a curved slit, its edges were crimped together around the shape of her thumb, and it was sprinkled with milk and strewn thickly with sugar. Then the whole disappeared into the oven of the kitchen range upon which, in partnership with Grandma, the comforts and pleasures of the kitchen depended.

When the pie was drawn forth, it was baked to flaky perfection, browned to the color of toast on its sugary humps and oozing brownish juice from the steaming slit on the top. Surely no shape is more pleasant to the eye than the plump roundness of a newly baked pie cooling on the lowered oven door and sending up couriers of fragrance to alert appetites that a feast is in the offing.

When the tide of bubbling juices had cooled slightly and receded again into the depths of the pie, Grandma would carefully lift the fragile edge of the slit and pour in a small measure of the contents of a tall amber bottle that was seldom taken down from the top pantry shelf. After the pie had been anointed with the spirits the aroma that filled the kitchen brought pure intoxication to the senses.

Fragrant tendrils of steam were still rising from its robust filling when Grandma lifted the hot pie off the oven door and whisked it away to cool on a shelf of the pie safe.

"Stay for supper," Grandma invited. "You can sample the mince pie."

I didn't need to taste the pie to know that it was wonderful. It was replete with flavors of the day, which I savor still at moments when my memory transports me back to that pleasant time. I have only to open the doors of the old pie safe that my sister-in-law, Pat, has kept in its place in the same kitchen where Grandma rolled out countless rounds of pie dough many years ago.

LAMPLIT EVENINGS IN COZY KITCHENS

When darkness came, Grandma took down two kerosene lamps from their places on a shelf on the kitchen wall, where they were kept beside a golden oak clock that ticked away for eight days without rewinding.

She lit these with a flaming torch made from a piece of tightly rolled paper, called a taper. She set the taper afire by touching the end of it to live embers in the kitchen stove.

"No need to light a match," she would say.

Sometimes the flame flared up and burned rapidly toward Grandma's fingers before she managed to light the wicks.

"Fiddlesticks!" she would exclaim, dropping the taper gingerly into the stove to let it burn up. Then she would roll another strip of paper into a taper and try again.

Lighting lamps was one of those everyday chores too dangerous for young children to have a hand in, and therefore fascinating to watch. It was a job to grow into.

When the lamps were lit, Grandma turned the wicks low and replaced the fragile glass chimneys. She adjusted each flame so that it would burn brightly but not blacken its sparkling chimney.

One lighted lamp was placed back on the high shelf next to the clock, where it cast a good light down on the stove below and dimly illuminated most of the kitchen. The other lamp was placed in the middle of the kitchen table or carried to wherever light was needed to work by.

Carrying a lighted lamp from one place to another was also too dangerous for children to do. Even grown-ups had mishaps. One night when I spent the night at Grandma's, Grandpa was carrying an oil lamp and holding my hand to help me down the steep shadowy stairway when he made a misstep at the landing and knocked off the lamp chimney. The shattering glass cut my forehead and left me with a tiny scar that I treasured for years afterward.

I loved lamplight and the way it transformed the daytime appearance and feeling of familiar rooms. Whenever I recall scenes from Grandma's kitchen—or Mother's—they are cozy, lamplit memories. Grandma placing a mince pie on the pie safe shelf and closing the heart-adorned doors; Grandpa still grinding sausage long after dark; Jewel getting out the popcorn popper and stirring fudge after supper; Dad telling bedtime stories about bears; all of us doing schoolwork around the table while Mother graded papers; all of us cousins crowded together on the bench in Grandma's summer kitchen, eating homemade ice cream with soda crackers; getting undressed for bed by the stove on cold nights, then making a dash upstairs to dive under the feather bed: each treasured vision raised before my mind's eye is cast in the ambient glow of lamplight.

SLEEPING WARM IN GRANDMA'S FEATHER BEDS

To sleep *on* a feather bed and *under* one in cold weather in an unheated bedroom is a luxury I knew because Grandma Buse kept geese and supplied us with feather beds and pillows.

Our upstairs bedrooms were unheated except for that which rose up the stairway from the heating stove in the living room downstairs. Sometimes my room was cold enough to freeze ice in a glass of drinking water beside the bed. We had flannel sheets, top and bottom, and I had flannelette nightclothes, neck to toe. Often I took a flatiron, heated on the kitchen range and wrapped in newspapers, to warm the bed and my feet. And on the coldest nights, I also wore my long underwear to bed. Then, ensconced between Grandma's feather beds and Mother's wool comforters, I slept warm!

GRANDMA'S GEESE

Grandma kept chickens, ducks, turkeys, and geese. In the springtime, when the geese began to lose their feathers in the chicken yard, Grandma plucked their feathers and down to make stuffing for pillows and featherbeds. The molting geese were penned up in the chicken house in advance of the plucking event to make sure the feathers would be dry and clean.

The rest of the time the geese ranged freely in the barnyard, where they could be near the pond.

When Grandma was ready to pluck the geese, she sat in a straight-backed chair in the yard. She held a big goose on her aproned lap, much as she would a baby, with its head on her upper arm and its stomach up. The hand of the arm that supported the goose's back firmly held its yellow leg just above its webbed foot. With her free hand Grandma plucked soft feathers and fluffy down from the white breast and fat underside of the goose. Most geese were remarkably well behaved when Grandma held them, considering how sassy and nasty-tempered certain geese could be when I came too close to them out in the barnyard, or bravely dared to tease them. Grandma's geese had mastered the art of intimidation, and I was always prepared to run. When Grandma had to pluck a mean goose who wanted to nip her with its beak, a cotton stocking was slipped over its head.

When the plucking was finished and the naked goose released, it honked loudly, waggled its tail, hissed, and retreated indignantly to the barnyard. There it rejoined the gaggle and fussed the rest of the day.

TOLLIE KIRKMAN'S GOOSE

Grandma's geese were funny looking without their feathers. They seemed even more insulted when we stood around laughing at their bad tempers and their nakedness.

"If you think that's a funny-looking goose," Dad said when a big white goose flounced and flapped away after losing its feathers on Grandma's lap, "you should have seen Tollie Kirkman's goose.

"Tollie's mother had a jar of strawberry preserves go bad, so she emptied the jar out into the backyard somewhere a little way from the back door. The chickens and geese were ranging free, the way ours do at times, and a big old goose came along and ate the spoiled strawberry preserves. When Miz Kirkman looked out in the yard and saw that old goose, it was stretched out flat on the ground, limp as a goose can be.

"Miz Kirkman went out to the fence and called Grave to come and get the dead goose and take it away, and when she walked back past it, laid out there on the ground, she thought: 'There's no use to let those good feathers go to waste.' So she knelt down and plucked that goose right there, and took the feathers into the house.

"A little while later she looked out the door again, and doggoned if that goose wasn't up and walking around— weaving back and forth across the yard, honking and hissing—drunk as could be on those fermented strawberry preserves!

"When Grave came in to bury the goose, Miz Kirkman said, 'You'll have to bring that goose in the house. It's too cold for her to stay outside with no feathers.' It was wintertime.

"So they kept that naked goose in a box behind the kitchen stove. Miz Kirkman felt sorry for it, having no feathers, so she got busy and made it a dress out of one of her old dresses. One day when Miz Kirkman opened the kitchen door, that goose saw its chance, and it ran right past her and out of the house.

"They never could catch that goose again, and it walked around the barn lot all winter, wearing a dress."

FEATHER "TICKS" AND DOWNY PILLOWS

There was no need to make dresses to keep Grandma's geese warm because she plucked their feathers when the weather was warm and saved them until it was time to get the beds ready for winter.

The downy-soft feathers were separated from the coarser

ones and saved for pillows. The coarser feathers went into feather ticks, which we used on our beds in wintertime.

Flattened feather beds and pillows were replenished and plumped out every season. Extra goose down was saved for new pillows and feather beds, which took two or three years to make. The covers for the pillows and feather beds were sewn out of stout blue and white striped ticking fabric, which was stiff with sizing when new, but soon softened.

We appreciated the soft, downy bedding we had because Grandma kept geese. But feathers were not the only unusual commodity provided our families by Grandma's geese.

GOOSE EGGS

The free-roaming geese hid their nests and eggs near the pond, in the barn, under the strawstack, and in the tall weeks in corners of the split-rail fence around Grandpa's barn lot. Sometimes we would find the hidden down-lined nests and rob them of one or two large eggs. Then, off to the kitchen we would go, whatever the time of day, to have our bounty made into an enormous fried-egg sandwich. A single large goose egg filled the frying pan, and it was a curiosity just to see it broken open and slipped into the skillet. The flavor of goose eggs was distinctly "egg-y," and the yolk was rich, golden yellow.

At Easter time, a few goose eggs, miraculously colored blue and red and purple, appeared in grass nests hidden outside in the front yard among clumps of "Easter" flowers, or daffodils.

GOOSE GREASE

Grandma also made a dish called "goose grease." It sounded bad and it tasted bad, as far as I was concerned. But my grandfather relished it, so goose grease was a necessity in

Grandma Buse's kitchen. This old-fashioned concoction was made of fat rendered from a goose and mixed with caraway seed or marjoram to make a spread for Grandpa's German rye bread.

A goose yielded lots of fat for whatever use Grandma had. Whenever she intended to stuff and roast a goose, she first placed it in a hot oven to fry out the excess fat. After about a half hour, she took it out, drained off the fat, and then completed the stuffing and roasting. The drained-off fat was the goose grease.

Goose grease could also be used as a shortening for pie crusts and biscuits, in the same way that chicken fat was used. Not a bit of it was wasted.

Plain goose grease, without herbs and spices, had medicinal uses in old-fashioned German homes in our community. In the Broeker household, it was put on cuts and sores as a soothing and healing salve. Grandma maintained that it was the best cold remedy, beneficial when used both inside and out.

A croupy cough brought out the goose grease and a flannel cloth to be warmed at the kitchen stove. The miraculous balm was rubbed on the chest and neck and back, and the patient, willing or unwilling, was swaddled in warm flannel. A coughing spell was relieved by a spoonful of warmed goose grease mixed with honey.

I may owe my life to an adaptation of Grandma's goose grease remedy forced down my throat when I could no longer breathe during a severe attack of croup. Although I was only a little over two, I still remember being laid across my grandmother's knee with my head back, and the choking, coughing, and gasping-for-air sensation that accompanied my crisis. A spoonful of Vicks Vapo-Rub mixed with sugar, used in lieu of goose grease (which my mother did not have on hand), somehow relieved my constricted throat and breathing.

I had good reason to respect Grandma's home remedies, no matter how old-fashioned they seemed. But I was glad Mother rubbed Vicks Vapo-Rub on us when we had colds, and that we were given black cherry-flavored cough lozenges or horehound candy to ease coughing and tickling throats.

THE CHRISTMAS GOOSE

The Christmas goose was another matter.

The usual bird at Grandma Buse's Christmas dinner was a fat goose. Somehow a roast goose seemed to be the most grand and suitable bird for the holiday meal. I knew the old English rhyme:

> *Christmas is coming*
> *The goose is getting fat*
> *Please put a penny*
> *In the old man's hat*
> *If you haven't got a penny*
> *A half penny will do*
> *If you haven't got a half penny*
> *Then God bless you!*

When the goose was on the ironstone platter, browned and crispy, stuffed with sauerkraut, apple, onion, and caraway, and ringed with spiced crab apples, Christmas dinner became a feast. It did not matter that youngsters were not fond of sauerkraut and mince pie. To fill the void, there were Grandma's brown-crusted yeast rolls shaped from kuchen dough and spread with apple butter, and hartshorn Christmas cookies, and lebkuchen in shapes of hearts, stars, birds, and horses.

HARTSHORN CHRISTMAS COOKIES

At Christmas time, Grandma Buse baked old-fashioned German cookies—lebkuchen, springerle, and hartshorn. All were leavened with ammonium carbonate, which was the "hartshorn." Hartshorn was supposed to have been scraped from the horn of a hart, or male deer, in old Germany. When the cookies baked, the scent escaping briefly, and somewhat unpleasantly, from the oven was of ammonia. It wasn't too difficult to make the association with the horn of a hart.

After the cookies were taken from the oven and cooled, there was not a hint of ammonia in their flavor. Lubkuchen and hartshorn cookies were delicious. Springerles, which means "lively little horses", were brittle and hard, but fragile and shell-like. My cousins and I all helped imprint the deliciously anise seed–flavored dough with festive symbols and pictures embossed on Grandma's old carved wooden springerle board—birds, candles, cherries, and flowers.

Grandma put the baked springerles away in a closed tin in the pie safe. They lasted long past Christmas because they were hard as rocks and flavored with anise. At mid-morning, Grandma would have one with her coffee. She would dip the paper-white cookie into the coffee to soften it before taking a bite, then dip another edge in the coffee before the next bite. Grandma had a slight touch of palsy in her hands and chin, and I could see the little trembles when she delicately dipped the springerle and raised her coffee cup carefully to her lips.

JANUARY READING: ALMANACS AND SEED CATALOGS

Christmas seemed far away when the new bank calendar was hung on the kitchen wall on New Year's Day. At Grandma's, *The Old Farmer's Almanac* was hung, along with the calendar, on a nail near Grandpa's rocker by the kitchen window. On dark January days, he would sit there studying the almanac, often reading parts of it aloud to anyone who was near, and commenting:

"Year of snow, fruit will grow."

"Last frost by April 5."

"The drought will break this year."

Grandpa read the almanac cover to cover in January, and spent the rest of the year verifying the accuracy of its weather predictions. Grandpa had concluded it paid to give attention to the moon and the planting tables in the almanac when planting his field crops and vegetable garden.

The novelty of the new almanac had not worn off when the seed catalog arrived. Grandpa saved some of his own seeds from year to year, but there were others he ordered from Burpee Seed Company. It was a sign of spring when Grandpa ordered garden seeds.

SASSAFRAS TEA—GRANDPA'S SPRING TONIC

Another harbinger of spring, even before the calls of spring peepers from the ponds and creek, was the pot of sassafras tea that simmered on the back of the kitchen range during Lent— Grandpa's spring tonic. Sassafras tea seemed modern compared to the sulphur and molasses choked down by certain of our schoolmates from "backward" homes. And the pungent odor of sassafras roots was easy for a child to enjoy.

When Grandpa prepared the roots and bark for the teapot, the whole house smelled of sassafras. In February, before the sap started, Grandpa dug the roots of red sassafras (*Sassafras albidum*) from the small trees that grew on the road bank near the house. He carried the muddy roots to the barn well, in a gunnysack slung over his shoulder, where he washed them in a tub filled with water. Then he brought the roots into the kitchen and scraped away the dark, thin outer bark, preparing them for the brewing.

This was a task requiring the use of Grandpa's most fascinating and untouchable possession—a multibladed, sharp-honed pocketknife that he always kept safely buttoned in the bib pocket of his overalls—"over-hulls," he called them. The soft hiss of the blade being honed into readiness always brought his many grandchildren running to the bench behind the kitchen table, where we would line up like screech owlets on a limb to watch him use the awesome knife—whether he was peeling an apple in one long red curl, whittling for pleasure, or splitting sassafras roots into short, precise pieces for the springtime brew.

When the sassafras roots were cut into pieces that would fit into a large enamel kettle, Grandma made sassafras tea. Using a generous handful of the roots, four or five chunks to a quart of water, the kettle was set on the kitchen range and brought to a boil. Then it simmered for fifteen or twenty minutes at the back of the stove, until the water was a pretty rosy color. The color of the brew indicated its strength: a delicate rosy pink was mildly flavored; a rich orange-red was strong. When the tea was ready, it was poured into cups and sweetened with sugar or honey. Milk was then added—enough to make the tea whiten.

Sassafras tea has an unforgettable flavor, and I shall always associate it with the coming of spring.

SPRING GREENS—GRANDMA'S SPRING TONIC

While Grandma and Grandpa did not use as many home-made tonics and remedies as some of our neighbors, they still relied upon several old-fashioned practices to guarantee their well-being.

In the spring, Grandma would cook a pot of mixed wild

greens for the same reason Grandpa made sassafras tea—"to thin the blood."

It was fun to go with Grandma into the greening fields as soon as wild lettuce, dandelion, narrow dock, and black mustard were the right size for greens. Grandma settled down in a fencerow, tucking her long skirts up into her waistband, while the cousins scattered out across the fields. Grandma gave us each a sample leaf to hold in hand during the hunt, and we tumbled about, shouting out our discoveries to one another.

"Woolly britches!"

"Dandelions!"

"Narrow dock!"

It was as exciting as an egg-hunt at Easter.

When the greens were in the pot, with a piece of ham or salt pork for flavor, being gently coaxed into tenderness on the back of the kitchen range, and a big flat pan of yellow cornbread was swelling to lightness behind the oven door, we knew the end of winter had finally come.

Grandpa drank the green broth taken from the pot, called pot liquor. He cooled it in a very deep saucer, then lifted the saucer and drank from it, just as he sometimes drank his hot coffee. It was a sight of wonderment to the row of grandchildren lined up on the bench behind the long table in Grandma's kitchen. And we knew winter was over when the spring tonics appeared in Grandma's winter kitchen.

GRANDPA'S KITCHEN GARDEN

Grandpa always had lettuce seeds planted in his cold frame by Valentine's Day. Sometimes he managed to get them in the ground as early as January, if a warm spell came along.

Less than two weeks later, delicate green sprouts could be seen through the moisture condensing on the sheltering windows protecting the cold frame.

"Don't take the glass off," Grandpa cautioned when we rushed out, eager for a glimpse of the first green leaves of spring. "Just look, now."

The cold frame was a raised bed sided with rough boards. The dark soil inside it was enriched with rotted barnyard manure. Unaged "green" manure and straw piled up along its sides gave off heat and helped keep the cold frame warm. Old windows covered the top of the cold frame. Their glass panes attracted the sun and warmed the little plants inside, even on cold days. On warm sunny days, when the temperature was well above freezing, Grandpa lifted the windows off and let the sun shine directly on the new plants.

In a month or so, the lettuce began to leaf out in the cold frame and needed thinning so the plants could develop fully. The first "mess" of fresh lettuce of the garden season came from the excess delicate baby lettuce plants thinned out of the cold frame. The plants were still spindly and the leaves small, but none of the later pickings of larger ruffled leaves were as tender, buttery, and succulent as the first "thinnings" of the lettuce bed.

Grandma always made wilted-lettuce dressed with her own unique "brown gravy," which was both sweet and sour. She prepared a "water gravy" of "2 tablespoons bacon grease, 1 tablespoon flour, $\frac{1}{2}$ cup water, salt and pepper. Add 2 tablespoons sugar, 2 tablespoons sorghum, and 1 to 2 tablespoons vinegar."

Many recipes jotted down by good cooks contained only measurements and ingredients as an aid to memory. They didn't need to be told to make a roux of the bacon fat and flour; or to stir it over medium heat until the mixture was browned; or to stir in the water, sugar, sorghum, and vinegar, mixed together in a cup. Or to stir until the mixture thickened, season with salt and pepper, and pour over a bowlful of fresh leaf lettuce, tossing to coat the leaves with the dressing. The number of servings a recipe yielded was not necessary, either, because everything depended upon who was eating at the table. A half-cup serving on a hungry farmer's plate would have been thought a joke. Cooks in country kitchens *knew* how much it took to feed their families.

As for the first "mess" of lettuce from a cold frame, the bowl needed to be generously sized, and full. Getting fresh lettuce to the table was the first major milestone in a summer's gardening. Having new peas and tiny new potatoes was another highlight of the season.

NEW PEAS AND POTATOES BY DECORATION DAY

The first peas from the garden were considered a delicacy, and Grandpa's goal was to have them on the table on Decoration Day, cooked with nuggets of new potatoes in Grandma's delicious green pea soup.

In order to accomplish this gardening feat, Grandpa started early. He plowed the garden spot in the fall to make the soil dry out quickly in the spring. Fall plowing also reduced the number of garden pests and weeds the following summer. He spread manure over the ground before plowing it. After years of careful nurturing, his garden soil was fertile and rich.

There was a small area apart from the main garden, south and west of the grape arbor, where Grandpa planted his "early garden" of peas, potatoes, radishes, and onions. There, too, were the perennial plants: rhubarb (Grandma called it "pie plant"), sage, horseradish, and gooseberry and raspberry bushes.

As soon as he could work the ground, in mid-March, Grandpa planted peas. If peas were up and growing when a late-spring snow came along, they were not hurt.

"Peas can stand the cold," Grandpa said.

When the first really warm spell came along a few weeks later, Grandpa put in a few potatoes, onion sets, and radish seeds.

"The radishes will be up in five or six days," Grandpa promised.

The miracle occurred on schedule. And before long the temptation to pull up a small prickly-leafed plant came, and it was always too much to resist—and too soon. There was never anything below the soil but threadlike roots. Furtively, the uprooted plant would be pressed back into place, and finally another covert investigation would yield a rosy, marble-size radish, hot and crisp and earthy on the tongue.

The peas were pampered and petted. When the plants were a few inches high and tendrils appeared under their leaves, short wooden stakes were driven into the rows a few feet apart. Strings were strung at different heights between the stakes. Then the plants were laid over the strings and the tendrils encouraged to wind around them until they caught hold. Soon delicate white blooms appeared, like tiny sweet pea blossoms, only white. Then green pods formed in their places.

At first the pods were flat and limp and empty when opened, but, in a few days, there was a row of tiny round peas inside, all alike. They were sweet, juicy, and tasty when eaten raw.

Almost overnight the pea pods filled out. They became long and fat and bumpy with peas inside, and they had to be picked at once, before they got "old." Peas pass their prime quickly and "turn to starch." As they age, their crisp green pods turn leathery and yellow.

Grandma and Mother donned bonnets and sat down in the rows all morning, picking the first crop of peas. More blooms would come, and more peas.

Later, we all sat about—on the steps, in the porch swing, under the maple tree—with pans in our laps, shelling peas. The pods snapped crisply, the stem end first, with its small string, then the other end, and the pressure of two thumbs together popped open the pod. Inside the neat package were five or six moist green emeralds to be nudged out with the handiest thumb. Into the pans rolled the peas, five or six at a time, until very slowly a quart or more of the tiny sweet peas were shelled.

Then, quickly, the peas went into the cooking pan, already bubbling on the stove, fragrant with a piece of salt pork, making a rich broth. They cooked slowly, their bright green color gradually cooking off into the broth, their round outsides dimpling. Toward the last half hour, Grandma added a few tender pea pods for more flavor, and some rosy scrubbed new potatoes the size of pullets' eggs.

By Decoration Day, the row of early potatoes had grown lush and bushy with green leaves. The white star-shaped blossoms had long since dropped off, and the sides of the potato rows had been hilled up. While the peas were being shelled, Grandpa carefully scraped the soil away from the side of a potato hill, to avoid cutting into the tiny potatoes. Then, using his hands, he brushed the loamy soil away from a few small potatoes clinging to the main root. Only the largest ones were taken off the cluster, and the roots were covered over again with the hope that the tiny baby potatoes left behind would grow some more. The next hill was plundered of its buried treasure in the same way, and soon Grandpa had enough new little potatoes to add to the pea soup.

The thin, fragile skin of new potatoes is tender and rosy, and it can be scrubbed off with a brush, or even rubbed off, when washed. New potatoes are too small to peel, with peeling as thin as parchment and rosy cheeks all speckled with "eyes." Each was a delicious bite that tasted as different from old potatoes as new peas from canned peas when Grandma served them up in the pea soup on Decoration Day. Ham, green onions, radishes, wilted lettuce, new peas, and potatoes in a generous broth, and rhubarb pie and fresh strawberries— only the beginning of the "from-Grandpa's-garden" dinners to follow.

SUMMER'S SPECTRE

No children at Grandma's table had to be told to "eat your peas." Rather, moderation was required.

"You eat too many, comes the summer complaint," Grandma warned.

Summer complaint was a spectre awaiting us if we ate too many green apples, drank too much cider, or ate too many green peas. Summer complaint was in the realm of the proverbial dragon to be braved, the goblins who will "git you ef you don't watch out," and the nebulous "Booger-man" who lurked outside our upstairs bedrooms at bedtime.

Our elders did not worry about giving children complexes or phobias in those days. If anything, a little fear instilled was a sensible measure. And there were stories to carry every warning or moral, most of them true and about people we knew or knew of.

"Your Great-grandpa Gerhart ate two big bowls of pea soup at supper," Grandma told us. "The next day he took sick and died."

When we visited the cemetery in Stendal on Decoration Day and placed a bouquet of pink and white peonies, purple irises, and white mock orange branches at the headstone of Great-grandpa Gerhart Buse, I asked my mother if her grandfather had *really* died because he ate too many new peas.

"Your grandma always laid it on the pea soup," Mother said, "but there is no way of knowing with someone that old. He was eighty-nine."

As youngsters, we were very familiar with the inhabitants of the cemetery on the hill in our small town. The cemetery was one of our favorite places to walk to, to wander among the tombstones reading the inscriptions, to visit graves of members of our families and those of people who had lived in the community, mostly before our time. Even so, we knew them. We knew the stories of their lives and deaths, especially those that were extraordinary in some way.

Death was certainly dreaded and feared, but the ceremonies surrounding it were a real part of our lives when we were growing up in that small community. Whenever anyone in the community died and the funeral was held in the Methodist church in town, school was dismissed. The church was only a block away from the school, and often the pupils who wanted to attend the funeral walked in a group to the church when the bell started tolling. Any young girls who were present carried flowers into the church from the hearse, then back out to the hearse after the funeral, then from the hearse, following the casket, to the grave in the cemetery.

The Selvin cemetery was always well cared for, but on Decoration Day families made sure the graves of their kin reflected their devotion to the departed. Sinkholes were filled in, burdock shoots and dandelions dug out of the grass, sod placed over bare spots, and tombstones set straight. Some graves were covered with bouquets of flowers to show that numerous family members had remembered their dead. Small flags waved over the graves of veterans from all the wars since the War of 1812. There was a Civil War grave of a soldier from the south, who died and was buried on enemy ground. Then there were veterans of The Great War (World War I), in which our fathers and uncles had served before we were born.

On Decoration Day, even while the new peas were simmering on the stove, all the young girls around town met at the cemetery to carry flowers to the graves of the war veterans who were buried there. The VFW members held a service at the graveyard: a long extemporaneous prayer, a brief commemoration, a wavering trumpet call, an opening and closing hymn, sung a cappella by the Methodist choir and the people gathered around the flagpole at the cemetery entrance.

On Decoration Day, many of the irises, peonies, and roses planted around the cemetery were in bloom. In addition, we brought extravagant bouquets in glass canning jars—honeysuckle, roses, daisies, irises, peonies, pinks, bachelor's buttons—and we decorated the graves of our relatives and neighbors. The cemetery was a pretty, peaceful place on a small hill overlooking the old town, and there was nothing spooky about it for us as children.

But no one at dinner ate two bowls of Grandma's pea soup.

GRANDMA'S SUMMER KITCHEN

Mince pies and mincemeat, roast goose and sauerkraut dressing, goose grease, and hartshorn Christmas cookies are only a few of the foods I remember when I think of winter days in my German grandmother's kitchen.

Summer days recall a different kitchen. All the summer cooking was done in the summer kitchen to keep the heat out of the house. It was a room at the west end of the back porch, which was next to the winter kitchen. The summer kitchen was smaller, lighter, and more airy than the winter kitchen. Its walls were sided with white-painted poplar boards, run sideways, and the ceiling was low and slanting.

The summer kitchen had its own cooking stove—a black cast-iron one, similar to the one in the winter kitchen, but smaller and with more shiny chrome trimmings and handles and fancy curlicues embossed on its body. Grandpa ordered it from a Montgomery Ward Company catalog and it cost thirty dollars.

The stove stood over to one side of the kitchen, with a window to the back of it and one to the side. The heat could go right out the windows. Next to another window, a small wooden shelf held the water bucket and dipper. There were a table, chairs, a bench, and a small, long-legged pie safe to hold the dishes and foods.

The kitchen range in the summer kitchen was fired up three times a day to cook meals, and more during canning

season. Good ventilation and air circulation were needed to keep the house cool.

The south wall of the back porch was almost entirely of screened windows. The breeze from the windows helped circulate the air through the summer kitchen, and when the door to the winter kitchen was open, as well as the bedroom door and windows which also opened off the porch, there was good cross-ventilation.

The kitchen table from the winter kitchen was moved out to the enclosed back porch. Besides the table, there was very little other furniture in the simple, gray-painted porch room. A tall safe stood against one wall; a washstand against another, with a wash pan, soap, and a towel on a roller hanging above it. There were some hooks by the door for hats and jackets, and a rocking chair in one corner. Grandma did not have anything around that was not useful.

When seated at the table, the barn, barn lot with grazing cows, the pond, the cornfield beyond, sloping toward the tree-lined creek bank, were all in view. Just outside the back door a maple shaded the porch; the big cousins' swing hung from a limb on one side of it, the baby's swing on the other. The cistern and the woodshed were only a few feet from the back door. A long walk made of flat stones from the creek bed led straight from the back door past a chicken house, the woodpile, and a corncrib, to the barn.

Here the meals cooked in Grandma's summer kitchen were eaten. They were meals from summer gardens and orchards and berry patches. New potatoes, sliced and fried; wilted lettuce; ripe tomatoes; summer squash; cottage cheese; strawberry shortcakes; rhubarb and gooseberry pies; damson preserves; grape jelly; butter beans; deviled eggs; German potato salad; summer sausage; watermelon and "mushmelon"; and summer's choice dish—platters piled high with corn on the cob cooked only minutes after it was brought in from the garden. And our "roastin' ears" were spread with butter as yellow as the corn itself, which Grandma churned from cream given by Daisy, the "butter cow," and the lead cow in Grandpa's small herd of *milch* cows.

BRINGING IN THE COWS AT MILKING TIME

On most days, clocks could have been set by the cows' homeward journey at four o'clock. The herd might be leisurely grazing, with some cows standing under trees or lying down in the spring sunshine blissfully chewing their cuds, limpid eyes mirroring contentment, when the lead cow would suddenly start toward the trodden cowpath and head for home. The rest of the herd lumbered to attention at once and fell in behind her, as if given a silent command to get up and go.

On other days, if Uncle Roy or Grandpa went out to the barn and began pitching down hay and portioning out grain before the cows had come home, they would walk out to the split-rail fence and call out, "Hoo-ey! Hoo-ey! Hoo-ey!" That was a word reserved for herding cows from one place to another, and it usually worked whether one was driving them or calling them.

If calling failed, bringing in cows was a job that fell to younger family members, whoever was handy. Feeding was the men's job, washing milk buckets and getting the separator ready was women's work, and herding in the cows was child's work.

Once the cows were started toward home, single-file on the grass-bare cowpath, one plodding after another, tails switching and udders swinging and full of milk, there was nothing more to do except follow along behind them. The closer they got to the gate, the faster they walked until, finally, they broke into a run and galloped wildly toward their stables and the waiting grain and hay in the mangers.

GRANDPA'S BARN

The barn was a place of great allure on Grandpa's farm. We went there to hunt for hidden kittens and egg nests, and to swing on a rope swing suspended from a tie beam. We liked to be there when it was fragrant with just-mowed hay in the haymows, and when there was a newborn calf in the stable with its mother.

It was pleasant in the barn any time of day, but when the cows were all out to pasture and the horses were in the fields pulling the plows and planters, the barn sometimes seemed deserted and lonely. Unexpected noises were momentarily frightening and memorable, like those heard when one was all alone in the house at night. Pigeons sitting high up on rafters above the haymow crooned unexpectedly in the dreamy afternoon quietness, or beat their wings noisily when they flew in the open hay door under the rooftop gable. Swallows, glimpsed briefly, swished in and out opened shed doors. Mice skittered under the grain bin. Sudden, inexplicable noises rose from under the creaking floorboards. The cobwebbed interior of the dusky barn became chillingly mysterious.

At milking time, the barn changed and suddenly became vibrantly alive and hospitable. Buckets clanked, pitchforks whisked hay aloft, ears of corn bounced in horse feedboxes, big teeth grated across hard kernels and munched noisily. Animal bodies bumped and rubbed against stable walls. Whinnying, lowing, cooing, flapping, and the first metallic pings of milk streams hitting empty milk buckets filled the barn with friendly, familiar sounds.

To this rich, rhythmic harmony of the fragrant barn at milking time, we farm children added our laughter. We jumped from the upper loft into the hay-filled lower loft and wallowed in a sea of fluffy, dusty, sweet-smelling hay. For greater thrills, we grasped the end of a long rope tied around an overhead beam, swung out from the high hay mow, let go the rope, and landed in the middle of the hay. Our acrobatics stirred up dust and clouded shafts of sunlight angling through cracks in the west wall of the barn with dancing dust motes.

Taking turns, we swung in a board swing Grandpa had suspended from a tie beam. We explored the walkway behind the feeding mangers above the cows' stables. The cows had to put their heads through openings in a double-slatted partition between their stables and the manger in order to reach their hay and grain. As soon as they were happily munching their suppers, the second partition was locked around their unsuspecting necks, forcing the cows to stand in one spot at milking time. While they were captive in stanchions, we could rub their velvety brown noses and pet their heads. If there was a calf in the stable with its mother, we held our hands out, palms up with fingers extended, and coaxed it to give us "calf licks" with its slobbery, prickly tongue.

We laughed at unpleasant calf licks, and we laughed at little kittens begging for milk. They would sit up on their hind legs, paws held up off the ground, mewing and mewing until Grandpa and Uncle Roy would direct streams of milk from a cow's teat at their mouths. And what farm child has not tried to match the kitten's skill, and found it not so easy as it looks to drink the stream of warm milk?

Grandpa's "milch" cows were treated with special care. The small herd of a dozen or so cows, Jerseys, Guernseys, and Holsteins, was the hub around which family life revolved. The cows were fed and milked morning and evening. All other activities were carried on around these necessary tasks. Whatever was going on, Grandpa could not leave to go anywhere until after the morning's milking was finished, and if he was away during the day, he had to be back home by four in the afternoon.

The herd provided the milk supply, butter, cottage cheese, cream, beef, and veal for the table, and a cash income from the sale of milk and cream.

Cream was sold to Holland Creamery and milk to the cheese factory in Dale. The milk cans came back from the cheese factory filled with whey, which was fed to the pigs.

Every cow had a name and a distinct personality, with idiosyncracies that distinguished her. Some were rogues, prone to breaking out and plundering the garden or cornfield. They often had to wear yokes. Others had distinctive voices that could be picked out of a chorus of mooing. Cows with horns were given a wide breadth because they had the wherewithal to do damage, if incited. Some kicked the milk buckets over if given a chance, and others switched their tails so fiercely when being milked that the hairs at the end of their tails were separated and used to tie their own tails to their legs. Muzzles were put on calves who could not be weaned easily, lest they steal milk from cows in the pasture. But the most significant characteristic of a cow was her individual capacity to produce milk.

Holsteins gave lots of milk, but it was not very rich.

"This must be some of that blue-leg Holstein milk," Grandpa would say if he thought he detected it in his glass.

Guernseys were middle-of-the-road, giving a medium amount of milk with a medium amount of butterfat in it. And Jerseys gave the milk with the highest butterfat content.

CHURNING BUTTER IN GRANDMA'S KITCHEN

Jersey cream was what Grandma wanted when she made butter in her old-fashioned wooden churn once each week. The Jersey milk was kept separate from the rest at milking time until Grandma had gathered all the cream she needed for the week's churning.

The Jersey milk was carried from the barn directly to Grandma's kitchen as soon as it was in the bucket. She strained the rich milk through muslin cloth into large milk crocks and covered them with clean dish towels. The cream rose to the top of the milk overnight.

The next morning, Grandma skimmed the cream, with its thick, wrinkled yellow top, off the milk and put it into a cream pail. If there was not enough cream for churning, it would again be saved that morning and night.

When enough cream was collected, it was poured into the cedar churn with a smaller amount of the skimmed milk to make the buttermilk during churning. The churn needed to be filled halfway, or slightly more, with rich cream. Then it was set aside so that the cream could "turn" or clabber. In the summer this could happen quickly, in twenty-four hours or so. In the winter, the cream-filled churn was set near the kitchen range.

When it turned, the cream had to be churned at once or it wouldn't make good butter. To churn, Grandma sat on a kitchen chair at the side of the churn and worked the wooden dasher up and down, sloshing the cream until it thickened and the butter separated from the whey. The butter had to go through three stages. First it had to swell, then it broke, and then it gathered. Butter-making, like so many farm chores, had a language of its own.

Sometimes in hot weather, the churnful of cream was slow to "come" to butter. There was a chant to go along with churning that all children knew. We said it whether the butter was "slow" or not. It was chanted in time to the up-and-down movements of the churn dasher.

Come butter come!

Come butter come!

Peter's standing at the gate

Waiting for a butter cake

Come butter come!

After the frothed-up cream curdled and the smaller granular particles gathered into yellow lumps, Grandma would pour out the buttermilk and put in some cold water. A few more churns with the dasher and the butter was practically "washed." Then Grandma could put the butter into a large blue crock, wash and work out the rest of the buttermilk, and work in the salt, using two butter paddles.

BUTTER—YELLOW AS GOLD

In summer, the butter was golden yellow because the cows were eating tender, green grass. (In the winter it was pale yellow; a similar change occurred in the color of egg yolks.) It was "as yellow as gold" when it was pressed into a butter print to mold it into a round shape and imprint the top with a pretty design.

When the butter was unmolded—it came out smoothly because the mold was dipped in hot water, then in cold, before the butter was put in—a sheaf of wheat stood out in low relief on top of the yellow pat. Then it was put into a butter crock with a cover, placed inside a large bucket, and lowered at the end of a rope into the cistern until the bottom of the bucket touched the cool water. The rope tied to the bucket was secured to a spike nail driven into the wooden well cover.

The butter was left suspended down in the cistern until it was needed for butter cake or butter cookies or to butter Grandma's good apple kuchen—or for a "sugar bread" snack for a hungry grandchild.

Sugar bread was sure to follow butter churning. Grandma would cut a slice of white bread, spread it with freshly churned butter, and sprinkle a teaspoonful of sugar over the buttered bread. To taste as it should, the butter and bread has to be fresh and homemade.

The first grandchild favored with sugar bread would wander off, holding the treat on the palm of an upturned hand, carefully eating around the edges to avoid spilling sugar, and before long the kitchen was swarming with grandchildren waiting for sugar bread sandwiches.

AUNT HELEN'S LEMON SUGAR COOKIES

For a few years, Grandma had a house full of grandchildren to make sugar bread for. For a period during the Depression, Uncle Roy and Aunt Helen, with their growing family, lived with Grandma and Grandpa Buse, sharing the house and farmwork.

My brothers and I felt lucky to have cousins living just across the road from our house. There were seven of us all together, and we were "stairsteps" from the oldest cousin, Annabelle, down to her baby sister, with no more than a year or two's difference between our ages. I was right in the middle.

Aunt Helen was young and beautiful, with wavy bobbed hair. She wore pretty dresses, cracked out nutmeats in unbroken halves to decorate cakes, put bananas in homemade ice cream, and read *True Romance* and *Photoplay* magazines. She was lively and entertaining when she could get a little time away from housework and caring for baby Virginia. But when the dishes piled up, and Annabelle and Buddy were scrapping, and little "Sister" was crying, and beans were burning on the stove, it was of no use to wait around for smiles and laughter to return. Better to come back in the afternoon when the baby napped and dinner was over. Then I would dare to ask my favorite aunt, "Would you play the piano?"

Aunt Helen played classical music. Her nimble fingers flew up and down the keyboard, playing scales and elegant pieces unlike any we heard in church or on the player piano rolls.

"Did you like that?" she would ask when she closed the keyboard. "Well, you run home and practice your pieces and you'll be able to play, too."

So I would run home and practice my piano lesson, even if Jewel was trying to listen to her daily soap operas on the radio. I would drown out "Helen Trent" with my fresh new inspiration.

Then I'd have a reason to scoot back across the road to tell Aunt Helen that I had practiced—and perhaps to cadge a cookie out of Aunt Helen's cookie jar.

Sugar cookies were standard in farmhouse cookie jars. They were simple and plain, made of butter, eggs, sugar, leavening, salt, flour, and vanilla. They were cut in large rounds with the rim of a baking powder can, sprinkled with plain white sugar, and baked until just barely browned on their undersides. They were staple lunchbox fare, and old hat—nothing to be excited about. Unless . . . Aunt Helen had given them her "touch." Aunt Helen made sugar cookies with *lemon* flavoring! Sometimes she frosted them with a thick layer of icing, and she cut them out in shapes of hearts and triangles and crescents.

When Aunt Helen was in charge, the commonplace was transformed to the exciting.

BUYING UNBREAKABLE POTTERY

One summer, a traveling salesman with a truckload of pottery came to our community. He came to our house first, driving a rattle-trap truck and arriving in a swirl of dust. He parked under the huge oak tree in our front yard. I was outside in the yard and could tell at once that he was not anyone we knew.

I ran in the back door with the news. "Someone's here!"

Mother smoothed her hair, removed her apron, and was walking to the door even as he knocked, as composed and dignified in her cotton work dress as if she were dressed in her school clothes.

The man on the other side of the screen door was dressed in tacky clothes and he looked down on his luck, as many of the itinerant salesmen did during the Depression. He was carrying a pitcher and some bowls. They were made of heavy pottery with a mottled green, brown, and yellow glaze that resembled spongeware.

A rush of words assailed Mother. Her innate politeness always compelled her to hear out the brashest of drummers, even when she was not interested. But this time she opened the screen door and stepped out on the porch. She was interested.

The man went out to his truck and brought back additional pieces. He spread the pottery out on the porch steps and on the flat-topped pillars at the bottom and top of the steps. He went into his spiel. The dishes were ovenproof. They were unbreakable.

"You can put them right in the oven and bake in them. They won't break," he said.

Mother picked up one piece and then another, looking at them, but she was unresponsive. The price was high.

Pretty soon the salesman began to drop his price. But Mother didn't attempt to bargain. It was not her style.

Then the salesman offered to convince Mother the dishes were indestructible.

"You can't even break 'em with a hammer," he boasted, "and I'll prove it."

He took a hammer out of his basket and walked around hitting first one bowl, then another with the hammer. And none broke.

He offered the hammer to Mother, but she declined.

So he came down on his price again.

What the salesman did not know was that Mother was never effusive, always reserved. She made careful, well-considered decisions. And she was deciding—I knew that stance. She stood back, looking the dishes over, one arm folded across her waist, the other resting on it, hand curled under her chin, with her head tilted slightly to one side.

He had dropped his price almost to the bottom when Mother finally said, "All right."

She picked up a nested set of mixing bowls and set them on a tall pillar on one side of the porch. She added a large, fat pitcher and a lidded casserole to her selections.

"Run and get my pocketbook," she said.

I was tickled because we had new dishes that would *never* break. Mother just said, "Let's wait and see." And she got busy and baked macaroni and cheese in the new casserole for supper, to try it out. And it did not break.

"Not yet, anyway." Mother said.

After he left our house, the peddler drove over to Grandpa's house. Aunt Helen was more enthusiastic than Mother. Grandpa said, "She went overboard. She must have bought the whole truckload."

Poor Aunt Helen had to defend her purchases and counter the skepticism of Uncle Roy and Grandpa.

"He cheated you," Uncle Roy said. "He had a trick. You can't drop dishes on the floor and hit them with a hammer without breaking them."

So Aunt Helen dropped a bowl on the floor to show Uncle Roy and Grandpa that it wouldn't break. But it did!

"That must have been an accident," she said, and she dropped another bowl on the floor. And *it* broke!

She she got a hammer and tried it. Needless to say, another bowl shattered into pieces.

"Better stop," Uncle Roy said. "You won't have any left." Everyone had a good laugh—except Aunt Helen.

The story of Aunt Helen being taken in by the traveling salesman's "unbreakable pottery" follows her still.

In truth, the pottery proved very durable. We used ours for years, losing it piece by piece through normal breakage. The pitcher became our regular iced tea and lemonade pitcher. The first dish of baked macaroni and cheese led a succession of casseroles across our table. And the mixing bowls were well used for creaming and mixing and beating and whipping every imaginable batter.

None of us had an inkling that the "unbreakable Indian pottery," now known as "peddler's ware," would become valuable and be sought by collectors. If Aunt Helen still has any of hers, she has the last laugh.

LIGHTNING STRIKES THE BARN

Aunt Helen redeemed herself when lightning struck Grandpa's barn and burned it to the ground during a summer thunderstorm.

Lightning seemed always to be striking on our farms during the first decade of my life. Every time there was an electrical storm with loud thunderclaps and awesome jagged streaks of lightning stabbing earthward—we could tell when it hit— Grandpa, Uncle Roy, and Dad went out over the farms afterward to find the victim. It was usually a tree, often a huge old friend in the woods or about the farm. A majestic tall oak in Grandpa's front yard fell to lightning, and I remember the wide-eyed amazement I felt as we watched it from our windows, crashing down across the road in front of our house.

Once lightning struck the cow herd, and we all trooped out after the storm to see the carnage in the pasture where they had taken shelter under a tree. The creek was bank full and running swiftly, and all of us, including several children under ten, walked across it on a huge log laid bank to bank.

The dead cows, feet up and tongues hanging, were a sobering sight, but we were up to it because we had never been sheltered from the harsh realities of life and nature.

When lightning struck Grandpa's barn and it began to burn, we heard shouting coming from Grandpa's as everyone, except Grandma, ran to the barn to try to save the animals and the farm equipment. I ran as far as Grandpa's front yard when I was seen by our hired man and sent inside to stay with Grandma. We watched Grandpa's wonderful barn go up in flames from the window of Grandma's kitchen.

When it was all over, we learned that Uncle Roy had saved Grandpa's Model T Ford, but he hadn't been able to start the motor of his heavier automobile, and it burned. The hay rake stood in the burning rubble, but the harness that hung close to the door had been saved.

The cows had been caught out in the pasture which, this time, proved safer than the barn. Aunt Helen went to turn out a stabled cow, her calf, and the horses, while Grandpa and Uncle Roy tried to push out the automobiles and machinery.

Cows will leave a burning barn, but horses will run into one, trying to reach their stalls. When Aunt Helen could not get the horses to leave their stalls, she took off her apron, covered the head of the first one, and led him out. She tied him to a tree and went back into the barn and used her sweater for a blinder for the second horse. Her petticoat saved the third horse.

When Dad told the story about Aunt Helen's bravery, he would make the story funny at the end.

"It's a good thing Grandpa didn't have any more horses," he'd say, "or Aunt Helen wouldn't have had any clothes left."

And any time anyone told the story about Aunt Helen buying the unbreakable pottery, someone would balance the scale by telling how she saved the horses. Aunt Helen was truly a romantic heroine of the highest order.

NUTTING—A SHARED FAMILY OUTING

It was good to have our three families living directly across the road from each other. There were always plenty of relatives to depend on in times of emergency, such as when Grandpa's barn was struck by lightning. By the same token, there were always relatives to share our everyday lives, not just the dramatic, once-in-a-lifetime happenings that were in themselves unforgettable. With grandparents, cousins, and Uncle Roy and Aunt Helen living so near us during those years, many commonplace activities were lifted out of the ordinary because they were shared family activities.

Nutting in the autumn, usually on an October Sunday, was always an afternoon's outing, shared by members of our three families. The wild-growing trees from which we gathered hickory nuts and black walnuts grew in Grandpa Buse's woods on a hill at the back of his farm. The woods were not far from the farmhouse and we could easily walk the distance, and often did, but we usually rode in the farm wagon when we went nutting. One reason was that we always took a picnic; another was that the gunnysacks filled with nuts were quite heavy. But the real reason we needed the wagon and horses was because we always found things we were not looking for and brought them home.

The wooden farm wagon was painted green, yellow, and red, and it was pulled by Fan, our spirited chestnut mare, and old, faithful Tony, who had the "heaves" and was (we loved to say it) "part Percheron."

"I hate to hitch up the horses on Sunday, as hard as they work all week," Grandpa said, "but we will need the wagon."

During October, Grandpa and Uncle Roy worked at husking corn, cutting the fodder, and shocking it. As we bumped off down the lane toward the woods, a few stray ears of yellow field corn bounced around in the wagon bed, where a half-dozen cousins, Aunt Helen, and Mother were riding. Uncle Roy and Grandpa sat up front on the wagon seat, with Uncle Roy holding the reins.

There were rows of corn shocks standing in the fields along the creek (called "bottoms") that we passed through on our way to the woods. Drifts of orange pumpkins of all sizes lay scattered across the fields, waiting to be picked up and hauled to the house for winter storage. With a field full of pumpkins, we could have all we wanted to make jack-o'-lanterns. Uncle Roy stopped the horses and we scrambled out of the wagon to select our own pumpkins for Halloween. Looking forward to carving out pumpkin faces—and to the pumpkin pies and pumpkin butter Mother would make from those she picked up—added to the excitement of our nutting excursions.

At the fencerow we stopped again, and Uncle Roy guided the horses under the branches of a tree where wild fox grape clusters vined over a low-hanging branch. Standing in the wagon bed, Grandpa and Mother could easily reach the dark grapes that garlanded the tree.

The grapes were tart and juicy and their flavor was foxy and wild. They were half as large as the Concord grapes in Grandpa's garden and not worth eating raw. But they made delicious jelly, and Mother was delighted that we had found them.

"I might make some spiced wild grape jelly in case Charles brings home some venison or wild duck this fall," she told Aunt Helen.

Next we stopped where we knew the wild bittersweet grew on a black cherry tree, and Mother and Aunt Helen gathered armloads of the orange-berried vines to fill our flower vases for the autumn season. The wagon was beginning to fill up around us before we ever reached the nut trees in Grandpa's woods! A dozen orange pumpkins, some as large as a half-bushel, a basket of wild grapes, a pile of bittersweet, and a half-dozen cousins made a colorful, boisterous wagonload wending its way through Grandpa's cornfields.

As we bumped along in the horse-drawn wagon on the way to the woods, we gathered more than the wild harvest that surrounded us. The cawing flocks of noisy crows; the crisp edge of October air; Buddy and Harold pelting sassy red squirrels with pungent green-hulled walnuts; the foliage of the trees kindled to the peak of their autumnal brilliance and swirling downward around our heads; the sounds of our own laughter and shouts echoing across the fields—all the sights and sounds that are characteristic of nutting excursions are scrambled together in a sensory collage of memory. They have no chronology, and they span the autumns.

Standing out in bold relief among those images is one particular day I remember when we took a picnic and ate our lunch under the spreading, leafless branches of an old black walnut tree on a high hill overlooking Grandpa's house. We all sat around on the crisp leaves under the bare tree: Uncle Roy leaning his back against the thick-trunked, rough-barked walnut tree and Grandpa resting against the opposite side; Mother and Aunt Helen sitting on opposite ends of a fallen log on which the picnic was spread, handing out fried chicken and pickles and deviled eggs and lemon-flavored sugar cookies; and the rest of us scattered around, sitting on rocks, on stumps, and on lumpy, half-filled gunnysacks that held the harvest of nuts.

While we ate, a red squirrel in the tree barked and chattered at us and my brother Jimmy teased him more by throwing nuts into the branches. Every so often a walnut broke its bond with the tree and plummeted straight to the ground, rolling to rest nearby. This was a game to little cousin Ginger. At each *thump!* she was off for the fallen walnut, rummaging in the leaves until she found a nut to add to her small sack. The boys were always looking for mischief, and they ground the pungent husks of fallen walnuts underfoot to split the hulls, then rubbed the dark oily stain on their fingers and tormented us girls by trying to smear it on our faces. It was exuberant fun until someone was successfully smeared and the game was called to a halt.

Such a day, so rich in the feeling of family solidarity and so blessed with the riches of nature, deserves to be remembered among all the rest. The bounteous old walnut trees, the beauty of the farmstead dressed in the luminous golds, fiery reds, rich magentas, and warm browns of autumn leaves, the blue-hazed, familiar hills, the unusual charm of dried weeds and grasses, the serendipitous discoveries of wild grapes and bittersweet, the trampled leaf-color underfoot, a high-flying skein of geese—these were the scenes we gathered along with the wild harvest of black walnuts and hickory nuts from Grandpa Buse's woods.

Grandma's Light Bread and Coffee Kuchen

1 package dry yeast or 1 cake compressed yeast	2 teaspoons salt
	1 tablespoon shortening
$\frac{1}{4}$ cup water	$6\frac{1}{2}$ to $6\frac{3}{4}$ cups sifted enriched
2 cups milk, scalded	flour
2 tablespoons sugar	

Soften dry yeast in warm water (110°F) or compressed yeast in lukewarm water (85°F).

Combine scalded milk, sugar, salt, shortening. Cool to lukewarm. Add 2 cups flour and stir well. Add softened yeast and stir. Add more flour to make a moderately stiff dough.

Turn out on a lightly floured surface. Knead for about eight minutes, until smooth and satiny. Shape dough into a ball. Place in a lightly greased bowl, turning once to grease surface. Cover. Let rise in a warm place until double in volume, about $1\frac{1}{2}$ hours. Punch down, and let rise again until doubled, about 45 minutes.

Divide dough into two portions. Let rest for 10 minutes. Shape one portion into a bread loaf. Place loaf in a greased $9\frac{1}{2}''$ x $5\frac{1}{4}''$ x $2\frac{3}{4}''$ loaf pan. Let rise until doubled, about 1 hour. Bake loaf at 375°F for about 45 minutes.

To Make Kuchen: Return second portion of bread dough to floured surface. Make an indentation in dough and break 1 egg into it. Knead the egg into the bread dough. Then, in the same manner, add $\frac{1}{4}$ cup sugar and 2 tablespoons melted butter. Knead enough to mix ingredients into dough thoroughly. Divide dough into two portions and pat into two greased 9'' pie pans. Brush the top of each portion with beaten egg yolk. Top with brown sugar, butter, cinnamon, and nuts, or sliced peaches or apples, fresh or canned. Let kuchens rise until doubled in volume. Bake at 375°F for about 30 minutes.

Grandma's Mincemeat

$1\frac{1}{2}$	pounds lean beef, boiled	1 cup pitted sour cherries (canned or frozen)
1	pound beef suet	
$2\frac{1}{2}$	pounds tart apples, peeled, cored, and chopped	$1\frac{1}{2}$ teaspoons each nutmeg, ground cloves, mace, cinnamon, and salt
$1\frac{1}{4}$	pounds raisins	3 cups cider (more to taste)
$\frac{1}{2}$	pound chopped citron or chopped pickled watermelon rind	1 cup sugar
		1 cup tart jelly
		1 cup brandy or grape wine

Put the boiled beef and the beef suet through the medium blade of a food grinder. Add the apples, raisins, chopped citron or rind, cherries, spices, salt, and cider. (Boiled cider may be used if desired.) Mix to combine.

Transfer the mixture to a large heavy pan and simmer over low heat for about two hours, or until thick. Add cider as needed during cooking; stir frequently to prevent burning. Remove from heat, stir in jelly, and let mincemeat cool. Add brandy or wine. Store the mincemeat, covered, in refrigerator for at least one week before using. MAKES ABOUT 1 GALLON.

Mincemeat Pie

4 cups mincemeat
$\frac{1}{2}$ cup boiled cider or fruit juice

$1\frac{1}{2}$ tablespoons butter
Pie dough for two crusts

Preheat oven to 400°F. Combine the mincemeat with the boiled cider or fruit juice.

Make a double recipe of Grandma's Lard Pie Dough (page 231), using 4 teaspoons of sugar instead of the salt. Roll two-thirds of the dough into an 11″ round on a lightly floured surface, drape it over the rolling pin, and fit it into a 9″ pie tin. Trim off the excess dough, leaving a 1″ overhang, and chill the shell for 30 minutes.

Transfer the mincemeat mixture into the pie shell, and dot it with butter.

Roll the remaining dough into a 10″ round, moisten the edge of the shell, and fit the round over the shell, pressing the edges firmly against the rim. Fold the overhang over the round, crimp the edges decoratively, and make several slits in the top round. Brush the top with milk, sprinkle it with a small amount of sugar (1 tablespoon), and bake the pie on the lowest rack of oven for 1 hour, or until the crust is brown. Transfer the pie to a rack, lift open the slits in the top crust with the tip of a knife, and spoon in a small amount of apple brandy, if desired. Serve warm.

Grandma's Lard Pie Dough

1½ cups sifted flour   ⅓ cup lard
¾ teaspoon salt   ¼ cup cold milk

Sift together the flour and salt. Add the lard, chilled, and blend the mixture until it resembles meal, using the fingers or a pastry blender. Add milk by tablespoonfuls, sprinkling it over the flour mixture and tossing the mixture with a fork until the milk is incorporated. Form the dough into a ball, kneading it lightly against a smooth surface or the side of the bowl for only a few seconds, until a smooth ball forms. Wrap the dough in waxed paper and chill it for 1 hour before rolling it out on a lightly floured board. Makes one single 8" or 9" pie shell.

This recipe may be doubled or tripled.

Lamb's-Quarter with Little Dumplings

1½ gallons lamb's-quarter   1 recipe Little Dumplings
1 smoked-ham bone   Batter (p. 232)
1½ quarts water
1 pound potatoes, peeled
     and cubed

Gather a quantity of lamb's-quarter, at least 1½ gallons, in the springtime before the plants are six inches tall. Pick the entire plant. If you gather the lamb's-quarter later in the season, pinch out and use the tops. Rinse the greens well and drain.

In a large kettle, cook a meaty smoked-ham bone in 1½ quarts of water for about 1 hour. Add the lamb's-quarter to the broth along with the potatoes. Cover and simmer for 10 minutes. Remove the ham bone, cut off the meat, and cut it into ½" cubes. Return the meat to the cooking greens. With a teaspoon, drop Little Dumplings Batter on top of the lamb's-quarter mixture and simmer, covered, for 15 minutes.

SERVES 6 TO 8.

Little Dumplings Batter

$\frac{1}{2}$ cup flour

$\frac{1}{2}$ teaspoon salt

$\frac{1}{2}$ teaspoon baking powder

Pepper

1 egg, beaten

2 tablespoons milk

Sift together the flour, salt, baking powder, and pepper to taste. In another bowl, mix together the egg and milk. Add the flour mixture all at once and blend well with a fork.

MAKES 12 SMALL DUMPLINGS.

Pie Plant Pie

6 cups diced fresh rhubarb

2 cups sugar

$\frac{1}{4}$ cup instant tapioca

$\frac{1}{4}$ teaspoon salt

2 tablespoons melted butter

2 9″ pie shells

Combine rhubarb, sugar, tapioca, salt, and butter. Pour rhubarb mixture into pastry-lined pie pan. Cover with a vented top crust and seal and flute edges. Brush top crust lightly with milk and sprinkle with sugar. Bake at 400°F, for 45 minutes or until filling bubbles in the center of the pie and the crust is well browned. Cool before serving.

Corn Bread

$\frac{1}{4}$ cup shortening

1 cup flour

$\frac{1}{4}$ cup sugar

4 teaspoons baking powder

$\frac{3}{4}$ teaspoon salt

1 cup yellow cornmeal

2 eggs

1 cup milk

Divide the shortening between two round 8″ pie tins and put them in a hot oven (425°F) to allow the shortening to melt, about 5 minutes.

In the meantime, sift together the flour, sugar, baking powder, and salt. Stir in the cornmeal. Beat the eggs and milk together until mixed well, then add to the dry ingredients. Beat until just smooth. Remove the hot pans from the oven and pour the hot fat into the cornbread batter. Stir quickly. Pour the batter into the sizzling pans and bake at 425°F for 20 to 25 minutes. Cut into pie-shaped wedges and serve from the tins.   MAKES 12 WEDGES.

Roast Goose

Clean goose and prepare, or thaw a frozen ready-to-cook goose. Prick the goose with a fork about the legs and wings. Place the goose, without stuffing, in a moderately hot oven, (425°F) for 30 minutes to fry out some of the fat. Remove from the oven, drain off the fat (save this for goose grease), and let cool. Rub cavity with salt and pepper, stuff with sauerkraut stuffing, and truss.

Place goose on a rack in a shallow roasting pan, breast side up. Roast uncovered at 325°F, allowing about 25 minutes per pound. Remove excess fat as it accumulates in the pan.

Sauerkraut and Apple Stuffing

¾ cup chopped onion
¼ cup butter
4 cups sauerkraut, drained
2 tart apples, peeled, cored,
    and chopped

½ cup chopped celery
1 tablespoon caraway seeds
Salt and pepper

In a large skillet, sauté onion in butter over moderately high heat until it is lightly browned. Add sauerkraut, apples, celery, caraway seeds, and salt and pepper to taste. Cook over moderate heat, tossing, for 5 minutes. Let cool to room temperature.

Stuff a goose, hen, or game birds with mixture, packing the salted cavity of the fowl loosely.

German Rye Bread

2 cups water	1 teaspoon anise
$\frac{1}{2}$ cup brown sugar, firmly packed	1 tablespoon shortening
1 teaspoon salt	1 cake compressed yeast
1 teaspoon caraway seeds	$3\frac{1}{2}$ cups sifted bread flour
	2 cups rye flour

Combine water, sugar, salt, caraway seeds, anise, and shortening in a saucepan. Cook for 3 minutes. Cool to lukewarm. Crumble yeast into lukewarm mixture and allow to soften. Add bread flour and mix to make a soft dough. Place dough in a bowl, cover it with a towel, and place it in a warm place away from drafts to let rise for $1\frac{1}{2}$ hours.

Add the rye flour to make a stiff dough. Knead lightly. Place in a greased bowl and turn once to grease the surface of the dough. Cover with a damp cloth and let rise until double in volume, about 2 hours.

Knead dough. Divide into 2 portions, cover, and let rest for 10 to 15 minutes. Mold into two loaves. Place in greased $9\frac{1}{2}''$ x 5'' x 3'' bread pans. Cover and let rise until doubled in size. Bake at 375°F for 35 to 45 minutes. Cool on a rack.

Springerle

2 cups sifted sugar	1 teaspoon grated lemon rind
4 eggs, separated	
1 cube ammonium carbonate*	4 cups sifted flour
	Anise seeds
20 drops oil of anise	

*Food-grade ammonium carbonate, or "hartshorn," may be obtained at your pharmacy.

Stir sugar into beaten egg yolks. Beat whites until stiff, add to egg yolks and sugar, and stir vigorously for 10 minutes by hand, or use an electric mixer on a low speed. Crush ammonium carbonate and add to mixture, along with anise oil and lemon rind. Add flour in several portions, combining well after each addition. Chill the dough.

Divide dough into 3 or 4 portions; turn one onto a floured board and keep the rest chilled until needed. Roll out dough to $\frac{1}{4}''$ thickness. Dust springerle roll or squares by tying a spoonful of cornstarch into a twist of cheesecloth and striking it lightly against the roll. Imprint the cookie dough. Cut cookies apart between the designs and transfer them to a lightly floured board or cookie sheet. Cover with a dry towel, and let stand overnight.

When ready to bake, brush flour from dried surface with a fine brush and rub underside carefully with cold water. Place cookies on a buttered baking sheet and sprinkle lightly with anise seeds. Bake at 275°F for 40 minutes or until cookies are a delicate straw color. Cool on the baking sheet, then store in a covered jar or box. Springerles may be eaten immediately, but they improve with age. They are hard cookies.   MAKES 6 TO 8 DOZEN.

Hartshorn Cookies

$\frac{1}{2}$ cup butter
$1\frac{1}{2}$ cups sugar
1 egg
1 teaspoon vanilla

2 tablespoons ammonium
    carbonate (hartshorn)
$\frac{1}{2}$ cup milk
5 cups flour

Cream butter, adding sugar gradually. Beat until creamy. Add egg and vanilla, and mix well. Pound the ammonium carbonate into a powder and then stir into milk until dissolved. Add ammonium carbonate and milk to creamed mixture alternately with flour. Add more flour if needed to make dough stiff enough to roll out. Roll out dough, cut cookies, and dip each one in sugar. Bake on a greased cookie sheet at 375°F for 8 to 10 minutes.

MAKES APPROXIMATELY 4 DOZEN.

Grandpa liked to drink the buttermilk on churning day, and he liked hot corn bread with it. When he had a dish of fresh, cooked greens to go with it, either mixed wild greens, or mustard greens, or lamb's-quarters, he was as satisfied with dinner as a man could be.

Grandma used buttermilk in baking. She made buttermilk biscuits and even buttermilk pie.

Buttermilk Biscuits

2 cups flour
$\frac{1}{2}$ teaspoon baking soda
1 teaspoon salt

3 tablespoons shortening
1 cup buttermilk (approx.)

Sift together the flour, soda, and salt. Work in the shortening with fingers. Add buttermilk gradually, using just enough to mix to a stiff dough. Place dough on a floured board, knead smooth, and roll to $\frac{1}{2}''$ thickness. Cut with a small round cutter. Bake 12 to 15 minutes at 450°F.

MAKES 12 BISCUITS.

Buttermilk Pie

1 cup sugar
3 tablespoons flour
$\frac{1}{2}$ teaspoon salt
3 egg yolks
2 cups buttermilk

4 tablespoons butter,
   melted
3 stiffly beaten egg whites
1 9'' pie shell, unbaked
Mace or freshly grated
   nutmeg (optional)

Combine sugar, flour, and salt, blending well. Beat the egg yolks slightly and add the buttermilk and cooled melted butter to them. Gradually add buttermilk mixture to the dry ingredients and blend thoroughly. Fold in egg whites. Pour pie filling into pie shell. Sprinkle mace or a grating of nutmeg on top if desired. Bake at 375°F for 45 minutes, or until a silver knife inserted in the center comes out clean.

Cottage Cheese (Schmierkase)

Place whole (unhomogenized) sour milk in pan to clabber. After clabbering, place pan on stove on low heat. Do not let the milk simmer or boil. While the milk is heating slowly, cut through the clabbered milk crosswise with a knife to separate the curd and let the milk heat evenly. When the curds of milk and the whey have separated, pour the mixture into a clean muslin bag. Tie up the top of the bag and hang it on a clothesline or in another suitable place. Let bag of curds hang until the whey has drained out, for several hours or overnight. Then turn the curds out of the bag, season with salt and pepper to taste, and add enough sweet or sour cream to add moisture. If desired, add a little sugar, about 1 teaspoon per pint or to taste.

How to Make Clabbered Milk To make clabbered milk, fresh, skimmed milk is allowed to sour at room temperature until it thickens. This will take thirty-six hours or more. The whey will separate from the solid curd, which rises to the top. Sometimes the soured milk needs to be set in a warm place (the back of an old kitchen range was perfect for this) to hasten the formation of curd and whey. The curd is the milk clabber, or clabbered milk.

Homogenized, pasteurized milk from the grocery will not produce clabbered milk. Fresh milk, straight from the cow, is needed. The sale of unpasteurized milk, however, is controlled by stringent regulations, so clabbered milk may not be readily available to everyone.

Thick dairy sour cream may be substituted for clabbered milk, in biscuits and baking recipes using $\frac{3}{4}$ cup commercial sour cream for $\frac{1}{2}$ cup of clabbered milk. Or, substitute an equal amount of buttermilk for clabbered milk in recipes.

Milk clabber was used in biscuits, certain cakes, and in making cottage cheese. It was a cooking staple in the country kitchens I remember, being used almost daily in preparing meals.

Butter Cookies

This recipe is over one hundred years old. Inez Hopkins gave it to Aunt Grace, and it was used for plain cookies or cut into decorative shapes for Christmas cookies.

$\frac{3}{4}$ pound butter	$\frac{1}{2}$ teaspoon baking soda
$1\frac{1}{2}$ cups sugar	$\frac{1}{4}$ teaspoon salt
1 egg	1 teaspoon vanilla
4 cups flour	

Cream the butter. Beat in the sugar gradually. Add the egg. Continue beating until the mixture is light and fluffy. Sift together the dry ingredients and add in portions to the butter-egg mixture, mixing well after each addition. Add the vanilla. This recipe makes a heavy dough when mixed. If necessary for handling, add a few teaspoons of milk. Roll cookies out to $\frac{1}{8}''$ thickness on a waxed paper—covered breadboard. Cut in desired shapes, using flour-dipped cutters. Sprinkle with sugar. Baked on lightly greased cookie sheets at 400°F for 8 to 12 minutes. Cool on racks, then ice if desired.

Grandma's New Pea Soup

3 quarts cold water
1 meaty hambone
1 small onion, minced
1 quart shelled new peas

12 new potatoes, scrubbed
   Salt and pepper
1 recipe dumplings
   (optional)

Add the cold water to the hambone and onion in a large kettle and boil over medium heat until the meat is almost tender enough to fall off the bone. Add the peas and potatoes and simmer for about 30 minutes, or until potatoes are cooked through.

Add the dumplings, if desired, 15 minutes before soup is ready.

Bread Dumplings for Pea Soup Break 3 or 4 slices of home-baked bread (or home-baked style) in pieces. Add milk and 1 beaten egg. Stir only enough to mix. Add $1\frac{1}{2}$ tablespoons flour. Drop onto gently boiling broth in soup kettle during the last 15 minutes of soup's cooking time.

German Egg Dumplings (Spaetzle)

2 eggs, beaten
$1\frac{1}{2}$ cups flour
1 cup water or broth

$\frac{1}{2}$ teaspoon salt
$\frac{1}{2}$ teaspoon baking powder

In a pan with a handle, combine the beaten eggs with the remaining ingredients and beat well.

Tilt the pan containing the dumpling batter over a pan of chicken broth, beef broth, pea soup, spring greens, or other soup or liquid. As the thick batter drips from the pan, cut off thumbnail-size pieces and let them fall into the hot broth. Simmer the dumplings until they are tender, 5 to 10 min-

utes. Drain and place in a bowl. If desired, cover the dumplings with bread crumbs that have been quickly tossed in a
small amount of sizzling hot butter. Serve dumplings with
chicken, beef, soup, greens, or sauerkraut.

Spaetzle were so named because they were supposed to re-
semble tiny sparrows' eggs.

Grandma's Chicken Soup with Homemade Noodles

1   2½ pound stewing
        chicken, cut up
5   cups water
2½ teaspoons salt
⅛   teaspoon pepper
¼   teaspoon marjoram

1 bay leaf
4 medium carrots
½ pound small white onions
1 cup homemade egg
        noodles*, uncooked

Wash chicken. Place in a large kettle and cover with water.
Add seasonings. Simmer for 1½ hours, or until the chicken is
just tender.

While the chicken is cooking, prepare the vegetables. Wash
carrots, peel, and cut in 1″ chunks. Wash and peel onions.

When chicken is done, remove it, along with the bay leaf,
from the stock. Skim off as much fat as possible from the
stock. Bring back to boiling; add carrots and onions, and
simmer for 45 minutes.

Remove skin and bones from the chicken, leaving meat in
large pieces. A half hour before the vegetables are done, add
noodles. Cook 20 minutes, then add chicken pieces. Cook an
additional 10 minutes.   SERVES 4 TO 6.

*Egg Noodles

Break 3 eggs into a 1-cup measuring cup. Add 1 teaspoon
salt and enough cream to fill the cup. Pour into a large bowl
and stir in enough flour to make a stiff dough. Form into a

ball and roll out to about $\frac{1}{16}''$ thickness on a floured bread-board. Let stand for 1 hour. Cut in narrow strips, about $\frac{1}{4}''$ wide.

To cook, drop noodles into boiling chicken broth or meat broth and cook for $\frac{1}{2}$ hour.

New Peas and Potatoes

10 small new potatoes	1 teaspoon salt
Boiling water	1 teaspoon sugar
3 cups shelled new peas	Pepper
2 tablespoons chopped	
onion	

Wash and scrape the potatoes. Place in kettle with water to cover, and add remaining ingredients. Bring to a boil, reduce heat, and cook until potatoes are tender.　　SERVES 6.

VARIATION

When the potatoes are tender, make a paste of 2 tablespoons of flour and a little milk. Add 2 cups of milk to the flour mixture and stir into the hot, simmering new peas and potatoes. Continue stirring and simmering until the mixture thickens and the vegetables are creamed.

German Potato Salad

5 pounds potatoes	$1\frac{1}{2}$ tablespoons cornstarch
2 medium onions, finely chopped	1 cup water
	1 cup cider vinegar
$\frac{1}{2}$ pound bacon	1 cup sugar
4 hard-cooked eggs, sliced	

Boil the potatoes with their skins on until tender, about 30 minutes. Cool, peel, and slice. Add the onions. Set aside. Fry bacon, chop, and drain on a paper towel.

To the bacon grease in the pan, add the cornstarch and cook until the mixture bubbles. Add the water, cider vinegar, and sugar. Cook until the mixture thickens, stirring constantly.

Pour over the potatoes and mix. Add the bacon and hard-cooked eggs and mix just enough to combine.

MAKES ABOUT ONE GALLON.

Country-Fried Potatoes

Peel 8 to 10 potatoes and slice thin. Heat lard to the depth of $\frac{1}{4}''$ in a heavy iron skillet. When the lard is sizzling hot, add the potatoes and begin frying them with the lid on, turning frequently. Season with salt and pepper to taste while frying. When the potatoes are almost done, uncover the pan and cook the potatoes long enough to brown them.

Sometimes Mother added a few onions to the potatoes to please Dad.

Milk gravy was often served with fried potatoes for supper.

Grandma's Camomile Tea

1 teaspoon dried camomile   1 cup boiling water
    flowers, or 2 rounded
    teaspoons fresh flowers

Scald the cup, add the boiling water, and steep the brew for 2 to 5 minutes. Add sugar or honey, and lemon if desired.

Funeral Pie*

1 cup raisins
1½ cups sugar
¼ cup flour
¼ teaspoon salt
2 cups water
1 egg, beaten

2 tablespoons grated lemon
    peel
3 tablespoons lemon juice
    Pastry for 9-inch double-
    crust pie shells

Rinse raisins and set aside to drain. In the top of a double boiler, mix together the sugar, flour, and salt. Add the water gradually, stirring constantly. Stir in the raisins. Bring to a boil over direct heat, stirring constantly, and cook for about 1 minute longer. Remove from heat. Add a small amount of hot mixture to the egg, then stir the egg into the mixture in the double boiler. Return to the heat and cook over simmering water for about 5 minutes, stirring constantly. Remove from heat and add lemon peel and lemon juice. Cool. Pour mixture into a pastry-lined 9″ pie pan. Cover with narrow pastry strips, crisscrossed. Bake at 450°F for 10 minutes. Reduce heat to 350°F and bake 20 minutes longer.

Aunt Helen's Lemon-Flavored Soft Sugar Cookies

1 cup butter at room
    temperature
2 cups sugar
3 large eggs
1 teaspoon lemon extract
¼ teaspoon vanilla
½ teaspoon nutmeg

¾ teaspoon cream of
    tartar
½ teaspoon salt
3½–4 cups sifted flour
1 egg white
    Sugar

*Funeral pie "carried" well, and its ingredients were always available, making it a popular pie for neighbors to bring to a bereaved family.

Cream butter with sugar until light and fluffy. Beat eggs and add, mixing well. Stir in extracts and nutmeg. Blend well.

Sift together the cream of tartar, salt, and $3\frac{1}{2}$ cups flour. Add to the creamed mixture, a little at a time, blending well after each addition to make a dough stiff enough to handle and roll out. Add remaining $\frac{1}{2}$ cup flour, if needed.

The dough will be very soft. Chill it for an hour or more. Roll out, in several portions, on a floured board, to $\frac{1}{4}''$ to $\frac{3}{8}''$ thickness. Cut out with a large floured cutter, using a large spatula to lift cookies onto greased cookie sheets. Beat egg white until frothy and brush on tops of cookies. Sprinkle with sugar. Bake at 400°F for about 10 minutes. Cool on racks.

Frost with favorite icing, if desired.

MAKES ABOUT 4 DOZEN.

Chapter 9

Grandma Marshall's Olden-Days Kitchen

SPINNING WHEEL IN THE KITCHEN— LOOM IN THE ATTIC

ONE DAY, I came into Grandma Marshall's kitchen and found her sitting beside a spinning wheel, which took sheep's wool from her hand and twisted it, magically, into a long strand of creamy white yarn.

I had never seen Grandma spinning before, but I had seen the spinning wheel up in the attic behind the room where she often sat weaving on her big old loom. The spinning wheel had gathered dust since the World War of 1914 to 1918, when she spun yarn and knitted stockings and mufflers for her soldier sons.

Now she had a sack of wool that Uncle Harry, who was visiting, had given her. So Grandma brought her spinning wheel down from the attic to spin on it for the first time in twenty years.

That afternoon Grandma taught me to comb wool, using her wide-toothed tortoise comb, and let me try my hand at spinning yarn on her spinning wheel. A lasting fascination

245

with spinning and weaving began there in Grandma's "olden-days" kitchen, with its green-enameled cast-iron kitchen range and its network of woven rag rugs, some as long as the room, stretching this way and that, making pathways across the gray linoleum-covered poplar floors.

Grandma's rag rugs and runners were darker, not as bright and gay, as ours at home. But they were beautifully woven with narrow, tightly packed rug strips and even, closely woven selvages. She used dark, serviceable warp and cut rug strips out of gray and blue work shirts and work pants. Her own small-patterned, dark print dresses added some variety. Sometimes she put narrow bands of light or bright warp at the edges of the rugs. Her rugs could be recognized any-where—they were originals.

Grandma was small and sturdy and strong. She came from pioneer stock, her family having been settlers in New York in colonial times. Her eyes were dark and lustrous, like buttons on the somber calico dresses she always wore. When she took out her tortoise combs and let down her gray hair from the knot she wore at the crown of her head, it was long enough to lie across her shoulder and down into her lap. She was practical and down to earth. As a child in a family of thirteen children, a bride at sixteen, the mother of sixteen children, and wife of a strong-willed individual, there was no other way to be.

GRANDPA'S OLDEN-DAYS BUGGY

Every day Grandpa hitched "Old Doll" to the buggy and drove to the mailbox at the end of the lane. Almost every day he would go on down the road to town, ostensibly on business.

"He'll think of something he needs," Grandma would say.

Grandpa would get some cornmeal ground, pick up some

chicken feed, take the cream off—then he would "loaf" a while. The general store had two loafers' benches flanking its doors, and another inside near the pot-bellied stove and the checkerboard.

Grandpa had a bad leg and couldn't walk without leaning on his homemade hickory cane, so he took horse and buggy almost everywhere. He was quite heavy, and he so often went by himself that the springs were broken down on the side of the buggy he sat on. It always looked as if it were going to turn over. People could see his buggy coming for miles, and they knew exactly who it was.

Very few people still had buggies in our community, and those who did were labeled "old-fashioned" in a rural area that was itself remote and isolated and behind the times.

It was fun for the grandchildren to ride to the mailbox in the olden-days buggy with Grandpa, behind Old Doll. And it was funny to watch Grandpa drive off toward town with his buggy comically listing to one side.

There was always someone visiting Grandma and Grandpa in the summer. It was a good place to go to see aunts, uncles, and cousins. More often than not, they had a full house. Thirteen of my aunts and uncles were teachers, not counting spouses, and one or another of them might be home for the summer, especially when they were changing schools or out of a job. During the Depression, different ones moved home until conditions improved for them. Once, Uncle John's entire family came from Nebraska, bag and baggage. An unmarried aunt, Grace, and a bachelor uncle, Walter, still had rooms at home. When school was not in session, Aunt Grace came back, and her nieces flocked to the Marshall farm to see her.

However many visitors there were in residence, the big old rambling farmhouse was never crowded. There were always empty beds and room at the table for more. In earlier days, Grandma always fed a multitude at her table—three times a day. It was still her way, from long habit, to keep plenty on the table to allow for unannounced visitors on the "home-place" at mealtime.

"Draw up a chair," she would invite. "Have some dinner with us."

GRANDMA'S FIVE LOAVES AND TWO FISHES

Grandma's legendary pot of beans and a big pan of corn bread were her five loaves and two fishes. When Grandma Marshall's big family of sixteen children lined up around the kitchen table, they ate a lot of beans.

"It took six or seven fifty-pound lard cans full of shelled dried beans to do us for a winter," Dad told me. "And your grandmother could cook a pot of beans that made the finest eating in the world. She would soak those dried beans in water overnight and then the next morning she would put them on the stove in a big black kettle with a piece of salt pork in with them, and they would cook along *very slowly* until they were tender, but not mushy. Sometimes she would add a few cut-up Irish potatoes toward the last half hour when the beans were almost done. Along about noontime, she would mix up a pan of corn bread. Now that was a pan that measured two feet long and a foot and a half wide and it took up one entire rack of the oven. And, by gollies, when dinner was over, there wasn't enough left over to feed the old dog, Strongheart. Those beans and corn bread made a meal as nourishing as a meal of meat."

Aunt Grace agreed. "We had beans almost every day. We liked them so well that we wanted to take them to school in our dinner buckets, if there were any left over."

While the young boys of the Marshall family were concerned with growing and harvesting the bean crop, the little Marshall girls spent every Saturday picking over the beans to remove the chaff and slivers of broken beans, and to get them ready for their mother to cook during the coming week.

"I can still remember how my neck would get tired from bending over that pan of beans when we would sit on the back porch, hand-picking the trash out of the beans," Aunt Grace said.

"Yes sir," Dad said. "We ate a lot of beans in those days. Most folks did."

Not by Beans Alone

There was plenty of good food on Grandma Marshall's table to go with the ever-present beans. Two fertile gardens, one near the house and one on the old Marshall homeplace nearby, where my great-grandparents lived, provided vegetables. Grandma made tomato preserves from both yellow and red tomatoes. She grew pole beans that vined up bean-pole tripods and transformed them into green teepees. Parsnips, salsify, sweet potatoes, acorn squashes, cushaws, and butter beans were hearty vegetables Grandma made use of in her unique way. She grew huckleberries in the garden—and she kept bees.

One day, Grandma sighted a swarm of bees swirling through the air. She ran into the house and got a bucket and went outside and banged on it to bring the bees down, something she knew to do because her father kept bees. The bees gathered in a clump on the fence that went around the garden, and they settled down and stayed there.

"Hurry and build me a bee box," Grandma told Dad when he was a boy. "I'm going to catch those bees."

The beehive was mounted on the fence post, the queen bee went in, and her swarm followed her. From then on, Grandma had honey for her table and for cooking. She kept a dish of comb honey on the table at every meal.

It was impressive to see Grandma in her bee veil and bee gloves, with a smoldering fire in the bee smoker, preparing to go out to tend to the bees. Grandchildren watched from the screened-in back porch, although Grandma went around the bees without protective clothing other than the veil and gloves, and Uncle Walter tended the bees bareheaded and bare-armed.

"The bees know us," Grandma said.

HONEY FOR GRANDPA'S SWEET TOOTH

Grandpa had a terrible sweet tooth. It took more than a spoonful of honeycomb to assuage it. Grandpa liked honey and he liked Grandma's honey cake. So he poured honey on top of it!

Grandma always had cake or pie, or both, on her table. The sweets were left in the center of the table, along with the nonperishable pickles, jellies, condiments, and honey, and covered over between meals with a small tablecloth that Grandma had woven on her loom. One might lift a corner of the tablecloth and find applesauce spice cake, angel food cake, honey cake, or cherry float. And there were always pies.

Grandma baked lots of pies, like all women of the community, but often hers seemed curious when compared to Mother's. Among the familiar pies, there were those that seemed old-fashioned and strange—green tomato, dried apple, huckleberry, cushaw, green (unripe) grape, and ripe grape pies. Her pies had originality, like her woven rag rugs.

GRANDMA'S GRAPE ARBORS

Grandma still had two grape arbors when I was growing up. The Concord vines were trained up over arbors made of tall posts. One of them was built over the cistern by the back porch, south of the smokehouse, and the other was down by the chicken yard. You could sit under the one by the house, on benches placed under its roof of leafy vines. It was that way when Dad was a boy.

"It made good shade," he said. "Lots of time was spent out there. When it came to peeling peaches and apples, things like that, they'd sit out there under that grape arbor to the south of the smokehouse. One thing Mother always made was lots of jelly. Sugar was cheap—the cheapest food we used. She'd can a lot of green grapes to cook and eat. She made pies out of green grapes that were just as good as gooseberry pies. Yes sir! She canned ripe grapes and she put up grape juice. She never did fool around making any grape wine, I can tell you that. But she'd put the grapes up—skin, seed, and all. Concord grapes is what they were. We had a white grape vine or two there at one time, but they didn't do any good, for some reason."

GRANDMA'S PIES

Not all of Grandma Marshall's pies were made of old-fashioned or strange ingredients. There were the familiar custard pies and cream pies with baked meringues towering above their milk-and-egg fillings. There were pecan pies made from the nuts from the trees in the bottoms by Pigeon Creek. And there were fruit pies.

Two pear trees and several old gooseberry bushes at the ancestral homeplace site still offered their fruits for Grandma Marshall's harvest, to be made into fruit pies, gooseberry fool, and pear honey. There were wild blackberries growing along fencerows and creek banks on the farm, and a strawberry patch at the end of the garden. Fruit trees grew near the house— apple, peach, plum, and red cherry. Grandma never ran out of fillings for pies.

A lot of people knew Grandma Marshall made good pies.

The word got around. Threshing dinners helped to verify a woman's reputation as a good cook.

"When I went to your Grandma Marshall's to help with wheat threshing," Effie Hargrave told me, "there was a table as big as a restaurant table full of pies she had baked to get ready for the threshing dinner. Your grandma taught me to make pie crust using just a little bit of shortening. She said to me, 'I can't afford to use very much, I have to make so many.' And this is how she showed me to do it: she took about a half cup lard—in those days we used lard—and she put it in a bowl. Then she poured into it one cup of boiling hot water and stirred it until that lard mixed in. Then she stirred in the flour, about three cups, I think, and then you could roll that out real thin. The hot water cooks the flour, you see, and the pie crust is very crisp."

I felt lucky to have *two* grandmothers who were famous in our community for their pies.

GREEN TOMATOES BY THE BARRELFUL

Grandma's green grape and green tomato pies seemed much more unusual to me than fried green tomatoes, which were standard summer fare at our house, too. Dad had grown fond of them when he was a boy. Not only did Grandma Marshall serve green tomatoes to her crowd of little Marshalls in summertime, but she salted them down for winter use. Everyone helped. Dad told us about it practically every time we had fried green tomatoes for dinner or supper at our house.

"We all picked and cut and sliced. Mother, or sometimes Dad, put them down in the barrels—we had two—with salt between the green tomatoes. Mother would soak them in water to get the salt out, then they were just like fresh. The salt goes out when they are soaked in water; it goes from dense to less dense—that's the rule. Then Mother dipped the tomatoes in cornmeal and flour—mostly in flour. We usually had gravy with fried green tomatoes, and sometimes we put it on them."

I liked to explore Grandma's smokehouse, which was a building just a few steps from the back porch and kitchen. The anteroom was still full of gray, white, and brown stoneware crocks and jars, some almost as tall as I was, and huge wooden barrels.

"I can just barely remember when Dad had those barrels made," my father told me. "There was a cooper in Selvin; that's all he did—make barrels. If a man wanted another barrel to put stuff in, he'd go over there and Bill Marshall would make a barrel for a dollar and a half, or two dollars. Dad's pickle-meat barrels were three or four feet wide so that a big side of meat could go down in there and be under the brine.

"When we had butchered and had meat to pickle, your grandmother would prepare the brine. She would put salt in the water to make the brine, then cook the salt and water together until it would float an egg. She had to cook it to get it down to the right weight and thickness. It took two barrels of pickled meat and two barrels of pickled tomatoes to get us through a winter."

MANY MOUTHS TO FEED—MANY HANDS TO WORK

Grandpa and Grandma Marshall's house was secluded, set back off the main road to Selvin at the end of a long tree-lined lane. They reared their family of sixteen children in the yellow poplar clapboard house that Grandpa built on land that had belonged to his father and grandfather. Next to the house, a large barn housed, at times, as many as eight teams of mules and several horses, and a dozen or more cows. The barn had a threshing floor where the Marshall children used to flail the grain, and there was still a flax brake there when I played in the barn as a child.

All their children had to work, even the little ones. The older boys worked in the fields, raising tobacco, corn, beans, wheat, and other crops, leaving the younger boys to do the barn and gardening chores as soon as they were old enough. The girls worked in the house and garden and helped to take care of the babies. And before long, Grandma had a row of daughters to help wash and cook and pick and peel and hoe and weed and sweep and sew. Running a large household, the division of chores was an exercise in management, and Grandma orchestrated it well. She had many hands to work as well as many mouths to feed.

Honey Cake

6   eggs
$1\frac{1}{3}$ cups honey
4   cups flour, sifted
$2\frac{1}{2}$ teaspoons baking powder
$\frac{1}{2}$ teaspoon baking soda

1   to 2 teaspoons ground
    cardamom, or to taste
$1\frac{2}{3}$ cups milk
1   cup butter, melted

Beat the eggs and honey for several minutes, until well blended. Sift together the flour, baking powder, soda, and cardamom. Add to the egg mixture. Add the milk and butter and mix thoroughly. Pour the batter into a buttered angel food cake pan and bake at 325°F for 60 minutes, or until the cake tests done.

Applesauce Spice Cake

$\frac{1}{2}$ cup butter	1 teaspoon cinnamon
1 cup honey	$\frac{1}{4}$ teaspoon salt
1 egg	$\frac{1}{2}$ teaspoon nutmeg or mace
1 teaspoon vanilla	$\frac{1}{4}$ teaspoon cloves
1 cup whole wheat flour, sifted	$\frac{1}{2}$ cup chopped pecans
	1 cup raisins
$1\frac{1}{4}$ cups all-purpose flour	1 cup unsweetened
1 teaspoon baking soda	applesauce

Cream the butter. Gradually add the honey, beating until light and fluffy. Add the egg and vanilla and beat well.

Sift together the dry ingredients. Coat the nuts and raisins with 2 tablespoons of flour mixture.

Add the remaining flour mixture to the creamed mixture alternately with the applesauce. Stir in the raisins and nuts. Pour batter into a greased and floured 9″ x 13″ x 2″ pan. Bake at 325°F for 35 minutes, or until cake tests done in the center. Cool and cut into squares. Serve with honey-sweetened whipped cream.

Sally Lunn

1 cup milk	3 eggs
1 package active dry yeast	1 teaspoon salt
$\frac{1}{2}$ cup butter	4 cups sifted flour
$\frac{1}{3}$ cup sugar	

Heat the milk until a film forms. Skim. Cool until lukewarm, then sprinkle in the dry yeast.

Cream butter. Add sugar gradually. Beat in eggs, one at a time, beating hard after each addition. Add salt to flour, then add the flour to the creamed mixture alternately with the milk. Mix well. Cover dough and let it rise in a warm place at about 80°F to 85°F until doubled in volume, about 1 hour. Stir the dough down and beat hard for 30 seconds. Pour into a greased Turk's-head mold or a 10″ tube pan. Cover and let rise again until double in size. Bake 25 to 30 minutes at 350°F or until browned on top.

Cherry Float

1 quart seeded red cherries	1 cup flour
1 cup sugar	$1\frac{1}{2}$ teaspoons baking powder
2 tablespoons butter	$\frac{1}{8}$ teaspoon salt
$\frac{1}{2}$ cup sugar	$\frac{2}{3}$ cup milk
1 egg	

Combine the red cherries with sugar in a saucepan and place on low heat until the cherries simmer in their own juice. Remove from the heat and set aside. There should be about $\frac{1}{2}$ cup of juice with the cherries.

Cream butter and sugar. Add egg and beat until fluffy. Sift together flour, baking powder, and salt. Add the dry ingredients alternately with the milk to the egg mixture, mixing until smooth after each addition.

Put the batter in the bottom of a greased $1\frac{1}{2}$-quart round baking dish. Spoon the stewed cherries and juice over the top of the batter. Bake at 400°F until the crust is golden and a toothpick inserted into the center comes out clean, about 1 hour. The batter rises up through the berries during baking.

Serve warm with cream.   SERVES 4 TO 6.

Green Grape Pie

$2\frac{1}{2}$ cups green grapes, picked before seeds develop	3 tablespoons flour
	$\frac{1}{4}$ cup water
	2 9″ pie crusts
$1\frac{1}{4}$ cups sugar	

Mix together grapes, sugar, flour, and water. Pour into bottom crust. Top with second crust. Brush top crust with milk and sprinkle with sugar.

Bake at 425°F for 15 minutes, then lower heat to 350°F and bake for an additional 45 minutes.

Pecan Pie

4 eggs, beaten
$\frac{2}{3}$ cup brown sugar, firmly
   packed
$\frac{1}{4}$ teaspoon salt
$1\frac{1}{3}$ cups light corn syrup

$\frac{1}{4}$ cup melted butter
1 teaspoon vanilla
$1\frac{1}{3}$ cup pecans
1 10″ unbaked pie shell

Combine eggs and sugar. Beat until blended. Add salt, corn syrup, butter, vanilla, and pecans. Mix well. Pour into pie shell. Bake at 400°F for 15 minutes. Reduce heat to 350°F and continue baking for 30 to 35 minutes or until cake is set in center.

Green Tomato Pie

3 cups sliced green
   tomatoes
$1\frac{1}{3}$ cups sugar
3 tablespoons flour
$\frac{1}{4}$ teaspoon salt
$\frac{3}{4}$ teaspoon cinnamon

6 tablespoons lemon juice
4 tablespoons grated lemon
   rind
3 tablespoons butter
Pastry for 9-inch double-
   crust shells

Combine tomatoes, sugar, flour, salt, cinnamon, lemon juice, and rind. Line 9″ pie pan with pastry, pour in filling, dot with butter, and cover with top crust. Bake at 450°F for 10 minutes; reduce temperature to 350°F and bake 30 minutes longer, or until tomatoes are tender and top of crust is browned.

Fried Green Tomatoes

Wash and slice green tomatoes crosswise, about $\frac{1}{4}''$ thick, and dip both sides in flour, or a mixture of flour and cornmeal. Fry in hot lard (or other shortening), about $\frac{1}{2}''$ deep, in a single layer until both sides are brown and the tomatoes are tender. Season with salt and pepper to taste.

Green tomatoes can be served with milk gravy, if desired.

Corn Oysters

1 pint fresh sweet corn, or whole-kernel canned corn

1 egg, well beaten

$\frac{3}{4}$ cup flour

$\frac{1}{2}$ teaspoon baking powder

2 tablespoons soft butter

$\frac{1}{2}$ teaspoon salt

$\frac{1}{8}$ teaspoon pepper

Combine all ingredients and mix well. Drop by tablespoonfuls into hot fat, $1''$ deep, which is hot enough to brown a bread cube in 40 seconds. Brown on one side, then turn. Serve with honey butter, sorghum, or golden syrup.

MAKES ABOUT $1\frac{1}{2}$ DOZEN.

Honey Butter Cream 1 cup of butter until fluffy. Add $1\frac{1}{4}$ cups strained honey, beating constantly (use an electric mixer on low speed). Serve with corn oysters or hot bread.

Grandma Marshall's Relish

1 quart green tomatoes, chopped into 1" chunks

1 quart ripe tomatoes, chopped into 1" chunks

1 medium-sized cabbage, coarsely ground

4 red bell peppers, chopped

4 green bell peppers, chopped

12 red apples, unpeeled, cored, and chopped

½ cup pure salt

½ gallon cider vinegar

4 tablespoons ground mustard

1 teaspoon horseradish

1 clove garlic, minced

2½ teaspoons celery salt (optional)

Combine the prepared vegetables and apples with the salt and let the mixture stand in a cool place overnight.

Drain the vegetable mixture and place it in a large kettle with vinegar and spices. Bring to a boil while stirring and boil gently for 20 minutes, stirring often. Ladle relish into hot, sterilized jars, leaving ¼" head space. Adjust lids. Process in a boiling-water bath for 10 minutes.

MAKES ABOUT 8 PINTS.

Grandma's Stuffed Mangoes*

12 green bell peppers (mangoes) or a combination of green bell peppers, red bell peppers, and yellow "banana" peppers

1 tablespoon salt

4 cups shredded cabbage

1 tablespoon salt

½ to 1½ cups sugar (according to taste)

2 tablespoons mustard seed

2 tablespoons celery seed

1 quart mild cider vinegar

½ cup sugar

*Bell peppers

Slice the tops from the stem ends of the peppers and remove the seeds and membranes. Put the tops and the whole peppers into a large crock and cover with cold water. Sprinkle with the 1 tablespoon salt and let stand overnight.

The next day, mix together the shredded cabbage, salt, sugar, and spices in a large bowl. Drain the peppers well, then fill their cavities with the cabbage mixture. Replace the tops of the peppers and tie or sew them into place with white cotton string. Place the stuffed peppers in a large, deep crockery jar and cover with the vinegar sweetened with the $\frac{1}{2}$ cup sugar. Put a weighted plate on top of the peppers to keep them under the vinegar. Cover the jar with a lid or foil and store in the refrigerator for 2 weeks before serving.

VARIATION

Green tomatoes may be used instead of bell peppers. Cut off the tops and scoop out their centers. Fill with the cabbage mixture, as above.

TO CAN STUFFED MANGOES

Sterilize 3 or 4 wide-mouth one-quart jars. Lift the peppers out of the vinegar and sugar mixture and place in hot sterilized jars. Heat the vinegar to boiling and pour it over the peppers. Leave $\frac{1}{2}''$ head space. Adjust the caps and process 15 minutes in a boiling-water bath.

Tomato Preserves

2 quarts ripe yellow plum tomatoes or ripe red tomatoes	4 cups sugar
	$\frac{1}{2}$ teaspoon cinnamon
	$\frac{1}{2}$ teaspoon ginger
1 quart water	1 lemon, thinly sliced

Scald, peel, and coarsely chop enough tomatoes to make 2 quarts. Place tomatoes in a heavy kettle with water and 2 cups of the sugar. Cook for 5 minutes, stirring to dissolve the sugar, then simmer for about two hours, stirring often. Add the remaining 2 cups sugar, spices, and lemon slices. Cook for 20 to 30 minutes more, until the mixture thickens, or reaches 221°F on a candy thermometer. Pack preserves in hot sterilized jars and adjust the lids. Process in a boiling-water bath for 10 minutes.   MAKES ABOUT 8 PINTS.

Note: If the red tomatoes are excessively juicy, halve each one and remove some of the juice by giving each half a turn on a juice reamer.

Grandma Marshall's Spiced Beets

"Select average-size beets. Wash and cook in the peel until you can pierce with a fork. Cool, then peel.

"Make enough pickling mixture to cover the beets. Use the proportions of: 1 pint cider vinegar; 1 quart water; $2\frac{1}{2}$ big cups sugar (size of a coffee mug); 1 teaspoon salt; $1\frac{1}{2}$ teaspoons cinnamon; $\frac{3}{4}$ teaspoon allspice, ground or whole. Bring to a boil. Add beets and let simmer 20 minutes. Seal hot. Cinnamon bark is what I use. This can be used for spiced pears or peaches."

Grandma Marshall's "Junket" Ice Cream

5 eggs	2 tablespoons vanilla
$1\frac{3}{4}$ to 2 cups sugar	6 Junket rennet tablets
2 quarts milk	$\frac{1}{4}$ cup cold water
2 cups cream	

Beat eggs well. Add sugar to taste, milk, cream, and vanilla. Pour into a one-gallon ice cream freezing container. Set container in a pan of warm water over low heat until contents are lukewarm (110°F).

Dissolve rennet tablets in cold water. Remove ice cream container from the heat, stir in the dissolved rennet tablets, and let stand undisturbed for 10 minutes.

Place the dasher in the freezing container and put on the lid. Pack the freezing container in crushed ice, using 4 parts ice to 1 part salt. Freeze until dasher is hard to turn. Remove dasher and repack in ice and salt. Let stand 2 hours to ripen.

A Time to Rest

By the time I knew her, Grandma was taking it easy. She had trained her family to work and she had earned the right to loaf.

She often sat in a chair to the back and side of the kitchen range and, with a great dignity, smoked a long-stemmed clay pipe. She smoked a pipe her entire life, and it was a sign you were family or had passed approval if she took out her pipe and smoked it in front of you.

"I had a toothache when I was a girl," Grandma explained to me one time when she saw me eyeing her pipe, "and I went to Uncle Doc Spradley. He said, 'If you get yourself a pipe of tobacco and smoke it, it might help that toothache.' So I got myself a pipeful of tobacco and smoked it. It didn't help the toothache and he had to pull that tooth after a while. So I got rid of my toothache—but I still had my pipe!"

Thus Grandma made smoking a pipe a joke on herself, but as a child, I thought secretly that it was out of keeping for a grandmother. But when Grandma reached up on top of the warming closet of her kitchen range, got down her pipe and tobacco, and sat down on her chair to rest and "smoke a pipe," I knew I would hear wonderful stories about the colorful past of our community and family.

THE COLORFUL PAST RETOLD

Oral storytelling was a tradition in the Marshall family, although some members leaned toward writing. Grandpa wrote political commentary in "Letters to the Editor" under a pen name, Enoch Arden, which he liked better than his own. (Grandma said he was afraid to say those things under his own name.) And Aunt Grace wrote childrens' stories to read to her elementary school classes. But, clearly, storytelling and sitting around just talking—and eating—were the family's main diversions when we all got together at Grandma's house.

"That's the Irish in them," Mother told me. "They all kissed the Blarney Stone."

Grandpa farmed and taught school. He was a "Hoosier schoolmaster" if ever there was one. He taught in one-room schools in our community for over thirty years. After he married one of his pupils, Cora Springston, and had a family, he taught his own children, too. In the one-room Wendel School, which housed all eight grades, with an enrollment of sixteen to eighteen, the Marshall children sometimes comprised as many as one-third of their father's pupils.

By the time I knew Grandpa, his teaching days were over, but they were immortalized in stories told when his large clan gathered. The stories were so captivating and colorful, it was easy for his grandchildren to visualize a straw-hatted, gray-haired, and mustachioed Grandpa as the schoolmaster and pistol-packing citizen of a frontier town.

When any of the Marshall family got together, it was a marathon story-telling event. They all liked to talk and loaf together. They would sit around the table on the back porch, or around the kitchen range, or in a circle in the parlor, or outside under the shade tree, and swap tales by the hour. There was no end to the stories. They loved to tell stories about each other, usually funny ones, followed by gales of laughter. Old stories about feuds and shootings and fires and shenanigans of one sort or another were all brought out and revived. Tales of school days and family legends were retold. The stories stretched all the way back to pioneer days when a relative was killed by an Indian in his front yard.

Grandchildren liked to hear the stories. We settled down where we would not be especially noticed, out of their line of attention and the smoke billowing out of their pipes and cigars.

Uncle Norman liked to tell how he was named:

"By the time they got to me, Mother and Dad had run out of names. There were three of us boys without names until we were of a good size. They called us Big Hon, Little Hon, and None. I was None.

"One day we had a family gathering here. Uncle Willis Marshall, Norman Spradley, and John Taylor were there. Norman Spradley called me over and asked me what my name was. I told him I didn't have none, so they called me 'None.'

"Those three men decided it was time for us boys to have names, so they made a bargain with Mother.

" 'If you'll name those boys after us, we'll buy each of them a suit of clothes.'

"Mother took them up on the bargain, and that was how the three of us were named.

"We still didn't have middle names—most of us didn't, unless we picked our own. So Willis and John and I decided we would only have one name until we needed another suit of clothes. When we outgrew our clothes, no one else came along and we finally had to go to work and buy our own suits."

Being singled out and summoned before a group of schoolteacher aunts and uncles could be an intimidating experience. You might be asked about your grades at school, quizzed about spellings of words and history dates. The Marshall aunts and uncles never forgot that they were teachers. And they all liked to tease. It was a way of conversing with us, of giving us some attention, of keeping us on our toes.

"Can you name all of the presidents of the United States yet? Let's hear you."

A mistake could follow the hapless one for years. Or until the entire list could be recited upon demand without an error.

We children were the subject of many anecdotes, ourselves. The suspense of waiting to hear the painful ending could make cheeks burn. Or praises could bring a swell of pride. We learned to endure with both grace and good humor.

"One time I was icing a fine applesauce spice cake when Marilyn came in," Grandma began. "She had her eyes on that cake. I finished icing it and put it up in the safe. She never said a word, but I knew she wanted some. So I asked her, along about time for her to go home, 'Marilyn, do you want a piece of that cake?' And she hung her head and said, in a little whiney voice: 'I don't know.'" So I said, 'If you don't know, then I won't give you any.' "

Peals of laughter followed Grandma's punchline. While I blushed, Grandma wound it up. "The next time I asked her if she wanted a piece of cake, she said, 'Yes!' "

You were lucky if you got off with only one story being told on you.

Aunt Grace was next. "One time when Marilyn was a little bit of a thing, about five, she was getting ready to go to school and she needed some dresses. I told Laura I would make her some, and Garnita and I were down on the floor cutting out some little print dresses with three-cornered pants to match. I said to Garnita, 'Let's go have a c-i-g-a-r-e-t-t-e.' Marilyn thought for a little bit, and she thought . . . then she said, 'I know what that spells! Cigarette!' "

Peals of laughter. That one was better.

We loved storytelling at Grandma's, even when the stories

were on us. But, sooner or later, the uncles and aunts would go on to more adventurous stories, maybe about the time their great-uncle Clarence shot Harry Miller, or the time Grandpa pulled Charlie Harter's chin whiskers out.

Dad liked to tell the story about his father's half-brother.

"Uncle Clarence got into trouble one time. He shot Harry Miller," Dad began. "Clarence had sold a load of tobacco. Harry Miller was riding home with him, and he wanted Clarence to pay him for some little things. Clarence said, 'All right. I'll pay you after you pay me. You always make your garden on my place.' And they got into it. Clarence jumped out of the wagon on one side and Harry on the other, and Harry came around the wagon with his pocket knife out.

"Clarence always carried a gun. He was a good shot. He could shoot a rabbit's eyes out. He could stand there and take those eyes out like his pistol was made for that.

"Well, Harry started chasing Clarence, I believe it was over The Graded School yard. But he couldn't catch him. Clarence could run like a deer. He had his pistol out, shooting over his shoulder, trying to scare Harry off, to make him quit chasing him. But he kept coming.

"Clarence had used all his bullets but one. It was a .38 revolver and the bullet was as big as the end of your finger, and he thought, 'I've got one cartridge left and I have to make that one count.' So he plugged old Harry with it.

"It didn't kill Harry, but it would have if he hadn't had so many clothes on. It went through his overcoat and the clothes he had on underneath and stuck on a rib, and lodged there.

"Well, Clarence ran home and left town that night for Missouri. He never came back."

Two generations later, it was hard for us to imagine that our quiet little town had been the scene of the exciting stories our aunts, uncles, and grandparents told over and over when they got together to talk and to draw up a chair at Grandma's bountiful table.

To us grandchildren, the present was as colorful as the past. Grandpa had a German shepherd dog named Strongheart who was trained to jump through a large hoop made of a buggy tire. He had a flock of speckled "Dominicker" hens that came running when he called them; they ran around and around him in a wide circle until he finally threw out their corn in a broadcasting motion as he himself turned around and around. It was great fun to watch Grandpa and the chickens in a merry-go-round at feeding time. Grandpa had a Seth Thomas clock on the mantel that he wound with great ceremony every day. He took us for rides in the buggy behind "Old Doll," cracking the long buggy whip just above her rump to start her trotting and urging, "Hop, Dolly! Hop, Dolly!" And, he played the violin.

Grandpa's violin playing was an entertainment to his children as well as his grandchildren. Dad would tell me about the evenings of violin music when Grandpa's friend came to talk and play the violin with him.

"Mr. Samples played the violin at Pleasant Hill church picnics. One day when they were having a picnic over there, I looked out across the bottom and I saw a man coming on a black mare. Dad told me, 'Run and tell Code [Code was Grandma's name for Grandma] to fix something. Mr. Samples will be here for supper.'

"Mr. Samples had red buffalo-hair. He carried his violin in a pillow slip. Mr. Samples jiggled and Dad played the long stroke. They talked and played violin all evening."

Mr. Samples' jiggling notes and Grandpa's long-drawn strains of "Old Dan Tucker," "Little Brown Jug," "Oh! Susanna!" "Carry Me Back to Old Virginia," and other old songs gave my father the tunes he played on his harmonica and sang to us in the evening in our home. I was always capti-

vated by the old songs and old stories and old-fashioned aura of my Marshall grandparents.

There was always something to transport me out of the present day into a time gone by in Grandma's house. The attic was a place to explore while Grandma wove on her loom in the next room. It was filled with Grandpa's school books. One day Grandma presented me with *The New Eclectic Series Complete Geography,* copyright 1883, and signed with Grandpa's name—James A. Marshall—and a book of fairy tales by Hans Christian Andersen that had been given to one of her little girls on Christmas in 1909. I was laden with treasures (which I have still) when I went home that day with my books and a graceful white china pitcher, hand-painted with lavender violets and banded with gold, which caught my fancy among all the old dishes in the attic.

"Do you want that pitcher?" Grandma asked when she saw me eyeing it.

"Yes!" I answered, with certainty.

"Then I'll give it to you."

When Grandma put the pitcher in my hands, she said: "You must always remember me every time you look at it."

And, to this day, I do.

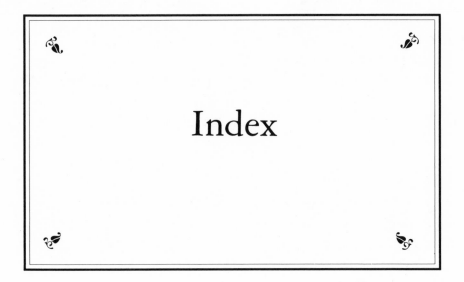

Index